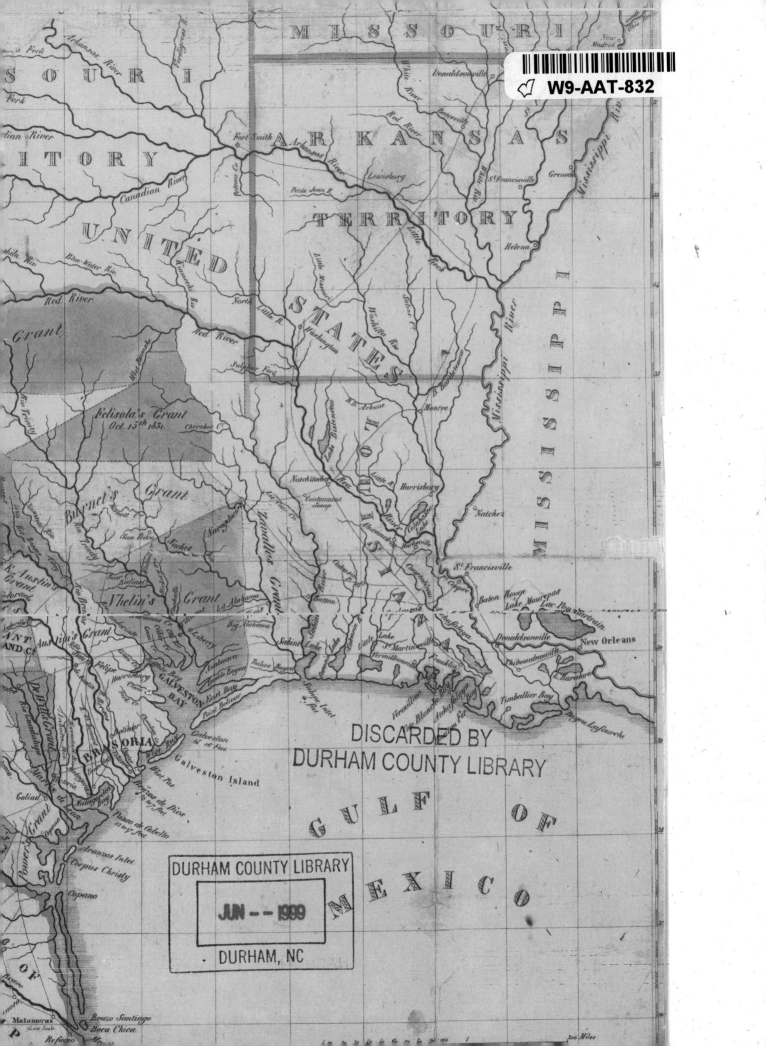

THEY RODE FOR THE LONE STAR

THEY RODE FOR THE LONE STAR

The Saga of the Texas Rangers

The Birth of Texas — The Civil War

THOMAS W. KNOWLES

TAYLOR PUBLISHING COMPANY
DALLAS, TEXAS

Book design by Mark McGarry
Set in Monotype Dante

page ii: The Rangers' tools of the trade included those of most Western lawmen.
Photo by Joe Griffin, Texas Ranger Hall of Fame and Museum

page vi: The legendary Ranger captains: (*clockwise from top left*) John Coffee Hays, John Salmon "Rip" Ford, Ben McCulloch, and Samuel H. Walker.
Library of Congress and the UT Institute of Texan Cultures at San Antonio; John N. McWilliams Collection; UT Institute of Texan Cultures at San Antonio; John N. McWilliams Collection

page viii: This 1851 map of the great state of Texas includes an inset of New Mexico, California, and Utah.
Texas State Library & Archives Commission

Published by Taylor Publishing Company
1550 West Mockingbird Lane
Dallas, Texas 75235
www.taylorpub.com

Library of Congress Cataloging-in-Publication Data:

Knowles, Thomas W.
    They rode for the Lone Star : the saga of the Texas Rangers /
Thomas W. Knowles.
       p.   cm.
    Includes bibliographical references and index.
    ISBN 0-87833-205-7 (hc.)
    1. Texas Rangers—History—19th century. 2. Frontier and pioneer
life—Texas. 3. Texas—History—1846–1950. 4. Texas—History—Republic,
1836–1846. I. Title.
F391.K69   1998
976.4'04—dc21
                              98–48988
                              CIP

10 9 8 7 6 5 4 3 2 1
Printed in the United States of America

As the old song says, this book is for "all you Texas Rangers," past, present, and future, who were, are, and always will be the true defenders of Texas and the West. And because they were, in every sense of the word, my "angels" while I struggled to put this story into print, I also dedicate it to Barbara Green and her parents, Wise and Billie Hollingsworth.

Acknowledgments

A great many people assisted and supported me in producing this book, but I'd like to extend special thanks to the dedicated people who maintain the Texas Ranger Hall of Fame and Museum in Waco—director Byron Johnson, curator Stewart Lauterbach, archivist/librarian Christina Stopka, and museum staff members Rebekka Lohr, Linda Rawls, Lisa Daniel, Jim Allen, Joan Warneke, Mable Fulp, Dusty Young, and Patricia Kelley. The Hall of Fame and Museum made my job much easier by extending resident historian status to me and providing me with an office while I researched this book. I owe a particular debt of gratitude to curatorial assistant Dan Agler for the personal time he devoted to researching my questions, for making his considerable store of Texas Ranger and South Texas folklore available to me, and for his assistance in photographing the artifacts in the Museum.

I also owe much to T. R. Fehrenbach, and not only because he agreed on short notice to read the manuscript and write the foreword for it. It was while I read his inimitable history of my native state, *Lone Star: Texas and the Texans*, that I began to understand just how important a part the Texas Rangers played in the cultural evolution of Texas and the American West.

The modern Texas Rangers played a large part in making certain this book got written. My thanks go out to all of them, but I'd like to particularly recognize the commitment made to this project by Sr. Capt. Bruce Casteele, and by the Rangers of Company F, who are stationed at Fort Fisher—Capt. Kirby Dendy, Lt. Cleete Buckaloo, Sgt. Christine Nix, Sgt. John Aycock, and Sgt. Matt Cawthon. Thanks also go to the Daughters of the Republic of Texas Library, the Eugene C. Barker Collection and the Center for American History, to the great Texas artist Bruce Marshall, historical photo collector John McWilliams, Sam Walker historian Jim Worsham, archivist Tom Shelton and photo librarian Chris Floerke of the Institute of Texan Cultures, Texas State Archives director Donaly Brice and archivist John Anderson, curator Ellen Brown of the Baylor Texas Collection, James Nowak of Specialties Photography, Waco photographer Joe Griffin, Taylor Publishing editors Fred Francis and Camille Cline, and my agent, Matthew Bialer. Without the able and enthusiastic assistance of all of these people, I could never have made this book a reality.

I'd like to recognize the fine folks at Barry's Coffee House and Common Grounds for the java that kept me jumping each morning while I was doing my research in Waco. Many thanks to the staff and management of Cadillac Jack's Texas Bar and Grill, who allowed me to turn their back booth into my second office while I filled the bar with pipe smoke, listened to great Texas music, drank Shiner Bock, and composed much of what follows here. They even ran an extension cord for my laptop computer!

As for the aforementioned computer system, without the timely intervention of its architect, my dear friend and colleague Nadine Miller, this job would have been next to impossible to complete—*gracias, amiga!*

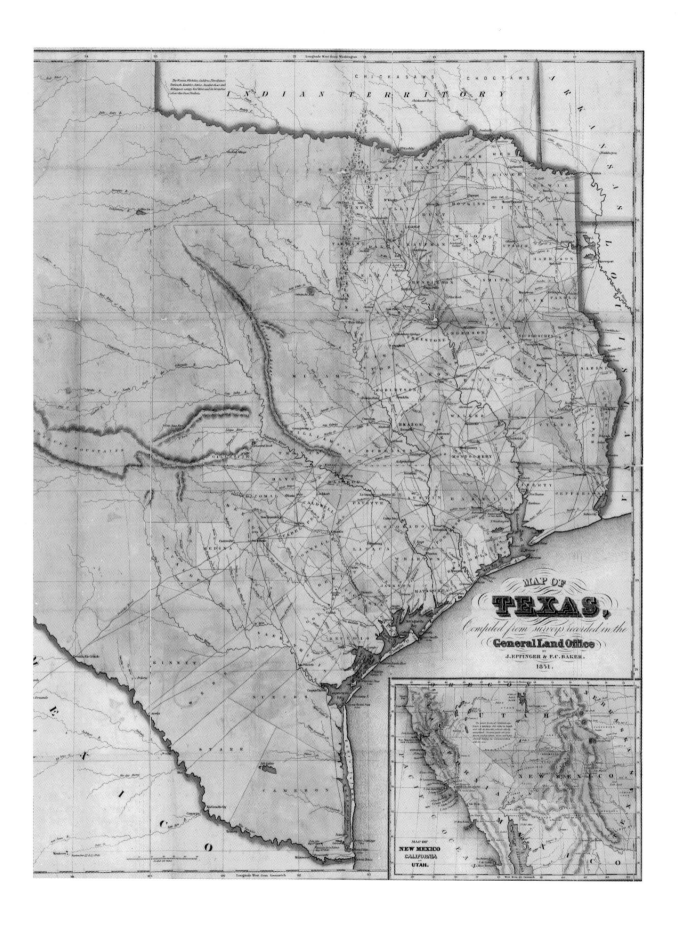

MAP OF
TEXAS,
Compiled from surveys recorded in the
General Land Office
J. EPPINGER & F. C. BAKER.
1851.

MAP OF
NEW MEXICO
CALIFORNIA
and
UTAH.

Contents

A Word from the Director of the Texas Ranger
    Hall of Fame and Museum   XI

Foreword by T. R. Fehrenbach   XIII

Introduction   "Where the West Begins"   XV

1   A Texas Genesis   I

2   Against All Odds   23

3   Rangers of the Republic   49

4   Defenders of the Lone Star   73

5   The Grand Constellation   103

6   The Cavalry of the West   149

7   In Blue and Gray   175

Afterword   From the Ashes   209

Appendix   In the Line of Duty: Texas Rangers
    Killed in Action in the Service of
    the Lone Star 1823—1865   215

Bibliography   221

Index   223

A bronze statue of George B. Erath, surveyor, soldier, Texas Ranger leader, stands at the entrance to the Texas Ranger Hall of Fame and Museum in Waco, Texas. He guards the time capsule sealed in the 175th anniversary year of 1998; the capsule contains letters written by the Texas Rangers of the 1990s to the Texas Rangers of the 2090s.

Photo by Tom Knowles

A Word from the Director of
the Texas Ranger Hall of Fame and Museum

The year 1935 was momentous for the Texas Rangers.

It was the centennial of the reorganization of the Ranger force under the Republic of Texas and preceded the state centennial celebration by a year. A few of the old-time Rangers were still living to tell tales of the frontier, and the Rangers were in the national limelight because Frank Hamer had recently ended the criminal careers of Bonnie and Clyde.

In New York, the Houghton Mifflin Company published Walter Prescott Webb's *The Texas Rangers: A Century of Frontier Defense*. The work drew international acclaim as a pivotal work in western American history. It would perpetuate the legend of the Texas Rangers for another sixty years and inspire countless movies, television programs, and novels.

In Austin, the fourth era of the Texas Rangers began. They had served as frontier minutemen, as lawmen around developing settlements, and as a state police force. Now, after a decade of political corruption and turmoil, the legislature reconstituted the Rangers and returned honor to the force. Their future would be with the new Texas Department of Public Safety serving as an elite investigative and major crime division. However, not everyone was pleased.

Walter Prescott Webb feared that this merger would mark the end of the "real" Texas Rangers. He knew and had become friends with such giants as Frank Hamer and Manuel Gonzaullas. He understood that their success was engendered by an intensely personal style, freedom of operation, and people skills. He doubted that such Rangers could exist if "department" became more important than "company," if "procedures" came to mean more than "success." His book was written, in many ways, as a eulogy for the Texas Rangers.

Webb was far too pessimistic. Six decades after he predicted their demise, the Texas Rangers are readying for their *third* century of service to the people of Texas. Under conservative and visionary Sr. Capt. Bruce Casteel, the 107 Rangers constitute one of the smallest, most effective law enforcement agencies in the world. Their wardrobe still includes boots, white hats, and pistols, but their tool kit now includes college degrees, networked laptop computers, cell phones, and blood spatter and DNA analyses.

Yet ask most Rangers what makes them successful and they echo Webb: people skills, perseverance, and an uncomplicated dedication to what is right. The Rangers know Texas and her people as no others do — their collective values are the traditional values of Texas. Honor, service, and self-sacrifice in the face of tall odds are traditions that still make children and adults line up at the Texas Ranger Hall of Fame and Museum to meet "real" Texas Rangers.

Interpreting the history, heritage, legend, and culture of the Texas Rangers is a daunting task. It takes a writer who knows Texas and the West and can absorb fragmentary documents, conflicting legends, oral history, and historical context, then weave them into a fascinating narrative.

Tom Knowles has captured the history and heritage of the Rangers in the first comprehensive work since Webb's *The Texas Rangers*. In the process of writing this narrative, he absorbed countless reports, autobiographies, government records, and folklore. As Webb did before him, he visited with serving Texas Rangers and was granted access to reports and opinions not often shared with those outside the service. The result is a landmark work that predicts a bright future for one of Texas's oldest and most cherished institutions.

The Texas Ranger Hall of Fame and Museum, the official state hall of fame and repository for the Texas Rangers, is pleased to endorse this work as the official history for the 175th anniversary of the Texas Rangers.

Byron A. Johnson, Director
Texas Ranger Hall of Fame and Museum
Waco, Texas

Foreword

BY T. R. FEHRENBACH

The Texas Rangers, second only to the Alamo, are a subject and symbol that serious Texans take seriously.

The Rangers, after all, are more than myth or legend and tales of law and order in the Old West; they made history on America's longest-lasting and bloodiest frontier. They were born in desperate times out of brutal necessity. Their purpose was to defend civilization as they knew it from dangerous and savage enemies. The fact that the Texas Rangers were largely successful in this goal is the reason that today both the name and organization survive.

Unlike United States Marines, who may change uniforms and missions but remain essentially the same Corps, the Texas Rangers present a very different aspect from age to age. As times and needs changed, they have changed—except for duty, devotion, and human valor, the stuff from which their legends are made. Both the Rangers and most Texans love those legends, although truth be told, they sometimes get in the way of the modern force. For example, in Hollywood's version of *Walker, Texas Ranger*, the legend of the Ranger as a one-man-army submerges the fact that today's Rangers form an elite investigative unit in which brains are more to be valued than brawn.

Texas Rangers are more than mere examples of "good guys" or men who "kept a-comin'"—as the state's best historians have noted, they also reflect, from the first, the enormous adaptability of the frontier breed. The early Anglo settlers took the name and notion of Rangers from American colonial history but adapted these to purely local circumstances and needs. As Walter Prescott Webb wrote, the Republic of Texas graciously permitted frontier communities to arrange and support their own defense, a course that quickly threw up a most remarkable body of men for that or any other age.

In the distinct phases of Ranger history, it must be remembered that the Rangers prior to the 1870s were in no sense a constabulary or police force. They were in fact something of a militia designed purely for the defense of Anglo-Texas's interminable Mexican-Indian frontiers, both of immense length and incalculable brutality. However, a patriot-style militia in which farmers took down their muskets and marched on short campaigns was totally ineffective on these frontiers. Faced with superb horsemen and long-ranging raiders, Rangers had to match and then best their foes in the same fields. This was adaptability at its best, or brutal worst—a lasting American trait. It also called for young, adventurous, often unattached men who passed in and out of the "service," such as it was. It is often overlooked that the early great captains, all born warband leaders, usually ended their Ranger careers by the age of thirty.

Several things about the first phase of Ranger history—the Republic and pre-Civil-War state—must be kept in mind. The Rangers were always an ad hoc force, raised according to perceived need. This often makes it difficult to define "Rangers" in the period. In one sense, nearly every able-bodied male along the whole breadth of the

Southwestern frontier at some time served with the Rangers. The core of the first Rangers, however, was composed of frontier-bred youth who chose their own leaders and were willing and capable of hitting the far-ranging, bloody trail. The term sometimes applied to these bands—"mounted gunmen"—is quite apt.

After 1845 Rangers were considered "state troops." Captains, appointed by governors, recruited their men. Much as good coaches attract good football players, great captains drew the best men for the job, a fact that colors most of Ranger history.

The reason Texas required such a unique, long-lasting paramilitary force was, simply, the Texas frontier. In most states, the true Indian frontier endured for a decade or less. The Army or militias subdued permanently settled, largely agrarian tribes with a few campaigns. In Texas different conditions prevailed. In no other part of North America did a numerous farming community live within the raiding distance of dangerous "neighbors" for two whole generations, sixty years. The Republic was too poor, the Federal government either too distracted, distant, or indifferent, to cure the running sores of the Indian and Mexican frontiers. In fact, Federal reluctance to solve the frontier problems was a major factor in the Texas frontier's (where there was no slavery) support for Secession.

So out of necessity, deeds were done and legends born. There is no understanding the attitudes of nineteenth-century Texans without the understanding that they waged a three-cornered war: against the Plains tribes on the west, hostile Mexicans to the south, and Yankee rule from the north. When Rangers mounted up, they rode to war, usually outnumbered and in most cases against enemies devoid of mercy. The rules of engagement were entirely different from modern policing. The man who asked questions before shooting might not survive. In wars, especially racial-cultural wars, hatreds and cruelty are easily aroused. Mexicans came to hate *rinches* (a term eventually applied to any Texas lawman) while Rangers treated them with contempt. But early Ranger-work was not abuse of despised citizen minorities; it was war to the knife against outside, perceived enemies of Texan destiny.

They rode superbly, shot splendidly, and were coolly courageous. These attributes were taken for granted: No man who did not fit this mold had any business on the Texas frontier. They were very few, but the Texas that sprang forth from the barren plains owes much to them.

This book details the facts of the early Ranger force. It does not attempt to judge. As for that, I think the Rangers can only be measured by results. Not that the end justifies the means, but no modern American can measure these men without having walked in their boots.

T. R. Fehrenbach
San Antonio, 1998

Introduction

"WHERE THE WEST BEGINS"

W E TEXANS HAVE A SAYING: "COWTOWN (FORT WORTH) IS WHERE the West begins, Dallas is where the East fades out." This statement accurately reflects the dual nature of the Texian character, the enduring ideological schism between the civilized world and the Wild West. Our spirits remain divided between what was and what is, between our allegiance to the past of our frontier heritage and the manner of our everyday life,

which is firmly rooted in the modern urban reality.

But the original geographical, psychological, and historical dividing line between East and West falls much farther east, where the thick East Texas piney woods give way to open country. There, in the early nineteenth century, pioneers from the youthful United States emerged from the sheltering woods, into the rolling hills and prairies that would lead them to the uncharted reaches of the Great Plains. It wasn't a "New World," except to the newcomers. An ancient land already long occupied by conflicting cultures and fraught with incredible perils, Texas challenged them and changed them, and the American character, forever.

For them, and for America, Texas was where the Wild West began.

In the land that would become known as Texas, three cultures met in a collision of moral highs and lows, of deeds glorious and ignominious, in excesses of greed and examples of selfless courage fired by both racial hatred and uncommon brotherhood. As in all such histories of human endeavor, pathfinders and leaders emerged from among the men and women who found the courage to face the challenge of adapting to life on the frontier. In combining the strengths of their own people with what they learned from the other cultures they met, sometimes in friendship but often in bitter rivalry and conflict,

Captain Brooks's Company of Texas Rangers, Frontier Battalion, Falfurrias, Brooks County, Texas. (*seated, left to right*) Tupper Harris, Sgt. John H. Rogers, Capt. J. A. Brooks, Charles Rogers, T. S. Crowder. (*standing, left to right*) Marcellus Daniels, Robert Bell, C. L. "Kid" Rogers, Jesse Bell, Jim "Nest Egg" Moore.
Dudlie Dobie Collection, Moody Texas Ranger Memorial Library

they formed the prototype of a new culture, of the people that would become known to the world as "Texans."

And in doing so, some of them became the stuff of legend and myth.

Capt. John S. "Rest In Peace" Ford said of the fighting companies of frontier Texans led by himself and Capt. John Coffee Hays that they could, "ride like Mexicans, track like Indians, shoot like Tennesseeans, and fight like the very Devil himself." To the casual observer they appeared to be a mismatched and unlikely lot, for their uniform was whatever rough clothes they chose to wear in the field. They followed no flag, no tune of fife and drum, wore no bright colors, and shunned pompous ceremony and official honors. They often served without pay, and

sometimes at the cost of their own lives. Until very late in the nineteenth century, they carried no official badges of office

A photo taken late in his life of John Salmon "Rip" Ford, Texas statesman and journalist, and the commander of the Cavalry of the West. He took over leadership of the Texas Rangers when Jack Hays moved to California.
UT Institute of Texan Cultures at San Antonio, Courtesy of Ford DeCordova

support and no communication from higher authority, they lived and often died by the motto, "Order first, then law will follow." They served first as citizen soldiers, then as the recognized authority of an independent republic, then as the police force for a fledgling state. They often functioned as the court of last resort, and if the justice they dispensed was of a rough sort, it was fitting for the times in which they lived.

except for the Colt revolvers they wore in their belts and the moral authority they carried in their hearts.

When called to duty in these companies, farmers and ranchers and laborers joined in an equal and elite brotherhood with physicians and politicians and military officers, teachers and clergymen and surveyors, Indian scouts and blacksmiths, and the descendants of Spanish grandees. They learned to remove themselves, at a moment's notice or less, from their peaceful pursuits and intents, to transform themselves into the fiercest of warriors, eager for battle, ready to lay down their lives in the defense of their new homeland.

They performed a unique blend of military service, frontier defense, and autonomous civil law enforcement. Charged with the mission of operating beyond the boundaries of civilization with minimal

Clayton Moore as "The Lone Ranger," with his horse, "Silver."
CBS Photo Archive

Capt. Samuel H. Walker, Texas Ranger and field commander of the 1st U.S. Mounted Rifles in the Mexican War. Photo by Mathew Brady, circa 1847.
Library of Congress

Tommy Lee Jones stars in *Lonesome Dove* as "Capt. Woodrow F. Call," a retired Texas Ranger.
Tony Esparza, CBS Photo Archive

In their struggle to win and hold Texas for their own people, their names became both respected and hated, dreaded by some and welcomed by others. To many of the Mexicans who found reason to oppose them, they were known as *El Rinche* or *Los Diablos Tejanos*, the "Devil Texans." To the proud Comanche and Kiowa and other Indians they fought to the bitter end of the terrible Indian Wars, they were certain death on horseback. To the cultured officers of the United States military whom they protected and guided during the Mexican War and then fought against during the American Civil War, they were "those damned frontier ruffians." To the outlaws they pursued, they were the most feared and hated of all lawmen.

Chuck Norris in *Walker, Texas Ranger*.
Tony Esparza, CBS Photo Archive

xviii

Texas Ranger Sgt. Lee Trimble, circa 1915. *Trimble Collection, Moody Texas Ranger Memorial Library*

They were the Texas Rangers, and in the truest sense, they were the first real Texans, the first true Westerners of the Wild West.

So like the stuff of legend and myth reads the saga of the Texas Rangers that indeed many modern Americans believe them to be nothing but a legend, the fantastic creation of pulp writers, novelists, and Hollywood scriptwriters. Mention Texas Rangers to baby boomer television addicts like me and the immediate image called to mind is that of the Lone Ranger and Tonto, riding through the video Wild West to dispense justice on a frontier that never really existed. To the average American on the street, the Texas Rangers are a powerhouse baseball team from that Southern state that has all of the oil wells and cattle. Ask any kid about Texas Rangers and the kid will tell you all about the latest spin-kicking exploits of Chuck Norris in his role as *Walker, Texas Ranger*. Some historians will tell you that the Texas Rangers are a closed chapter of regional American history, a mere footnote to the overall history of the American West.

Not so. That brotherhood of warriors endures in the modern-day Texans, the descendants of grim Scots-Irish borderers and Revolutionary irregulars, Apache scouts and the scions of Imperial Spain, and wanderers and immigrants from many other lands. In Texas, that sometimes still wild place where the West began, the Texas Rangers continue to serve the Lone Star as they have for 175 years. They were and they still are the inimitable Texas Rangers, true to the traditions of their Old West predecessors and devoted to the promise of the future.

This is their story.

THEY RODE FOR THE LONE STAR

1

A TEXAS GENESIS

Ranger. THE WORD FROM ITS EARLIEST USE IMPLIES THE EXERCISE of individual judgment, but a judgment tempered by duty to a cause or a calling, as well as by personal honor. In the purest sense, a ranger is one who defends the borders of the known against the unknown and so must familiarize himself with both to excel at that duty in either territory. To be a ranger, then, is to accept the challenge of crossing over the border into the dark unknown to learn its secrets, there to operate beyond the support or comfort of civilization in the service and defense of civilization.

The early Texas Rangers, in the words of one Ranger captain, were "the defenders of the West." Others bore the title of "ranger" before them, and some have carried it proudly after them, but the Texas Rangers have always redefined the title to fit their mission rather than allowing it to define them. Even today, at the threshold of a new millennium, at a time when the borders they defend are set by civil codes rather than by physical boundaries and wild frontiers, the Texas Rangers continue to carry the title, "Ranger," in a way that fits their mission, their calling, their personal honor.

To understand this, one must first understand the unique forces that molded a disparate group of colonists into a new nation and drew from among them the men who would become its defenders, the Texas Rangers.

Despoblado

In the beginning, the land itself shaped their destiny. Early Spanish explorers named it *Tejas*, using an Indian word for "friend," but the country that attracted first the Spanish treasure seekers and missionaries, then the Mexican settlers, and finally the Anglo colonists, was anything but friendly. Unforgiving in geography and climate to those used to tilling more civilized lands, homeland to a fierce race of nomadic warriors, Texas offered rich opportunities to settlers but often exacted

A group of Texas Rangers at Glen Springs, Texas, circa 1900.
UT Institute of Texan Cultures at San Antonio/Texas State Library & Archives Commission

a steep price for them. "Texas is heaven for men and dogs," one despairing pioneer woman said, "but it's hell on women and cattle." Like a blacksmith forging steel from raw iron, Texas reshaped the character of those who came to take what she could offer. She changed them all to fit her mold, or she broke them.

Imperial Spain had tried to extend her dominion into Texas, but for the most part, Spain, and her successor, Mexico, were unable to successfully establish more than a tenuous colonial foothold. In essence,

Texas served Spain as *un despoblado*, a buffer zone between civilization and the wild Indian raiders of the plains, as well as feared incursion from the expanding United States. Establishing expendable colonies of settlers as buffers in freshly conquered territory was a tactic the Spanish had employed to great effect centuries before in the process of retaking their homeland from the invading Moors.

The result of this policy was a halfhearted effort at true colonization. What counted for civilization in

Texas revolved around the Spanish military establishments, the *presidios*, and the mission system built by the Catholic Church in an attempt to convert the Indians.

Just to maintain the mission and *presidio* systems, the Spanish sometimes literally forced colonists from New Spain (Mexico) to settle in Texas. Such forced settlement, closely akin to banishment, made for unwilling and unreliable colonists and reinforced the negative perceptions most Spanish subjects had about Texas. To the civilized people of New Spain, Texas was that wild place "beyond the edge of the world," the *comanchería*, Comanche territory, a desolate land ruled by fierce human enemies and even more savage elemental forces of nature.

Only where the *presidios* offered protection to the citizens did the colonies endure, in part because the soldiers and officers of the *presidios* intermarried with the colonists, thereby providing some stability and sense of community. Other missions and settlements that lay unprotected by forts and soldiers failed; were looted and burned by the Lipan Apache, Kiowa, or Comanche; their people killed or driven away.

Some admirable individuals and groups among the Spanish settlers were tough enough to meet the challenges of the *frontera*, even to thrive upon them. To bolster the thin military line, political administrators

Kicking Bird, a Kiowa chief. Photo by William S. Soule.
UT Institute of Texan Cultures at San Antonio/Barker Texas History Center, University of Texas

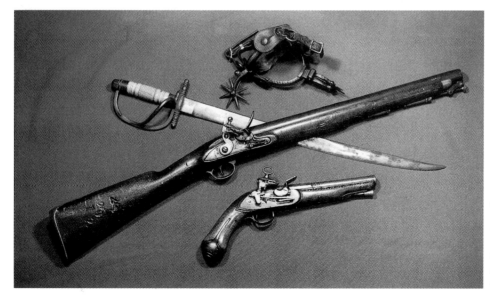

Spanish Colonial Era—The *espada ancha* (cavalry short sword), migulet pistol, *escopeta* (cavalry carbine), and Mexican spurs of the type used by Spanish colonial and Mexican lancers.
Photo by Tom Knowles, Texas Ranger Hall of Fame and Museum

of New Spain encouraged the colonists to arm themselves and provide for their own defense, a move radically different from the tradition of Spanish colonial oppression in Mexico. These *ciudanos armados*, or armed citizens, naturally began to develop a sense of self-reliance. Where they succeeded in nurturing colonial expansion, it was almost completely on their own, marginalized by Spanish society's negative attitude toward Texas and the crown's unwillingness to fund the military effort necessary to actually occupy the territory. As always, Texas never gave an inch of ground to those who were not strong willed enough to take and hold it.

Los Tejanos

A few Spanish colonies did hang on and finally begin to prosper to some extent, primarily in the Nacogdoches region deep in the eastern woods, in the Rio Grande area far to the south near the Mexican province of Coahuila, and in the Béxar-Goliad region of southern Central Texas.

The population of Nacogdoches, originally founded by the Spanish as a safeguard against territorial incursions by the French, fluctuated wildly because of epidemics and panic. More than once, officials traveling from Mexico arrived only to find the village nearly deserted. It took a growing trade with the United States in horses and cattle to stabilize the settlement. Eventually, Nacogdoches became the eastern gateway into Texas for American colonists.

In the southern border areas near the province of Coahuila, settlement coalesced around isolated *rancherias*, where the cattle ranchers built miniature *presidios* and created their own familial communities based on their vast holdings. The *rancheros* of South

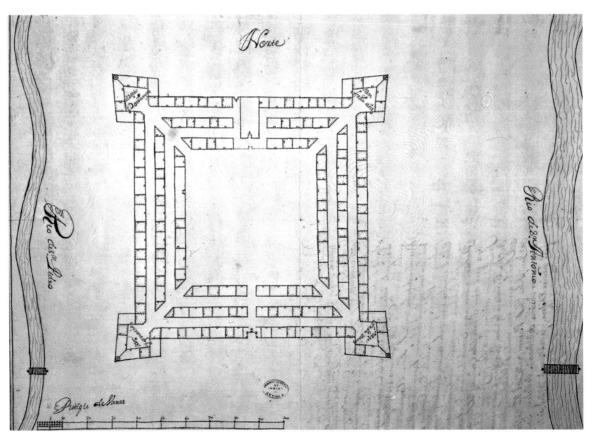

From the Spanish Colonial Texas period, *Plano del Presidio de San Antonio de Béxar de la Provincia de Texas* describes the fortifications and bridges at the presidio of Béxar as mapped out by the Marques de San Migel de Aguayo.
Texas State Library & Archives Commission

Texas called not upon the soldiers of the *presidios* but their own riders to defend their herds against Indians and other raiders. It was among these riders, the *vaqueros*, that the cowboy traditions of Texas had their origins.

Most of the settlers in Texas came from the northern provinces of Mexico; they were *mestizos*, people of mixed European and Mexican Indian heritage. Many of the soldiers sent to man the *presidios* were Tlascalans, descendants of the soldiers of the conquered Aztec Empire. As the colonists and the soldiers learned to depend on one another to survive, racial and social divisions between them grew less important. The civil and military populations of the colonies merged, Spanish with Indian, Aztec with their conquerors, finding in their mutual need a new sense of community separate from the distant society of New Spain. From the traders in the eastern woods to the *vaqueros* who rode the plains of the south, they began to think of themselves not as Spanish or as Mexican, but as *Tejanos*, a new people adapted to a new land.

A Light at the Edge of the World

Béxar, the most distant viable outpost of Spanish colonization, barely reached into the edge of the brush country of South-Central Texas. Although a series of missions the Spanish established in the area in the early 1700s failed to attract the Indian converts they sought, in 1731 one set of colonists from the Canary Islands succeeded in establishing a village near the *presidio* just across the river from Mission Valero. The town, San Antonio de Béxar, grew from the original settlement into the highest expression of Spanish culture in the wild province. Mission Valero, surrounded by the huge cottonwood trees that grew along the river, eventually became known as "the Alamo." (*Alamo* is the Spanish word for the cottonwood tree.)

Under Spanish rule, the Alamo was occupied by *La Segunda Compañía Volante de San Carlos del Alamo de Parras*, a company of one hundred colonial mounted lancers posted to Mission Valero in 1803 as scouts and support for the garrison of San Antonio. (See "La Compañía Volante.") Unlike garrison troops who defended a fortified *presidio* or a town, the *compañia volantes* or "Flying Squadron" did just what its name infers. It moved quickly and struck at the enemy, rather than waiting for the enemy to strike. Using the *caballada* principle, which meant maintaining a *remuda* of ten or more remounts for each man, the lancers always had fresh horses on which they could pursue and run down raiders. This allowed them to mount effective extended patrols (*cortadas*) and long pursuits. Each man was required to supply his own weapons (a rifle and at least two handguns), clothing, supplies, and other accouterments, as well as a suitable string of mounts.

As the flying squadrons expanded their numbers and their patrol areas, the colonists and civil authorities came to rely on them not only for protection against Indian raiders but to track down lawbreakers and to prevent border incursions by American freebooters (illegal settlers, slave traders, and outlaws). Although they were trained and led by professional military officers, the *compañias* often drew their members from local citizens. By introducing into *Tejano* culture this tradition of drawing a mixed volunteer and professional mounted force from the community, the flying squadron set the stage for the special orders by which colonial leader Stephen F. Austin would later create the early "ranging companies," the predecessors of the Texas Rangers.

Spark of Empire

Despite the way *los Tejanos* adapted to life on the frontier, in the three hundred years after Spain claimed Texas no permanent settlement had pushed much further north and west than San Antonio de Béxar. By 1820, when Missouri businessman Moses Austin began bringing Anglo colonists to his Spanish land grant, the entire *Tejano* population numbered only about 3,500. Even in San Antonio de Béxar, it wasn't unusual to see

LA COMPAÑÍA VOLANTE

Of the several *compañías volantes* (flying companies or flying squadrons) that the colonial Spanish deployed in Texas, *La Segunda Compañía Volante de San Carlos del Alamo de Parras* figured most prominently in Texas history. In 1803 this troop of one hundred mounted lancers under the command of Francisco Amangual joined the garrison at San Antonio de Béxar. They eventually established their headquarters in the old Mission Valero, near the San Antonio River.

This company originated from the San Carlos district of the Coahuila province, from the village of San José y Santiago del Alamo de Parras, which took its name from the grapevines (*parras*) of its vineyards, and from the cottonwood (*alamo*) trees that grew nearby. Cottonwood trees also surrounded Mission Valero in Béxar. From the *Alamo de Parras* company's long association with the mission, as well as from the graceful cottonwood trees that surrounded it, Mission Valero gained its more famous name — the Alamo.

The members of the flying squadron used a decorated leather shield (*adarga*) and a long lance as their primary weapons of defense and offense, although they also carried sabers, pistols, and military-issue flintlock rifles or carbines. Using a string of remounts (*remuda*), they served as a mobile strike force that could pursue and intercept Indian raiders and bandits. They also acted as scouts and couriers. Although they operated as a separate unit, they often provided support for the *presidios* (forts) and the soldiers who manned the static defenses.

The Spanish colonial government sent the *Alamo de Parras* company to Texas mostly in response to the fear of invasion from the United States. At times the company did end up pointing their lances at a few American freebooters, but they usually fought Indians and bandits. Veterans of many fights against Apache raiders and bandits in Mexico, in Texas they made effective use of the same light cavalry tactics in campaigns against the Lipan Apache, Comanche, and other Indians. Their actions against cattle thieves, bandits, and Indian raiders vastly improved the quality of life for the citizens of the small community of San Antonio de Béxar.

They also added to the population. Like the *presidio* soldiers, the flying companies also took their families with them to each new station and became a part of the community wherever they settled. In Béxar, Commander Amangual found the barracks at the old Plaza de Armas in such disrepair that he moved his entire company and their families, almost two hundred men, women, and children, into the partially completed, abandoned Mission Valero. They repaired and reinforced the structure's defensive walls, eventually enclosing the courtyard, the old convent (now known as the Long Barracks), and the chapel. Unmarried men bunked in the Long Barracks, while the married men and officers built *jacales* (huts) and houses outside the walls. The homes they built along the river near the mission became known as La Villita, the "little village," which exists today as a part of the Riverwalk park in San Antonio.

In the years between their assignment to Béxar and the beginning of the Mexican Revolution in 1810, the *Alamo de Parras* company became a part of the *Tejano* community. They came to share sense of a separate cultural identity, isolated from Spanish society, and so found themselves torn between old loyalties and new.

They helped to put down a rebellion led by the Texas y Coahuila governor in 1811, but just a year later, *Alamo de Parras* commander Lt. Vicente Tarin, many of his men, and the men of the Béxar *presidio* joined in the Gutierrez-Magee affair. This conspiracy to wrest control of Texas from

6

The "Long Barracks" at the Alamo were originally constructed for the enlisted men of the Spanish "flying company" stationed at the mission.
Photo by Tom Knowles

Mexico was staged from the United States by *Tejano* rebels, financed and aided by American free-booters. They sent an expeditionary force into Texas, but while the invasion itself succeeded in driving out most of the garrison troops, popular support for the rebellion failed to materialize. When Gen. Joaquín de Arredondo's loyalist forces put down the revolt in 1813, many of the *Alamo de Parras* company's men died fighting against Spain, were captured and executed, or were forced to flee to Louisiana.

The company disbanded for a time, leaving the Alamo and the *presidio* all but abandoned and the citizens of Béxar to fend for themselves against emboldened raiders and bandits. It wasn't until 1817, when seventy-five veteran lancers from Nuestra Señora del Carmen and new recruits from Béxar entered the Alamo, that the company *Alamo de Parras* again became an effective force. After Mexico won her independence from Spain in 1821, the company continued in its role as a part of the army of the Mexican Republic.

The *Alamo de Parras* commander under Mexican rule, Lt. Col. José Francisco Ruiz, became a good friend to Stephen F. Austin and a supporter of the Texian *empresario*'s colonial enterprises, but ill health eventually forced him to retire. Ruiz later joined the Texas Revolution and became one of the signers of the Texas Declaration of Independence.

Again, the *Alamo de Parras* company found itself split by revolution. In the fall of 1835, some of the company and their new commander, Capt. Francisco Casteñeda, became involved in the attempt to seize the famous "Come and Take It" brass cannon from the Texians at Gonzales. After that debacle, many of Casteñeda's men deserted him and went over to the cause of independence. Some of those who stayed with him defended the Alamo against Ben Milam's Texans during the bloody Battle of Béxar.

After Antonio López de Santa Anna's defeat at San Jacinto, *Tejano* patriot Col. Juan N. Seguín and several of his men who had once served with the *Alamo de Parras* company showed up to accept the final surrender of the Alamo from Casteñeda and the few members of his company who had remained loyal to him.

wild Comanches or Lipan Apaches riding unmolested through the city streets. By the early nineteenth century, the sparks of a nascent empire lay dormant in Texas like surviving embers in an otherwise extinguished campfire, waiting for just the right fuel to flare up into a flame of legendary proportions.

The American colonists were that fuel. Although Texas attracted colonists from all over the United States and many European nations, the greatest number of them were emigrant Scots-Irish "borderers" from Kentucky, Tennessee, and Alabama. The borderers were themselves the descendants of a conquered people who had been drafted to police another conquered people, the Irish, under their British overlords back in Europe. Their Celtic ancestors, Welsh and Scots and Irish, had engaged in centuries of clan warfare and cattle raiding as a way of life, and for generations they'd fought against their subjugation into the Roman and British Empires, even to the shores of the New World and the American Revolution. The colonists who came to Texas in the 1820s were a new generation of frontiersmen born in America, blooded in the ways of Indian warfare and yet steeped in the equally grim and vengeful traditions of their European fathers. In effect, these descendants of the old borderers carried within them the basics of "ranger" character.

They also brought with them memories of the early American antecedents to the Texas Rangers. Three quarters of a century before, during the French and Indian Wars, "Rogers's Rangers" and other irregular troops of colonial America had studied the tactics of the Indians and had applied them to great success against their native enemies. (See "Rogers's Rangers.")

Most of the Americans had only a vague idea about what awaited them in Texas, beyond the promise of open land and a chance at a new life. In increasing and often alarming numbers, so far as many of the Spanish officials were concerned, they forged their way across the frontier to settle in Texas. They settled by permission of the crown as Spanish subjects on legal land grants under the authority of *empresarios* like Moses Austin and the Baron de Bastrop, or as illegal freebooters in their own little enclaves. No matter how they got there, the American colonists started to think of themselves as a people apart, even as had *los Tejanos* before them. They began to call themselves "Texians."

Into the Crossfire

These new Texians were fighters, but they were used to the kind of Indian fighting done in the woodlands of the East. In Texas they ran into the same barrier, other than the land itself, that had stopped Spanish expansion dead in its tracks — Indians. To settle in Texas, they had to contend with the cannibal Karankawa of the coast, the veteran Apache warriors of the Southwest, and the proud Kiowa to the north. Their deadliest enemy would be the wild raiders of the southern Great Plains, the fierce Comanche. Culturally, the American colonists were unprepared for what Texas had to offer them. They were woodlands farmers and planters, merchants and builders, not cavalry or cowboys. The vast "emptiness" of the arid plains and the no-quarter warfare practiced by the Plains Indians were alien to them.

Indeed, to the emigrant Anglo with his Eastern sensibilities, the convoluted *Tejano* code of honor and the relentless Comanche wanderlust were as foreign as something from an alien world. Concepts of morality didn't easily translate across cultures, especially between three peoples that met in competition for the same country. The inevitable conflict that arose from this triangle of competition grew into implacable hatred, often identified in racial terms, and led to a century of bitter border wars.

By the time Moses Austin got his land grant from the Spanish crown and began bringing in American colonists in the 1820s, the Comanche had claimed much of Texas for nearly a century. Originally an off-shoot of the Shoshonean-speaking peoples of the northern plains and mountains, the Comanche had

ROGERS'S RANGERS

If the French and Indian Wars (1754-1763) can be considered a prelude to the American Revolution, the irregular units of colonists commanded by a colonial New Hampshire farmer named Robert Rogers could be considered as the first Americans to bear the name of "ranger." Beginning with the first company he formed in 1756, Rogers's Rangers used guerrilla tactics adopted from the very Indians they fought. In an era of stylized warfare and parade uniforms, the Rangers wore drab green camouflage fatigues and mastered the art of surprise attack. They operated under a set of unconventional guidelines called "Rogers's Ranging Rules," tactics similar to those used by modern special forces such as the U.S. Army Rangers and the Green Berets.

Robert Rogers was a British officer and frontier soldier who served in the French and Indian Wars. His ranging company provided a model for those in Texas.
Dictionary of American Portraits

Rogers's Rangers won fame for the forced march through the wilderness into Canada to attack the stronghold of the Abenaki St. Francis Indians. The Abenaki, vital allies of the French, had killed more than six hundred colonists and attacked a group of British soldiers and colonists even while they were withdrawing under a truce flag (as fictionalized in James Fenimore Cooper's novel, *The Last of the Mohicans*). Under Rogers's command, two hundred rangers lived off the land as they secretly navigated through enemy-held territory. Outnumbered, without support, almost starving and worn out by the journey, they successfully attacked and destroyed the Abenaki and burned their village.

Rogers's Rangers also participated in Gen. James Wolfe's expedition against Quebec, in the 1760 Montreal campaign, and in the campaigns to seize Detroit and other northwestern posts. In the West in 1763, the Rangers fought in Pontiac's War and the Battle of Bloody Bridge.

In his own lifetime, Rogers never received much praise for his innovations in guerrilla warfare or his contributions, and he was much derided for his obsession with and search for a "Northwest Passage" through North America. Despite the sacrifices the Rangers made in His Majesty's service and the results of their unconventional tactics, regular British troops and officers had always regarded the Rangers as uncouth and irrelevant. Penniless and forgotten, Rogers had retired to England, but he returned to America when he heard talk of the revolution there.

John Stark, a Revolutionary general, served as lieutenant in Rogers's Rangers during America's colonial period.
Engraving by Alexander H. Ritchie, Dictionary of American Portraits

Rogers might have recognized his own handiwork at play in the spark of rebellion. His lieutenant, John Stark, who had been one of the finest officers to serve in the French and Indian War, had been severely mistreated by the British military establishment. When the colonists met British troops with force at Lexington and Concord in 1775, former members of Rogers's Rangers, Stark's embittered comrades and friends, fired the first shots of the conflict.

Fearing that he might be a secret loyalist, George Washington rejected Rogers's offer to reform the Rangers for Colonial service. Stung by Washington's snub, Rogers took service with the British, for which action he was branded a traitor. He organized and commanded the Queen's Rangers, mostly made up of Carolina Tories, and the King's Rangers, Scots Highland regulars he trained in unconventional warfare. Neither of these units succeeded in matching the record of the original Rangers, perhaps because the old warrior's heart was weakened by his divided loyalties.

Standing Orders, Rogers's Rangers (Major Robert Rogers, 1759)

1. Don't forget nothing.
2. Have your musket clean as a whistle, hatchet scoured, sixty rounds powder and ball, and be ready to march at a minute's warning.
3. When you're on the march, act the way you would if you was sneaking up on a deer. See the enemy first.
4. Tell the truth about what you see and do. There is an army depending on us for correct information. You can lie all you please when you tell other folks about the Rangers, but don't never lie to a Ranger or officer.
5. Don't never take a chance you don't have to.
6. When we're on the march we march single file, far enough apart so one shot can't go through two men.
7. If we strike swamps, or soft ground, we spread out abreast, so it's hard to track us.
8. When we march, we keep moving till dark, so as to give the enemy the least possible chance at us.
9. When we camp, half the party stays awake while the other half sleeps.
10. If we take prisoners, we keep 'em separate till we have had time to examine them, so they can't cook up a story between 'em.
11. Don't ever march home the same way. Take a different route so you won't be ambushed.
12. No matter whether we travel in big parties or little ones, each party has to keep a scout twenty yards ahead, twenty yards on each flank and twenty yards in the rear, so the main body can't be surprised and wiped out.
13. Every night you'll be told where to meet if surrounded by a superior force.
14. Don't sit down to eat without posting sentries.
15. Don't sleep beyond dawn. Dawn's when the French and Indians attack.
16. Don't cross a river by a regular ford.
17. If somebody's trailing you, make a circle, come back onto your own tracks, and ambush the folks that aim to ambush you.
18. Don't stand up when the enemy's coming against you. Kneel down. Hide behind a tree.
19. Let the enemy come till he's almost close enough to touch. Then let him have it and jump out and finish him up with your hatchet.
20. Don't use your musket if you can kill 'em with your hatchet.

This drawing by George Catlin depicts a Comanche village near the Red River. The illustration comes from Catlin's 1876 book, *Illustrations of the Manners, Customs, and Condition of the North American Indians.*
UT Institute of Texan Cultures at San Antonio

been one of the first groups of Indians to get the horse from the Spanish and the French. They took to the nomadic life of raiders and buffalo hunters as did no other tribe. They excelled at it, even eclipsing the great Lakota and Cheyenne in their horsemanship. In 1839 in his *Travels in the Great Western Prairies*, Thomas J. Farnham wrote of them as the "Spartans of the Prairies," noting their "incomparable horsemanship" and their ferocity in battle. After the Medicine Lodge Creek Council of 1867, a treaty meeting where Comanche warriors put on a spirited display of their skill on horseback for the attending members of the U.S. Army and negotiators from Washington, one observant officer deemed them "the finest light cavalry in the world."

Unequaled in battle, armed with lance and shield and short *bois d'arc* bow, the Comanche rode, hunted, and raided where they willed, from the High Plains into the heart of Mexico, from Nacogdoches in East Texas to Santa Fe in New Mexico. They often took captives, some to trade, some as slaves, some to raise as members of their bands in order to offset an unusually low birth rate caused by genetic disease. As they swept in from the north like a Texas thunderstorm, they forced even the powerful Apache to retreat into the Southwestern deserts and the sheltering mountains. Their own name for themselves, *numanu*, meant "the people," and their sign for themselves was that of a snake wriggling backward.

The Spanish used the name the Apache and the Utes had given to these fierce horse lords, *Komántcia*. To other Indians, to the Spanish and the Mexicans and *los Tejanos*, and eventually to the Texians, Comanche meant "enemy." When someone other than a Comanche made the snake sign, it meant, "Back up, quick!"

Running Bird. *Gonzaullas Collection, Moody Texas Ranger Memorial Library*

The American colonists and the Comanche met peacefully in some of their early encounters, for the Comanche at first considered the Texians possible allies against the Spanish, whom they had come to hate. But friendly relations didn't last, couldn't last between such dissimilar peoples. As the Texians advanced into the *comanchería* and began to put up civilized barriers in the path of the free sweep of Comanche wanderlust, the newcomers soon found out how true and deadly an enemy the Lords of the Plains could be.

The same condition often held true for the other side of the triangle, as well. Even though some *Tejanos* welcomed the Americans as fellow pioneers, many feared them as the vanguard of a long-threatened avalanche, a cultural invasion from the United States. The racially mixed *Tejano* society, with its altered but still strong Spanish tradition of maintaining the status quo, its more liberal political and racial philosophies, and its Catholic background differed significantly from that of the American emigrants.

Artifacts of the Plains Indians—The beaded vest and belt, the tomahawk pipe, the turquoise handle bowie knife, and the silver flask inlaid with coral and turquoise are typical "trade" items that might have been used by any tribe. The stone implements are pre-Columbian spear and arrow points used by the Plains and mountain tribes before the Spanish brought the horse and iron to the Americas. The metal-tipped arrows, moccasins, and medicine bags were recovered by Frontier Battalion Rangers (1874–1900) from actual battlefields where they fought the Plains Apache, Kiowa, and Comanche.
Photo by Tom Knowles, the *DeGraffenried and Gillett Collections, Texas Ranger Hall of Fame*

Comanche chief Quanah Parker and his wives. *Gonzaullas Collection, Moody Texas Ranger Memorial Library*

Moses Austin planned a colony in Texas that his son, Stephen, later settled.
Texas State Library & Archives Commission

and then Texas broke away from Mexico, many *Tejanos* fought beside the Texians as brothers in the cause of liberty. Some opposed the obliteration of their hard-won cultural identity by taking up arms against Texas. Like Juan Seguín, a hero of the Texas Revolution and leader of an early Texian ranging company, many *Tejanos* would find themselves at odds with the very Republic they'd fought to establish. Either way, it's a sad twist of history that *los Tejanos*, who contributed so much to the traditions and culture of Texas, for a long time lost much of their cultural identity in doing so.

An inevitable collision took place, there in the wild place at the edge of the world where the West began. Three peoples — the Texians, *los Tejanos*, and the Comanche — met in the contest for Texas, a bitter and deadly crossfire. Only one among them could emerge as the victor.

Most of the Anglo colonists came from the southeastern United States; they were a homogenous group, predominantly Protestant in their religious leanings and somewhat racially isolated in the clannish nature they'd inherited from their largely Celtic ancestors. Population pressure and a sense of what would later come to be known as "Manifest Destiny" fueled their desire to expand into new territory. Their strong cultural identity resisted what they considered "foreign" influences.

In interacting with the culturally stable but somewhat stagnant society of *los Tejanos*, the dynamic and adaptable Americans naturally adopted some *Tejano* customs and influences, but these influences could not prevent an inevitable conflict. When an expanding culture meets another, more traditional culture, the more dynamic group will almost invariably absorb or supplant the other. Whatever they learned from *los Tejanos* about living in Texas, the Texians put their own inimitable stamp on it. They remained for the most part culturally distinct.

When Mexico gained its independence from Spain

A Texas Genesis

It was in the early settlement period of the 1820s that an evolution in the character and nature of the American colonists began. At first, before the colonists moved into the plains and came into conflict with the Comanche, their defense was limited to hastily formed, highly temporary forays in response to specific raids by the Karankawas and others. These disorganized and unprepared attempts often ended in disaster. Far from the protection of the Spanish and then the Mexican armies, menaced by bandits, thieves, and Indians, the colonists realized that they would have to adapt or die, even as had *los Tejanos* before them.

That adaptation, the evolution of American colonists into the Texians, took far more than the effort of an individual or of any one group of colonists, but the spark that ignited it came from the mind of a single visionary leader.

Stephen F. Austin, known as the "Father of Texas," was the son of *empresario* Moses Austin. Moses Austin died in 1821, shortly after he'd secured from Spanish Governor Antonio Martinez a colonization land grant

An engraving of Stephen F. Austin, the "Father of Texas."
Texas State Library & Archives Commission

of 200,000 acres in Texas, land on the Colorado and Brazos Rivers on which he planned to settle three hundred families. With earnest good will, the younger Austin threw himself into the task of making his father's vision a reality. He studied Spanish until he became fluent in the language; he made influential friends in Mexico City and learned to navigate the treacherous and convoluted currents of Mexican politics. In the midst of the Mexican Revolution against Imperial Spain, Austin managed to convince the politically unstable elements in the new Mexican government to allow him to continue with his colonization plan. By swearing to restrict emigration to approved colonists who would become Mexican citizens, and by pointing out to the Mexicans that the Anglo colonists would serve as a buffer between the Indians and Mexico, he gained their trust and admiration.

He also exercised his diplomatic abilities among his own colonists to ease their transition into Mexican cit-

izenship. He secured assurances from the Mexican government that the requirement that all colonists convert to Catholicism would be enforced in name only, as long as Protestant activities were observed discretely. In applying Mexican laws and traditions, he sought to find American equivalents — equating the Spanish term *alcalde* with the Anglo "mayor" or "sheriff," for example. He sent detailed reports back to Mexico in literate and fluent Spanish but translated legal pronouncements and public proclamations into English so that his colonists would understand them and feel comfortable with them.

Despite the many adversities it faced, Austin's colony thrived. Other *empresarios* came to look upon Austin as the acknowledged leader of the American colonists in Texas, as did the Mexican authorities. In 1823, the Mexican government appointed him its chief officer in Texas, with the title of Civil Commander. This gave Austin not only the authority but the mandate to raise militias to defend the colonies between the Brazos and the Colorado.

As in the *Tejano* tradition, the civil leaders in each community, the *alcaldes* or mayors, were responsible for forming local civil defense units. By 1824, the colonists had formed militia groups in six districts; most often, the members of such a company chose their officers informally, from within their own ranks.

These groups of citizen soldiers, usually all of the able-bodied men in a settlement, didn't stand as a permanent force. They did train to take the field at a moment's notice to defend their families and farms. Unfortunately, when they went on a campaign or assembled to track down Indian raiders they had to leave their settlements mostly defenseless. Austin had parceled out most of the land grants to married men with families, and only later did he make a provision for single males who could serve longer, more standard military service. Although the militias did perform their duties bravely and to the best of their ability, they could not possibly defend all of the settlers against the highly mobile bands of raiding Indian

THE LONG RIFLES

The primary weapons used by the Texas Rangers and other Texans prior to the advent of the revolver and the metal cartridge were the different versions of the Pennsylvania long rifle. Often called the Kentucky rifle or the Tennessee mountain rifle because it came to Texas with immigrants from those frontier American states, the long rifle was actually designed by the German craftsmen who settled in Pennsylvania. From the template of the hunting rifles used in Europe, Colonial American gun makers created this heavier, longer weapon that was more suited to frontier use. The weapons produced from their designs remained basically the same for over a century.

Spiral grooves, or rifles, cut at a particular twist (usually one complete revolution in four feet) into the barrel of this weapon spun the projectile, thus greatly improving its accuracy. Muzzle-loading rifles used a fabric patch between the powder charge and the ball; the patch not only sealed the charge but gripped the grooves to impart the spin to the bullet. The rifleman had to exert a considerable force to seat the bullet and patch into the grooves, and as powder residue fouled the grooves with each shot the task became more difficult.

During the American Revolution, irregular forces (the most famous of which was Rogers's Rangers) and some regular military rifle companies on each side of the conflict used the greater accuracy of the rifle for long-range fighting and sniping. The legendary effect American riflemen had on British troops was mostly psychological; the majority of the soldiers on both sides used muskets because of their greater rate of fire. While they were far less accurate, smoothbore weapons were much easier and faster to reload. It required a certain amount of skill to properly measure the charge and seat the bullet in a rifle. Military muskets were designed to use premeasured paper cartridges that contained the powder load and the bullet. If troops armed with smoothbores got close enough to a rifle company, they could easily massacre the riflemen while they attempted to reload.

Mexican troops used military muskets similar to the "Brown Bess" supplied to British troops during the American Revolutionary War. In fact, the Mexican government often purchased surplus British weapons and even shortened them into *escopetas* (cavalry carbines). Long muskets were marginally accurate up to about fifty yards, while the carbines were limited to much shorter ranges. By sacrificing accuracy for rate of fire, musketeers could load and fire four to six times as fast as most riflemen. The smooth bore of the *escopeta* allowed the Mexican lancer to insert a charge, seat the load, and fire it without dismounting. To achieve the full effect of the rifle, to reload it, and to fire accurately, the Texan had to dismount.

The Comanche bowman, trained from a young age as a mounted warrior, could fire his bow from over, under, or around his horse while riding at top speed. At combat ranges of fifteen to twenty yards the Comanche could accurately fire six or more arrows in the time it took for a Texan to reload his rifle a single time.

Although the rifle limited the Texan to a slower rate of fire, it was far more accurate and deadly at much greater ranges than the bow or the musket. Pennsylvania rifles could deliver consistently accurate kill shots at ranges of one hundred yards; the best marksmen could hit a man-sized target at two hundred to three hundred yards. When the Texans held discipline and staggered their fire, they could make nearly every shot a kill shot, delivering a devastating and effective response to any attack. If the

Hawken St. Louis Plains Rifle (circa 1840), percussion, in .54 caliber; with hand-decorated leather hunting pouch, brass shell-design powder flask, and Sheffield hunting knife.
Photo by Tom Knowles, Texas Ranger Hall of Fame and Museum

Texans broke discipline and fired all of their weapons at once, musketeers, lancers, or bowmen could move in and finish them off before they could reload.

The original Kentucky rifle's heavy barrel could measure up to forty-six inches in length and up to .45 caliber in bore size. Gunsmiths decorated the Kentucky rifle's polished cherry wood or maple stock with engravings, brass fittings, brass-plated locks, and metal or bone inlays. The Kentucky's stock "dropped" or curved downward behind the lock to meet the rifleman's shoulder at an angle. While similar in basic design, the Tennessee mountain rifle used a shorter stock and a shorter barrel that made it easier to carry on horseback. It usually fired a heavier bullet that proved more suitable for bringing down larger game and for penetrating the buffalo-hide shields of the Plains Indians.

In the 1830s, western gunsmiths altered the basic design to produce the Plains rifle, a simpler, straight-stocked design. It was also known as the St. Louis-style rifle because the first Plains rifles were manufactured in St. Louis, Missouri, the jumping off point for pioneers traveling into the American

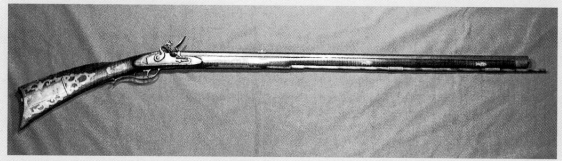

A Hawken half-stock St. Louis Plains rifle, .50 caliber, (1849–62).
Photo by Tom Knowles, Texas Ranger Hall of Fame and Museum

West. The makers of the Plains rifle constructed them for hard service, generally leaving off the decorations used on the earlier styles. Bored to fire bullets up to .58 caliber, a Plains rifle could bring down a buffalo. The well-made Hawken rifle, so named for the gunsmith who first produced it, became the most sought-after of the Plains rifles; many of them made their way to Texas.

The percussion cap, a superior method of igniting a firearm's powder charge, first came into use in the 1820s, but it took time for the new technology to filter out to the frontier. Percussion caps were expensive and difficult to obtain, and frontiersmen were reluctant to deviate from familiar methods. They also believed in using a tool until it wore down to nothing. Rather than discarding a perfectly good flintlock rifle, a Texan would have a gunsmith convert the lock to use percussion caps.

The ranging companies of the 1820s went armed with an assortment of weapons, from Pennsylvania rifles to smoothbore muskets and shotguns. The Rangers of the Republic period, 1836-1845, carried long rifles and Plains rifles, some flintlock and some percussion; after 1839, a few of them used Colt's Paterson revolving rifles. In the Mexican War period, 1846-1848, the Texas Rangers of the Mounted Texas Rifles and other Texas companies carried everything from old flintlocks to caplock military carbines and rifles. Although the Republic and Mexican War era Rangers immediately adapted the Colt's Paterson and Walker revolving pistols to use as their sidearms, they continued to rely on the Pennsylvania and Plains-style rifles up into the Civil War era of the 1860s. Not until the 1870s, when the State of Texas formed the Frontier Battalion of Texas Rangers, would the Rangers adopt new primary long-range weapons — the Sharps single-shot carbine and the Winchester repeating rifle.

warriors. Austin and others began to see that the colonies required something different, a radical departure from their traditional methods of defense.

The Mexican government was not completely indifferent to the problems that the colonists faced, but caught up as it was in constant civil strife, Mexico had neither the funds nor the political will to provide the kind of military force that would do the job. In 1823 Austin, perhaps harkening back to stories he'd heard of Rogers's Rangers, conceived a plan to hire a group of special scouts and pay them out of his own pocket. His original letter probably dates from sometime in 1823, because his handwritten draft appeared on the back of a proclamation made April 4 of that year by the Baron de Bastrop, one of his fellow *empresarios*. In a Spanish-language version of the letter he sent back to the Mexican government for approval, he spoke of his proposed group of irregulars as a *compañía volante*, a flying squadron similar to *La Segunda Compañía Volante de San Carlos de Parras*. In the English version, he spoke of them as "rangers." In his usual diplomatic way, Austin drew upon archetypes from both cultures to explain his idea to each.

His concept was far more than just the sum or a simple amalgamation of the flying squadron's *caballada* principle with Rogers's guerrilla tactics. Perhaps even Austin didn't realize how revolutionary an idea he'd introduced.

Austin proposed that he employ these ten mounted riders as "rangers" on a permanent basis and attach them to Lt. Moses Morrison's militia. As rangers, these men were to act not only as scouts but as a rapid deployment force designed to pursue raiders while at least part of the militia remained behind to protect the settlement. The concept was a radical departure for the colonists — rangers, as Austin saw them, weren't militia or citizen soldiers but professionals dedicated to fighting the enemies of his people.

Perhaps it was *too* radical a concept for the colonists, who were an independent lot and didn't see much use in supporting any kind of standing army or

A drawing depicting a "ranging company" of Texas colonial frontiersmen preparing to set out on a scout.
UT Institute of Texan Cultures at San Antonio/Texas State Library & Archives Commission

police force. Austin's original proposal met with no success in formally recruiting men for this company, so it fell to the individual *alcaldes* and militia commanders of each settlement to muster scouting parties for patrol duty. Even so, it was the first documented use of the word ranger in connection with Texian forces, and Austin didn't abandon the idea — he applied it, without formal approval, as he took an active role in leading successful expeditions against the Karankawas and other Indians in the following two years. He began training elements of the colonists under his command in ranger tactics, detailing small groups of militia as "ranging companies" to screen his volunteer troops and to scout the Indian opposition.

Even though he continued to meet resistance to the idea of establishing a formal ranger organization, Austin's idea did begin to disseminate through the militia forces. Some of them began to detail special units, ranging companies of well-mounted men who could ride out to combat Indian raiders and other lawless elements. The members of these early ranging companies provided their own mounts and equipment, and often rode without pay or support. Some older men joined ranging companies for the time they could afford to be away from their farms and families, then others joined to replace them as they dropped out. Most of these early rangers, even their captains, were young men who could stand the rigors of the wild lands beyond the frontier.

Still, the Texian found himself at a disadvantage when he faced native enemies. The Mexican raider and the Comanche warrior knew the land and fought from horseback and according to their own rules. When confronted with a mounted enemy, the Anglo dismounted and took a defensive position that favored his single-shot rifle. (See "The Long Rifles.") In the time it took him to reload, a Comanche could fire six or more arrows, from under, around, and over a running horse, with deadly accuracy. The Indians would charge to draw fire, and ill befell the party of Texians who fired all their loads at once — they wouldn't have a chance to reload before the Comanche rode in with arrows and lances ready to finish them. For a generation, this disadvantage confined major Anglo settlement to the eastern woodlands in the Nacogdoches region and Austin's colony in the central area.

Despite this disparity in firepower, the early rangers operated far beyond the boundaries of civilization, and so became almost self-contained in their traditions and methods of operation. Over time, they would evolve into as deadly and efficient a mobile paramilitary force as had ever existed. They would study their opponents, the Mexicans to the South and the Indians to the West, would learn from them, and eventually surpass them in technique and ferocity. By the time of the Texas Revolution and the founding Republic, the new nation would formally establish a Texas Rangers force of three companies. Austin would live to see his dream of the Texas Rangers become reality, even as his dream of a peaceful Texas as a state in a democratic Mexican nation fell to ashes and dust.

Before that could happen, before the ranging companies could become the Texas Rangers of Stephen F. Austin's visionary concept, the Texians would have to survive a revolutionary war and come to terms with the challenges of independence. As *Tejanos* and Texians joined to face bandits, raiders, and the growing shadow of the dictatorship that threatened to supplant the fledgling democracy of Mexico, the forge of the West would be readied to test the resolve of the men who called themselves "rangers."

2

AGAINST ALL ODDS

T HE TEXAS RANGERS HAVE A REPUTATION FOR VALOR AND
tenacity in the pursuit of their duties, for the ability to face the dangers and
hardships of their calling without flinching. That tradition endures,
handed down from the earliest ranging companies to the six companies
of today's modern Texas Ranger organization, but it didn't emerge
overnight. It stems from the many sacrifices made by a long line of frontier
warriors who dedicated their lives to the defense of the Lone Star.

Faint echoes of the warrior spirit did reverberate in
the bloodlines of the early Texians. The Anglos
brought with them the grim legacy of their old bor-
derer ancestors, as well as more recent memories of
the American Revolution and the Indian wars of the
East. The blood of Spanish conquistadors and Aztec
warriors ran in the veins of *los Tejanos*. Even so, most
of the American colonists of Stephen F. Austin's time
had no firsthand experience in frontier warfare. Even
the experienced Indian fighters and frontiersmen
among them were ill-prepared to face the kind of challenges they'd meet in Texas, paramount among them
the vast expanse of the land itself.

They had yet to learn the most draconian truth of
frontier warfare: If you couldn't take the fight to your
enemy, if you couldn't make him pay dearly for the

least transgression, you rated as little better than prey
on the food chain. To take the fight to the enemy in
Texas, you had to be well-mounted, well-armed, and
quick to respond. You had to be willing to do whatever
was required to take your enemy at a disadvantage.
Even if it didn't meet the standards of civilized
behavior, you had to be willing to do whatever it took
to win the fight.

The towns and settlements of *los Tejanos* and the
Texians, and even the camps of the Comanche, Kiowa,
and Apache, stood as isolated islands of human civilization in the savage wilderness of Texas. To survive
in a wild place where they'd always be outnumbered
and often alone, the Texians would have to learn to
navigate the physical and moral wilderness that was
Texas. They would be forced to leave certain of the

graces of "civilized" warfare behind them, to become warriors themselves. From that need, in the dark metamorphosis from colonist to warrior, the Texas Rangers were born.

The Tumlinson Legacy

One colonial leader who favored Stephen F. Austin's proposal for ranging companies was John Jackson Tumlinson, the *alcalde* of the Colorado River colony under Austin's authority. While Austin was away in Mexico resecuring his colonial grant from the new government, the nautical and overland supply lines to the colonies broke down because of storms, financial shortfalls, and raids by Indians, outlaws, and deserters. Tumlinson knew that the survival of the colonies depended on reopening those supply lines.

In January 1823, along with another prominent settler, Robert Kuykendall, Tumlinson petitioned Coahuila y Texas Gov. José Trespalacios to assist the colony in setting up a permanent mounted force. Tumlinson received permission and promises of aid from Trespalacios, including support by detachment of regular Mexican troops from San Antonio de Béxar. That summer he enlisted a company of ten men under the command of his militia lieutenant, Moses Morrison. Morrison, influenced by Austin's use of the term in his famous letter of 1823, described his men as a "company of rangers."

With Morrison as major, the company at first scouted the area of the lower Colorado River near Trespalacios Creek for sites where they could construct a series of fortified blockhouses. They found the site on the lower Colorado unsuitable, the timber insufficient to build fortifications; they found no ready supply of fresh water. The company eventually camped at the mouth of the Colorado River, but the promised financial and military support from the Mexican government failed to materialize. To fend off starvation, the men were forced to use up their powder and shot in hunting for food.

In June 1823, after an incident in which bandits plundered the supply depot on the Colorado, John Tumlinson joined Morrison's company at the mouth of the river. Tumlinson and his aide, Joseph Newman, decided to make the trip back to San Antonio in an attempt to secure badly needed ammunition and supplies for the beleaguered company. At the Guadalupe River crossing near the present-day town of Seguin, they ran into a party made up of Spanish deserters and Karankawa and Huaco Indians.

The Karankawa warrior in the lead acted friendly; in any case, the Texians had no ammunition. Despite Newman's warnings against trusting the Indians, Tumlinson reached out to shake one warrior's hand. The Karankawa grasped Tumlinson's wrist, pulled him off his horse, and stabbed him to death.

So it was on July 6, 1823, that John J. Tumlinson, the founder of the first effective company of rangers in the Texian colonies, earned the unfortunate honor of becoming the first member of a ranging company to be killed in action. His companion barely escaped with his life to carry the story of the *alcalde*'s murder back to Austin's colony.

Tumlinson's death also set the stage for a personal feud that his family would carry out for generations. His sons, John J. and young Joe, led a mounted militia force in an attack against a band of Huaco raiders they thought might have been responsible for their father's murder. They caught the raiders at ease in their camp, attacked without warning, and killed all but one of the fourteen Huacos. The man who killed Tumlinson probably wasn't with that particular group of raiders, but the attack did drive home the intended message. In their ride to vengeance, the Tumlinsons and their foes had learned a valuable lesson — an ambush can cut both ways.

Kuykendall and Morrison continued to run patrols with ranging companies whenever possible. In their mission reports to San Antonio, they asked to be resupplied and relocated farther north on the Colorado. They included detailed descriptions of predatory raids by increasingly hostile Indians. Despite the lack of support, they stayed active and attempted to fulfill their mission to the best of their ability. They retired from the field only when Austin returned from his trip to Mexico and ordered them to do so.

John Tumlinson's legacy to Texas reached far deeper than just his death in her service or his participation in founding the early ranging companies. His oldest son, John J. Tumlinson, served in the Texas Revolution and later as captain of the first formally recognized Texas Ranger company. Members of the Tumlinson family and their descendants served Texas as soldiers and peace officers up through the 1950s. At one time or another during that period, sixteen of John Jackson Tumlinson's direct descendants held commissions as Texas Rangers.

The warrior spirit of Texas took root in the hearts of the Tumlinsons and of those who followed them; there it would flourish.

Austin's Dilemma

Upon his return from his diplomatic mission to Mexico in August 1823, Austin immediately began working to secure the supply lines for his colonies, to provide for their defense until the expected military support could arrive from Mexico. In 1824, he led a campaign against the Karankawa, who had been devastated even more by imported disease than by military action, forcing the remnants of the tribe to sign a peace treaty. He was also able to raise larger militia forces as the population of the Texian colonies increased. He began training some of those militia members to conduct ranging operations to scout for militia forces and to provide some protection along the major supply routes.

Unfortunately, even after the men of Morrison's company proved their effectiveness in the field, and despite the obvious need for an established defense, Austin couldn't persuade his colonists to support a regular ranger force. Usually no more than eight to ten men in strength, the volunteer companies faced the impossible task of patrolling and defending an ill-defined and seemingly endless frontier.

The promised military support from Mexico didn't materialize. Instead, as the Anglo settlements increased in size, strength, and prosperity, officials of the Mexican government began to reconsider their decision to allow American colonists to settle in Texas. The growing predominance of Anglos alarmed conservative elements in Mexico who feared that the Americans might use a secessionist rebellion to allow the United States to annex the territory.

The great majority of Texians and *Tejanos* remained firmly committed to the idea of Texas as a Mexican province, but they resented the government's general indifference toward Texas, as well as its policy of lumping Texas in as part of the province of Coahuila. Those who volunteered for militia service expected the government to eventually take up the burden of frontier defense. They most often found themselves and their expectations derided or ignored, or even worse, interpreted as traitorous criticism of the government.

The man with the vision of a peaceful, progressive Texas, Stephen F. Austin, stood directly in the path of an approaching social and political revolution. He persisted in promoting the concept of a regular ranger force for frontier defense, despite the reluctance of the colonists to fund or otherwise support it. He continually exerted his considerable diplomatic skills to smooth out the political and cultural difficulties between the Texians, *los Tejanos*, the Indians, and an increasingly fragmented but authoritarian Mexican government.

There was only so much one man could do. The break with Mexico was inevitable. When war came, the experienced warriors of Austin's volunteer ranging companies would play a major role in the struggle for Texas independence.

The Seeds of Revolt

The Mexican Federalist Party modeled itself on Jeffersonian ideals and supported the democratic spirit of the Mexican Constitution of 1824, which was modeled on that of the United States. The Centralist Party favored a more European, autocratic approach to government. The power struggle and eventual civil war between these factions left Texas in a political limbo for years. At the same time, it also left the colonists free to conduct their day-to-day affairs untroubled by governmental interference.

When the Mexican government did finally act to extend its influence into Texas, it did so with the heavy and unwelcome hand of Centralist authoritarianism. President Anastasio Bustamante's government enacted on April 6, 1830, a series of edicts that banned further immigration by Americans into Texas and seriously restricted vital trade with the United States. Instead of providing support for defense against the Indians, the Mexican military established a series of garrisons to enforce the 1830 edicts and other laws that the Texians and *Tejanos* had long ignored. These garrison troops were mostly convicts, the barracks sweepings of the Mexican Army. The often arrogant and incompetent behavior of the officials charged with enforcing the edicts further interfered with the growing commerce and development of the colony. This led to several armed conflicts between Texian colonists and Mexican officials.

At a convention of landowners led by Austin in 1832, the delegates proposed resolutions to overturn the trade restrictions of the 1830 edicts, to bolster the militia companies, and to establish new ranging companies to protect the frontier. Because they couldn't agree on a course of action, most of their efforts failed to accomplish any actual results.

They did agree to send a message of support to the Mexican general who was fighting a civil war to wrest control of the government from Bustamante. The man upon whom the Texians pinned their hopes for preserving the Mexican democracy did have a fine military record, even if he did have a few personality quirks: an indulgence in opium; a weakness for a pretty face; a somewhat inflated ego; a severe phobia about river crossings. Christened as the "hero of Tampico" after his troops repulsed the 1829 Spanish

A painting of Gen. Antonio López de Santa Anna based on a circa 1850 daguerreotype. This portrait comes from Albert Ramsey's *The Other Side: or Notes for the History of the War Between Mexico and the United States.*
UT Institute of Texan Cultures at San Antonio

attempt to overthrow the revolutionary government, he preferred his self-conferred title of "the Napoleon of the West." He was none other than Don Antonio López de Santa Anna, the man who would eventually destroy the young Mexican democracy and would force the Texians into revolt. For more than a decade, he would exert a malignant influence on relations between Texas and Mexico.

The Texians celebrated in 1833 when news came to them of Santa Anna's victory over Bustamante, and they sent out a call to convene a new provincial convention. They decided to send the new leader of Mexico a petition lobbying for full-fledged Texas statehood, separate from Coahuila. Despite his failing health, the delegates chose Stephen F. Austin to deliver the message to Mexico City.

Even as an ill and weary Austin arrived in the capital city, Santa Anna used the confusion of civil strife to destroy his last Centralist enemies and his former Federalist supporters as well, thus securing his position as the virtual ruler of Mexico. Austin eventually got his meeting with Santa Anna. The persuasive *empresario* did win from him a promise to loosen the restrictions of the 1830 edicts and earlier regulations, but the general refused to consider a change in provincial status for Texas. Then, an unwise letter Austin had sent to friends in San Antonio when he had despaired of gaining an audience made its way back to Santa Anna. Santa Anna had Austin intercepted and arrested at the provincial capital of Saltillo, then brought back in chains to Mexico City.

Austin's arrest and imprisonment marked a major turning point in the fortunes of the *empresario*, and of Texas and Mexico as well. For two years, Austin languished in a Mexican prison as Santa Anna suborned the constitutional authority of the democratic government. Austin's imprisonment ruined his health, hastened his death, and left radical elements in charge of the colonies. It deprived Texas of the only statesman who might possibly have been capable of averting a civil war. Indeed, his unjust imprisonment converted the former peacemaker into a revolutionary. It convinced him that Santa Anna, once hailed as a hero of the Mexican Republic, was not only a bloody-handed tyrant but a deadly enemy to all Austin held dear.

Rangers, Rogues, and Revolutionaries

Austin's imprisonment in Mexico from 1833 to 1835 did cause some unrest in the colonies but occasioned no outright break with Mexico. Cholera and malaria epidemics swept through the settlements, drawing much of the colonists' attention from the growing strife with officials of Santa Anna's new regime. Indians and bandits grew bolder; their increasingly destructive raids diverted the militia and ranging companies to frontier duty.

Texas patriot James Bowie was one of the most famous of the Alamo's defenders. *Texas State Library & Archives Commission*

The epidemics took the lives of many prominent Texians and *Tejanos*; among the dead was Mariá Ursula de Veramendi, a daughter of the most prominent family of Coahuila y Texas. Her death, and that of their children, left her husband, famed duelist James Bowie, at loose ends. He found solace in drinking with Sam Houston, who had recently arrived in Texas. Houston, a hero of the Creek Indian War, the protégé of President Andrew Jackson, and a former rising star in American politics, had resigned from his office as Speaker of the Tennessee Senate in the wake of a disastrous marriage and the subsequent public scandal. Fleeing from the wreckage of his political career, he went to live in Arkansas with his adoptive Cherokee father, Chief John Bowles. Houston spent several months living in the bottle; the Cherokee nicknamed him "the flowing bowl." When his friends in Texas wrote to him to suggest he join them, the prospect of a new land to conquer, a new adventure, overcame his despair.

Bowie and Houston would soon find themselves at the center of a storm in which their inner torments would drive them to their separate but glorious destinies — Houston to victory over Santa Anna at San Jacinto and to the presidency of the new Republic of Texas, Bowie to victory in death at the fall of the Alamo.

Sam Houston won independence for Texas at the Battle of San Jacinto and served as the new republic's first president.
Gregory's Old Master Gallery

All of the people of the colonies, Texians and *Tejanos*, newcomers and first colonists alike, would soon find themselves caught between two prairie fires, one burning up from the South and one in from the West. In doing so, they would begin to rely on those men who had the experience to lead them. Some, like Bowie and Houston, had gained that experience in other conflicts. Some, like Juan N. Seguín, Erastus "Deaf" Smith, Henry Wax Karnes, and John Tumlinson, had grown accustomed to frontier service with colonial ranging companies. After the Texas Revolution, many of them would serve as the architects and commanders of the new Republic's Texas Ranger companies.

When the Texian leaders met at San Felipe de Austin to consider a protest to new trade restrictions, they intercepted a courier who carried orders from Santa Anna's brother-in-law, Gen. Martín Perfecto de Cós, to the *alcalde* of San Felipe. From those papers, they learned that Cós was marching to take Béxar. Santa Anna was already campaigning to crush the liberal government of the Central Mexican province of Zacatecas and intended to suspend the civil government of Coahuila y Texas. He planned next to lead a

massive force of Mexican regulars into Texas, there to put down what he considered a potential revolution.

All across Texas that fall season of 1835, men began to finish up their harvests, to clean and oil their guns, and to pack up supplies in preparation for war. They drifted in increasing numbers toward Gonzales, the center of the growing conflict, for a showdown with General Cós and his regulars.

Stephen F. Austin, the great peacemaker and diplomat, was released via a general amnesty and quietly returned to Texas in September. When he spoke at a convention convened by the War Party on October 15, the radicals might have expected him to promote compromise. Instead, the embittered Austin counseled them to prepare for "war in full" against Santa Anna, to whom he referred as "a base, unprincipled bloody monster."

The shooting war was already in progress. The first true battle of the Revolution took place on October 2, when the Mexican commander at San Antonio, Gen. Domingo de Ugartechea, sent a detachment of one hundred dragoons to confiscate a small brass cannon from the colonists. A gift to the colonists made by the Mexican government in 1831, the cannon

Andrew Jackson served as President of the United States during Texas's fight for independence from Mexico.
Metropolitan Museum of Art

was practically useless. It served mostly as a catalyst for Texian rebellion. The volunteers rallied around the cannon at Gonzales, raising a banner that read, COME AND TAKE IT!

One hundred sixty Texians and *Tejanos* armed with long rifles met the dragoons, defeated them, and sent them running back to San Antonio, just as some of their ancestors had sent British troops reeling back at Lexington and Concord. Even as the politicians debated at the convention, the Revolution had begun. Texas would need all of her warriors, revolutionaries, rogues, and rangers, to survive the storm.

The First Companies of Texas Rangers

Volunteers poured into Gonzales as the Texian leaders met in San Felipe de Austin to create a new civil government. This provisional government directed its first efforts to organizing the army against Santa Anna's promised sweep through Texas. Even as they prepared for war, the Texians also turned their attention to the problem of the frontier. With most of the men pulled away to join the revolutionary army, their farms, families, and homes lay vulnerable to raiders. When the Texian leaders realized that they needed a separate force to defend the frontier against the Indians, they turned to Austin's original scheme for organizing and funding ranging companies.

For the first time in the history of the colonies, a recognized legislative body followed Austin's plan — they authorized financing for the frontier defense force and set standards for service. Even as the first battles of the Revolution took place, the provisional government fashioned the laws that would reshape the old colonial ranging companies into the Texas Rangers.

To trace this legal genesis of the Texas Ranger service, it's best to step for a moment outside the direct timeline of Revolutionary events:

On October 17, 1835, the provisional legislature agreed on the first resolution: Silas M. Parker

---

THE BRIGADIER GENERAL

MARTIN PERFECTO DE COS,

Commanding General and Inspector of the Eastern Internal States.

IN THE NAME OF THE PRESIDENT OF THE REPUBLIC:

I MAKE it known to all and every one of the inhabitants of the three departments of Texas, that whenever, under any pretext whatsoever, or through a badly conceived zeal in favor of the individuals who have acted as authorities in the state, and have been deposed by the resolution of the Sovereign General Congress, any should attempt to disturb the public order and peace, that the inevitable consequences of the war will bear upon them and their property, inasmuch as they do not wish to improve the advantages afforded them by their situation, which places them beyond the uncertainties that have agitated the people of the centre of the Republic.

If the Mexican Government has cheerfully lavished upon the new settlers all its worthiness of regard, it will likewise know how to repress with strong arm all those who, forgetting their duties to the nation which has adopted them as her children, are pushing forward with a desire to live at their own option without any subjection to the laws. Wishing, therefore, to avoid the confusion which would result from the excitement of some bad citizens, I make the present declaracion, with the resolution of sustaining it.

Matamoros, July 5, 1835.

Martín Perfecto de Cós.

This circular, written by Mexican Gen. Martín Perfecto de Cós, warned Texans against revolutionary activities. It was issued July 5, 1835, from Matamoros. *UT Institute of Texan Cultures at San Antonio*

would recruit twenty-five men to cover the area between the Trinity and Brazos Rivers, D. B. Fryar would recruit thirty-five men to patrol between the Brazos and the Colorado Rivers, and Garrison Greenwood would supervise a company of ten men along the east side of the Trinity River. By November the frontier patrol line extended all the way from the Colorado River to the Cibolo River. Ten more men joined Parker's recruits, and George Washington Davis mustered in a new company of twenty men for service.

These men selected to recruit the Texas Rangers — Parker, Fryar, Greenwood, and Davis — were influential settlers and respected community leaders. As supervisors, they didn't command the forces directly; they recruited men, mustered them in, assisted them in securing supplies, and managed general operations and finances. The members of the new companies elected their own officers from among their ranks, carrying on the tradition that began with the ranging companies.

In a subsequent ordinance drafted on November 24, 1835, the military charter set forth formal rules to "establish and organize a Corps of Rangers," to organize the men recruited under the original resolution into a manageable unit. With a major as their overall commander, the Ranger Corps grouped into three companies of fifty-six men, each company commanded by a captain and his lieutenants. Rather than the regular military enlistment period of two years, Rangers signed up for one-year terms.

Even though these resolutions specified that the Rangers serve as guardians against frontier raiders, not in combat along with the regular armed forces, they did direct the Rangers to draw their weapons, munitions, and other supplies from the military stores at Washington-on-the-Brazos. The Texas Ranger force operated under the same military code as the regular army. The Ranger Corps made up a battalion force when combined under its overall commander, and it used military rather than police

rankings for officers and men. The Texian leaders intended it to serve a flexible paramilitary purpose, not only for frontier defense but as an emergency military support unit. Many of the men recruited for Texas Ranger duty did eventually end up in the fight for independence.

These resolutions also set the standard for Texas Ranger service in the century that would follow. They required each man to provide for himself a good horse and "suitable weapons," which eventually came to mean a rifle or a shotgun (or both), a brace (or more) of pistols, and a good knife. If a Ranger couldn't provide his own horse and equipment, his commander could provide them and deduct the cost from the Ranger's pay. Of course, that assumed that the Ranger got paid. Although the terms of Ranger enlistment specified a daily wage of a dollar and a quarter for a private and higher pay for officers, these first formally regulated Rangers, as would many who would follow them, often went unpaid and poorly supplied.

Although the 1820s colonial companies organized by Austin, Seguín, and others were historically the first "rangers" of Texas, the three-company battalion created in the resolutions of 1835 was the first formally approved, regular "Texas Ranger" service. Experience in the earlier ranging companies prepared some of the new Rangers for what they would face. When they picked their officers, John J. Tumlinson, the oldest son of the slain *alcalde* of the Colorado colony, took command of one of the companies as its captain. The other companies elected William A. Arrington and Isaac Burton as captains; Robert McAlpin Williamson (see "Three-Legged Willie") served as the commanding major for the entire battalion.

Finally, Austin's long-denied vision of a recognized, organized corps of frontier defenders for Texas had become a reality. With war against Santa Anna imminent, the survival of the Texian colonies and the fate of the new companies of Texas Rangers remained much in doubt.

THREE-LEGGED WILLIE

s Texas Ranger John S. Ford said of Robert McAlpin Williamson, "He did more than any one man to nerve out people to strike for liberty." One of the first to stand against official oppression and Santa Anna's tyranny, on July 4, 1835, he delivered the Texas equivalent of Patrick Henry's "Liberty or Death" speech to the convention at San Felipe. Even before Texas won her independence, his fellows chose him to lead the first official battalion of Texas Rangers.

Williamson assisted his friend and mentor, Stephen F. Austin, in setting up safety patrols for the San Felipe de Austin colony. He served at different times as the settlement's prosecuting attorney, *sindico procurador* (city attorney), and *alcalde*; won election as one of the first district judges to the Texas National Supreme Court and as one of the first Texas legislators in the United States Congress. As the major of the Texas Rangers he led his men in battle against the Comanche; as a Texas patriot he participated in the Battle of Béxar and the Battle of San Jacinto.

He was a literate, educated Southern gentleman and an astute judge of human nature, a man of the finest sensibilities, highest political acumen, and ultimate dignity. And yet, his best friends among the Texians who made up the rough society of frontiersmen in San Felipe de Austin nicknamed him "Three-Legged Willie." He took to the appellation with good humor, recognizing it as a sign of respect rather than of derision.

A painting of Judge Robert McAlpin Williamson, known as "Three-Legged Willie," the first major commanding the Texas Rangers in 1836. This painting by Duncan Robinson hangs in the Texas State Capitol.
UT Institute of Texan Cultures at San Antonio

Born in 1804 to an influential Georgia family, Williamson was abandoned by his footloose, many-times-wed father and brought up by his grandmother, Sarah. His other family ties made him a natural future politician and citizen of Texas — he was a direct cousin of Mirebeau B. Lamar and a distant cousin to Sam Houston.

At age fifteen, young Robert suffered an attack of "white swelling," likely a form of infantile paralysis caused by an infection, so acute that he was confined to his bed for months. The lower half of his right leg drew up at the knee and remained useless to him for the rest of his life. When he walked again, it was with the aid of crutches and a wooden peg leg fastened to his knee. Never willing to allow any obstacle to stand in his way, he set a strenuous pace for his own physical rehabilitation and eventually did away with his need for crutches.

David G. Burnet, president under the provisional government of Texas during the War of Independence, later vice-president under Mirabeau B. Lamar and secretary of state following annexation by the U.S. This photo comes from Lewis Daniell's *Personnel of the Texas State Government.* *UT Institute of Texan Cultures at San Antonio*

As a young lawyer he made his mark in the Georgia capitol, but in 1825 he suddenly gave up his practice and began to drift west, first to Alabama, then to New Orleans, and eventually to Texas. There were rumors that he'd "gone to Texas" because he'd killed his rival in a duel for the affections of a certain Georgia belle, who had then in turn spurned him for another. When Williamson arrived in San Felipe de Austin in June 1827, the first building he saw on the edge of the frontier settlement was Noah Smithwick's blacksmith shop. On the steps of the *Texas Gazette*, he met Stephen F. Austin.

Smithwick and Austin were only the first of many friends he made in Texas; in that rough pioneer society, Williamson formed lifelong friendships with many of the present and future leaders of Texas, including W. A. A. "Bigfoot" Wallace, William Barret Travis, Francis W. Johnson, and David G. Burnet, who would become the first president of the Republic of Texas.

As the commander of the Texas Rangers in 1835, Williamson wasn't required to stay in the field with his men, but he did. He had a good eye for a fast horse, as did the Indians whom he fought. Once, when a larger party of Comanche set to ambush Williamson and his detail of six Rangers to get their horses, the major set up an ambush of his own. When they camped for the night, he had his men build up a big campfire, then had them roll up their bedrolls around logs. The Rangers slipped out to hide in the brush, their rifles at the ready.

The Comanche warriors moved quietly into the camp, then stood up and with a fierce war cry plunged their knives into the slumbering forms. The Rangers opened fire; not a single warrior escaped with his life. Later, Williamson said that of the many battles he'd had with Indians, this one had the most satisfactory conclusion.

"He was a man of wonderful powers, an able and finished orator," wrote later Ranger leader John S. Ford of Williamson after his death. Indeed, Williamson's famous July Fourth speech to the convention at San Felipe closed with the words, "Liberty or Death should be our determination...." They were the words by which "Three-Legged Willie" lived, and they fired the determination of the Texians as had no other previous words.

When the retired Judge Williamson lay dying of a fever in the fall of 1859, in his delirium his mind turned back to the young adventurer he'd been. "Hark!" he called to his Texas Rangers, "to the right boys — quick to the right! Who follows? Now, come on!"

The Future in Question

Even as they moved to create the Texas Army and to recruit a new frontier defense force, the delegates to the convention in San Felipe debated the question of declaring independence versus remaining a Mexican state. Few of the delegates questioned the certainty that Texas would be forced to fight Santa Anna, either way. While Austin traveled to the United States to recruit volunteers and solicit funds for the war effort, Sam Houston took command of the armed forces. The provisional state legislature elected Henry Smith as governor.

In this daguerreotype, Sam Houston wears a cowboy duster.
Texas State Library & Archives Commission

mand of the most important gateway into Texas, Santa Anna would have an open road for invasion come that spring.

Ben Milam, a former Kentuckian who'd had his share of Indian fights and adventures in Texas even before Austin had founded his colonies, considered the situation even more appalling than did Burleson. His Republican views had once before earned him time in a Mexican jail, so he wasn't anxious to give Santa Anna a second chance to imprison him. He stepped out before the Texian volunteers, drew a line in the dust and called out, "Who will go with old Ben Milam into San Antonio?" (See "Ben Milam.")

The volunteers answered his call. Among them were Juan N. Seguín and the men of his ranging company, including Pedro Herrera, a former private from the *Alamo de Parras* flying company.

The bitter and bloody Battle of Béxar began on the morning of December 5, 1835, when Milam and

While the Texians debated the question of independence, the war continued to escalate. On October 27, a party of Texians under James Bowie soundly defeated a troop of Mexican cavalry near San Antonio de Béxar and captured several artillery pieces. Bowie's chief scout was a young Tennesseean, Noah Smithwick, who would later join the first authorized Texas Ranger company. General Cós took the city and reinforced the garrison at the Alamo with his 1,400 veteran regular troops. The Texians laid siege to the city, but Bowie wasn't so foolish as to attempt to roust Cós from such a strong position.

By late November the siege began to break down. Gen. Edward Burleson, an experienced veteran of the Indian wars in the East, found himself in command of a ragtag troop of Texian volunteers who mostly wanted to return home to get ready for spring planting. Burleson knew that if Cós remained in com-

1850 daguerreotype portrait of Gen. Edward Burleson, Sr.
Texas State Library & Archives Commission

"BEN MILAM"

It was four to one, not gun for gun, but never a curse cared we,

Three hundred faithful and fearless men who had sworn to make Texas free.

It was mighty odds, by all the gods, this brood of the Mexique dam,

But it was not much for heroes such as followed old Ben Milam!

With rifle-crack and saber-hack we drove them back in the streets;

From house to house in the red carouse we hastened their flying feet;

And ever that shout kept pealing out with the swift and sure death-blow;

"Oh, who will follow old Ben Milam into San Antonio!"

Behind the walls from the hurtling balls Cós cowered and swore in his beard,

While we slashed and slew from dawn till dew, and Béxar, how we cheered!

But ere failed each ruse, and the white flag of truce of the failing day was thrown,

Our fearless soul had gone to the goal in the land of the Great Unknown.

Death brought the darksome boon too soon to this truest one of the true,

Or men of the fated Alamo, Milam had died with you!

So when their names that now are Fame's — the scorner of braggart Sham —

In song be praised, let a rouse be raised for the name of Ben Milam!

A painting of Ben Milam, who was killed leading the Texians in the Battle of Béxar. *Texas State Library & Archives*

Francis W. Johnson led three hundred Texian and *Tejano* volunteers into the city of San Antonio. Milam's Texians, outnumbered more than four to one, assaulted the Mexicans with such ferocity that even Cós's hardened troops gave way before them. The battle lasted for five days as the colonials fought the Mexicans from house to house, rooftop to rooftop. They took possession of the central Military Plaza, the De La Garza house, and the Veramendi mansion,

home of Bowie's late wife's family. From these strong points they advanced steadily under heavy artillery bombardment and musket fire, pushing Cós's troops back toward the Alamo.

When a bullet to the head killed Milam during the third day of the battle, Johnson took command and led the vengeance-minded volunteers in a final push. As the colonials shelled the walls of the Alamo, even Cós's best officers began to desert him. On the fifth day of the battle, he raised the white flag to surrender his command.

Their victory against so strong a force of regulars, a battle so hard-fought and won at the cost of their gallant commander's life, had united the patriotic *Tejanos* and Texians as no previous event could have done. They had walked together, as brothers, through the fire. It had burned away their differences, at least for the time, and had made them one people — Texans.

Most of the Texans believed that they had fought the decisive battle there at Béxar, that their victory against Cós would force Santa Anna to back down. Reluctant to break completely with Mexico and the Constitution of 1824, to which they had sworn loyalty, the Texans didn't execute Cós on the spot. General Burleson gave Cós and his troops parole on the condition that they swear to uphold the Constitution and never again bear arms against Texas, then he gave them safe escort back across the Rio Grande.

Burleson's volunteers celebrated their victory and dispersed to their farms to prepare for the spring planting. Only a few men remained under arms, and the most adventurous of those went to the western frontier to join the newly formed Texas Ranger force.

Their victory celebrations were premature. To the south, Santa Anna prepared to invade Texas with an army he'd looted the Mexican national treasury to build. The "Napoleon of the West" rode at the head of a force of 6,000 well-disciplined soldiers and skilled mercenaries, freshly blooded from destroying Federalist resistance forces in the Zacatecas province. Even though his ego had bloated on his victories, Santa Anna was almost as good a military leader as he thought himself to be.

Knowing that Santa Anna would take great personal insult from his brother-in-law's defeat at Béxar, Sam Houston pleaded with the colonial leaders to prepare for war. For the most part, they didn't listen to him.

A Meeting of Warriors

Before he returned to Bastrop in the Colorado River country to join one of the new Texas Ranger companies, John J. Tumlinson had served with distinction in the 1835 battles around San Antonio de Béxar. He'd held the rank of lieutenant in those battles, but his men had begun to call him "captain" because their commander, Capt. John A. Coleman, had fallen ill and was unable to lead during most of the fighting. Tumlinson had served in a ranging company under Coleman before, during a summer 1835 expedition against the Tawokoni in the north. His reputation as an Indian fighter and his service at Béxar influenced the men of his Ranger company to elect him as captain.

Young Noah Smithwick, who had fought alongside Bowie in the battles around Béxar, had taken ill and had returned to Bastrop to convalesce. He missed out on the assault on San Antonio, but he did get to meet with the famous frontiersman, David Crockett, who was on his way to join the Texan forces at Béxar. Crockett suggested Smithwick remain at Bastrop until

David Crockett, a frontier scout and U.S. Congressman, was killed defending the Alamo.
Dictionary of American Portraits

he was well, then join another party of volunteers headed to Béxar.

The opportunity never presented itself. As an old man, Smithwick detailed his personal experiences in an excellent reminiscence, *The Evolution of a State*, and of his youthful disappointment at being too ill to travel with Crockett, he wrote, "I cursed my ill-luck, though it was doubtless fortunate for me, as otherwise I should probably have been with some of the parties who were exterminated the following spring." Instead of ending up at Goliad or the Alamo, Smithwick took Crockett's advice and stayed in Bastrop. After he recuperated from his illness, he joined Tumlinson's Texas Ranger Company as a private.

In January 1836, Tumlinson's company of sixty Rangers prepared to ride from Bastrop. Their mission was to set up a base camp at the head of Brushy Creek, about thirty miles north of the present location of Austin, from which point they could patrol the frontier. Even as the Rangers moved out, they stumbled on their first indication of a Comanche incursion; rather, it stumbled upon them. A young woman, bleeding from thorn wounds through her tattered clothing, fell exhausted into their camp at Hornsby's Station.

Sarah Hibbons gasped out her frightful story to the gathered Rangers. She had escaped from a raiding party that had attacked her group while they were traveling toward their homestead on the Guadalupe River. They'd killed her husband and her brother and had taken her and her two small children captive. The Indians, irritated by the infant's crying, had casually killed the child, "dashed its brains out against a tree," according to Smithwick. They had tied her three-year-old son on a mule during the day and tied him up beside her at night, figuring that she wouldn't leave him.

Mrs. Hibbons had reasoned that her only chance to save her son was to get help, and to do that she had to make an agonizing choice. She had waited for her chance, and as the warriors had grown careless, she had slipped away in the night. She had made her way through the thickets along the Colorado River until she had come upon some grazing dairy cattle, then had waited until evening to follow them to the Station.

It was the kind of tragic story that would become all too familiar to the Texans in the following years. An otherwise vigorous and dynamic people, through some accident of genetic drift the Comanche suffered from a low birth rate and an infant mortality rate unusually high even among Plains Indian tribes. They raided other tribes and took what they needed to keep their people strong. Other than horses and weapons, raiders most often took women of childbearing age and children old enough to survive but young enough to be retrained in the Comanche way.

Male children taken captive often grew up to win honors as warriors among the Comanche. Some captors treated "adopted" women and female children with compassion and honor, at least according to the harsh standards of Comanche life. Other captives, such as the Hibbons infant, weren't so lucky; some Comanche used captives as slaves and cruelly tortured them. In the highly individualistic structure of Comanche society, the decision between compassion and cruelty depended upon the whim of the captor.

The determined, resilient Mrs. Hibbons was a poor choice of captives. That particular Comanche band had chosen the wrong people to attack, at the wrong place, and at the wrong time.

Captain Tumlinson figured from Sarah Hibbons's description that he'd be dealing with the Comanche. The company ate a hasty meal, then rode out until they cut the raiding party's tracks. A sudden cold norther blew in, so the Rangers camped to wait for daylight so they wouldn't lose the trail. The next morning they surprised the Indians still in their camp, which Smithwick described as being at a point sheltered by a cedar break "on Walnut Creek, about ten miles northwest of Austin." Not expecting anyone to have so quickly cut their trail, most of the raiders lay sheltered against the cold in their buffalo robes, half asleep.

The Rangers fired their rifles into the camp. Taken by surprise and cut off from their horses, the Indians grabbed for their weapons and ran for cover instead of making a concerted effort to fight back. This gave the Rangers the chance to reload their rifles and pursue immediately, breaking the fight up into individual combats and keeping the Indians from gathering to use their arrows to full effect. As the Comanche warriors scattered into the surrounding cedar thicket, the warriors of Texas charged in among them.

Noah Smithwick got there first. A Comanche fired a rifle at him but missed; Smithwick dismounted and fired, dropping the warrior to the ground. The Comanche wasn't finished; he took aim at Captain Tumlinson and barely missed him. The bullet punctured the captain's coat and knocked his horse out from under him. Conrad Rohrer wrestled the wounded warrior's empty rifle away from him and crushed his skull with the butt. He stopped to scalp the Comanche, taking a gory memento that he would later present to Smithwick in recognition of his shot.

Reloading as he ran, Smithwick pursued the Indians into the cedar thicket, where he lost his hat to a limb. He almost lost his head when one of his comrades, seeing him bareheaded, mistook him for an Indian and took aim at him, but another Ranger knocked the rifle aside. The newly recruited Rangers were no doubt confused and exhilarated at the same time, both terrified and sanguine at the prospect of taking the fight to the enemy. To the Comanche, far more used to ambushing than being ambushed, the Rangers' sudden attack must have come as quite a shock. They fled, leaving the battlefield, their plundered goods and horses, their dead, and the captive child in the possession of the victorious Rangers.

The excitement of the moment caused Rohrer to lose his judgment, momentarily. Seeing a figure mounted on a mule and swathed in a buffalo robe, he rode up, pressed his rifle against the figure's back, and pulled the trigger. The rifle providentially misfired twice, and another Ranger, a bit more perceptive, pushed the weapon aside even as it fired on the third attempt. The robe concealed the Hibbons boy, the object of the rescue.

Tumlinson's company returned to Hornsby's Station in possession of the rescued child and almost all of the Comanche plunder and horses. Tied to Smithwick's saddle, the scalp Rohrer had taken served as a rather grisly proof of the Rangers' ability to take the fight to the enemy. The warriors of Texas had counted coup against the Comanche, and they had returned to their own lodges with not a man lost in the battle.

Smithwick said of the reunion between Sarah Hibbons and her son, "There was a suspicious moisture in many an eye long since a stranger to tears, when the overjoyed mother clasped her only remaining treasure to her heart...." It was not the last time that the Texas Rangers would return a kidnapped child safely into the arms of a grateful parent, but the Rangers wouldn't always succeed in such a mission without taking losses of their own.

Tumlinson's Rangers didn't realize that they'd won only the first battle in a bitter conflict that would rage between the Texas Rangers and the Comanche for another forty years. In high spirits, they headed out once more to build their blockhouse on Brushy Creek, out on the western frontier. They wouldn't stay there for long. By the time news of the massacre of the Texans at the Alamo reached Tumlinson's company and Sam Houston recalled the Rangers to duty in the south, the people of Texas would be in full retreat from Santa Anna's advancing army.

A Defender's Oath

Historians have written much about the Texas Revolution, about the fall of the Alamo on March 6, 1836, and the massacre of James Fannin's men from Goliad by Colonel Portilla on March 27, about the Runaway Scrape and the Texas victory at San Jacinto on April 21. Few histories of the Revolution mention the Texas Rangers because the Ranger companies didn't participate as a unit in the fight against Santa Anna's invading army.

A painting of Col. William Barret Travis, the commander of the Alamo. *Texas State Library & Archives Commission*

That is an oversight in that it ignores detail in favor of the overall picture. The individual members of the new Texas Ranger companies — the men who would serve as the Rangers of the Lone Star Republic — and the experienced men of the colonial ranging companies played a major role in the fight for independence. The Texas Army, little more than a ragged band of volunteers made up of Texian and *Tejano* patriots and new immigrants from the United States, eventually overcame Santa Anna's forces using the kind of tactics the fighting men of Texas had employed since the days of the *compañías volantes*. From the Battle of Béxar in December 1835 to the taking of three Mexican supply vessels by Isaac Burton's company at Copano Bay in June 1836, the warrior spirit of the Texas Rangers touched every battlefield of the Texas Revolution.

The first report of the arrival of Santa Anna's force at Béxar and the beginning of the siege at the Alamo, dated February 25, 1836, came from Maj. Robert M.

Williamson, the commander of the Texas Rangers. Upon receiving the news, the newly appointed general of the Texas forces, Sam Houston, ordered Col. William Barret Travis to destroy the arms stockpile at the Alamo and withdraw.

Travis refused Houston's order to withdraw from the Alamo, and in doing so set into motion one of the most controversial and mythologized military defenses in history. It is certain that after they heard Santa Anna's musicians play the opening strains of the *Deguello*, the anthem of "no quarter," Travis and the defenders of the Alamo must have known that their defense of the old mission would cost them their lives. They could have escaped earlier but chose not to do so. On March 3, Travis sent a dispatch to the members of the constitutional convention at Washington-on-the-Brazos. He ended it with the salutation, "God and Texas — Victory or Death!"

For the thirteen days of the siege, their challenge commanded the vainglorious Santa Anna's attention, effectively blocking his advance into Texas. Their long rifles held enemy forces at bay until March 6, when the Mexicans moved up artillery that could strike from beyond rifle range. Even as the walls crumbled about them, the riflemen continued to cut down the massed troops that crowded in upon them. At the final estimation, the 183 Texans killed perhaps a little less than a third of the attacking force of 5,000 men.

Captain Tumlinson's cousin, George W. Tumlinson, was one of the 183 Texans who died at the Alamo along with Bowie, William B. Travis, Crockett, and Almeron Dickinson. Like George Tumlinson, some of the other defenders of the Alamo had served in colonial ranging companies. One of Juan Seguín's men, José Toribio Losoya, was a former member of the *Alamo de Parras* company; he died defending the mission that had been his old company's headquarters since 1803. It's also likely that some former colonial rangers were among George Kimbell's thirty-two volunteers from Gonzales, the last men to answer Travis's desperate call for reinforcements. Despite the almost certain knowledge that answering the call would result in their deaths, those men from Gonzales slipped through the Mexican lines to join the defenders of the Alamo on February 29.

On February 25, as Santa Anna's noose tightened about the Alamo, Travis chose Juan N. Seguín (see "Man Without a Country") to carry his plea for help to Gonzales. The son of wealthy Federalist landholders, Seguín had formed his own *Tejano* ranging company to fight Indians and had led them against Cós at Béxar in 1835. When the call went out for volunteers, he led his men to the defense of the Alamo. As Travis's couriers, the *Tejano* captain and some of his men successfully bluffed their way past Mexican patrols to carry the message. His company got back to the Alamo too late to make the last stand with its other defenders. As he watched the smoke from the funeral

An engraving from D. W. C. Baker's *A Texas Scrapbook* of the storming of the Alamo by Mexican soldiers, 1836.
UT Institute of Texan Cultures at San Antonio

Recalled from the Frontier

After their rescue of the Hibbons boy from the Comanche, Captain John Tumlinson's company returned to Brushy Creek to build their blockhouse. They were patrolling the frontier when they got the news of Santa Anna's invasion and the fall of the Alamo. Their new orders recalled them to Bastrop and directed them to guard and assist the settlers who were beginning to flee in terror before the Mexican advance.

This flight, known as the Runaway Scrape, included not only the Texian colonials and anti-Santanista *Tejanos* but the government of the new Republic of Texas. Within a few days of declaring independence and signing the constitution for the new Republic of Texas, the government was itself forced to flee from Washington-on-the-Brazos one hundred miles southeast to Harrisburg on Buffalo Bayou.

Some of the Rangers, Captain Tumlinson and Lt. Jo Rodger among them, split off to see to their own families. Smithwick and sixteen-year-old Pvt. James Edmundson remained at Bastrop to guard against Indian attacks, but most joined up with Major Williamson and headed toward the Colorado River crossing to catch up with the refugees. Tumlinson's company never returned to Brushy Creek; as Smithwick later wrote of the headquarters blockhouse, "...it was burned by the Indians and never rebuilt."

The remaining Rangers found Bastrop deserted, the trail from Cedar Creek into the main settlement strewn with supplies and possessions the refugees had abandoned. According to Smithwick, the company was down to about twenty men by the time Major Williamson moved out to find the refugees they'd been ordered to assist. In the confusion of

"Retreat from Gonzales," a drawing of a Mexican Colonial-era lancer by Gary Zaboly from Stephen Hardin's *Texian Illiad*. He's armed with the long lance, *espada ancha*, and *escopeta*, the traditional lancer's weapons.
Stephen Hardin

pyres blot the sky over San Antonio de Béxar, he swore an oath of vengeance against Santa Anna. Seguín and the men of his company would later fulfill that oath, on the battlefield at San Jacinto.

Many Texans would swear such an oath upon hearing of the fall of the Alamo. The Texans would not forget that it was Santa Anna who had given the order for the Palm Sunday execution of Col. James Fannin's men after their surrender at Goliad. The Texas Rangers would remember Santa Anna's treachery and would one day carry their desire for vengeance into the very heart of Mexico.

MAN WITHOUT A COUNTRY

Many *Tejanos* served Texas in *las compañías volantes*, in ranging companies, as revolutionary volunteers, and as Texas Rangers, even as the dynamic Texian culture began to dominate their own. Juan N. Seguín's story typifies the loss of cultural identity many *Tejanos* experienced as they participated in founding the Lone Star Republic. Lauded as a Texas hero, later branded as a Mexican traitor, Seguín's sacrifices in the service of his native Texas in the end made him a stranger in the very nation he'd helped to found.

Seguín's roots lay deep in Texas, in the *Tejano* society of San Antonio de Béxar where his prominent and influential family had resided for a century before the first Anglos came to Texas. His father, the *alcalde* of Béxar, was a steadfast sponsor of Stephen F. Austin's colonization efforts and in his dealings with the Mexican government and other influential *Tejanos*. Juan Seguín also became a personal friend to the young *empresario*, and he signed on as an early supporter of Austin's "ranging company" concept of frontier defense.

Col. Juan Nepomucena Seguín, a Mexican patriot to Texas during the Revolution, appears in this photo from Dudley Wooten's *A Comprehensive History of Texas*.
UT Institute of Texan Cultures at San Antonio

One of the first Texans to answer the call for volunteers in the Texas Revolution, Seguín recruited a mounted company of *vaqueros* to join the fight against General Cós at the Battle of Béxar in 1835. Some of the experienced Indian fighters from the *Alamo de Parras* flying company also joined him in the cause of Texas liberty. As a lieutenant colonel in the Texas Army he led his troops to victory over Santa Anna's forces at San Jacinto, and at the bitter end of the war he accepted the final surrender of the Alamo from the last Mexican troops who held it. As the military governor of San Antonio de Béxar under the new Lone Star flag, it fell to him to perform the sad duty of officiating at the funeral service for those who died at the Alamo.

His place among the honored citizens of the Republic seemed assured, and he continued to serve his new nation as a senator and as the mayor of San Antonio. That began to change; unlike the early Texians, the new immigrants who flooded into Texas after the revolution didn't make the distinction between the loyal *Tejanos* and the defeated enemy to the south. To the greedy land speculators who'd come from the United States to make their fortunes in Texas, they were all "just Mexicans," a conquered people to be swept aside and ignored.

Seguín exerted all of his political power and prestige, and sometimes the threat of force, to protect *Tejano* holdings against freebooters and land thieves. His effective actions in this cause made him powerful enemies among the more influential newcomers.

Santa Anna also had a long memory for injuries done to him. Mexican agents began to circulate rumors that Seguín had turned traitor and intended to assist Santa Anna in his plan for retaking

The Alamo as it appears today, restored and preserved by The Daughters of the Republic of Texas.
Photo by Tom Knowles

Texas. To anyone who really knew of his abiding hatred for the dictator and of his devotion to Texas, the idea of Seguín aiding Santa Anna against Texas would appear laughable at best. To his enemies in Texas, the rumors presented them with an excellent opportunity to tarnish the *Tejano* leader's reputation.

In 1842, a mob forced Seguín to take an action he'd never before taken — he had to run away from a fight. Most humiliating of all, his only retreat lay to the south, to his relatives in Mexico. There Santa Anna took him prisoner and forced him to join in a raid led by Gen. Rafael Vásquez on Seguín's own home city, San Antonio. Seguín's critics pointed this action as proof of his treachery, but in 1848, after the end of the Mexican War, some of his old friends petitioned the new State of Texas to allow the *Tejano* hero to return.

Juan Seguín returned, a broken man, to the country he'd defended since "...the report of the first cannon which foretold her liberty." Despite the efforts of his detractors, his name lives on in the Texas city that bears his name, thirty miles to the east of San Antonio, a tribute to the brave *Tejano* who rode for the Lone Star.

events, many of the Rangers had decided that they'd better find out what had happened to their own families.

Williamson couldn't move the refugees, cattle, and supplies across the Colorado because the spring rains had so flooded the river as to make a crossing nearly impossible. Smithwick and Edmundson, who had decided they didn't want to be left behind at Bastrop, joined Williamson at the captain's camp at the Colorado River crossing.

When the Rangers awoke and the morning fog burned away, they were shocked to see Mexican soldiers on the opposite bank of the river. A full division under Gen. Antonio Gaona had moved up from the southwest in the night to take possession of the crossing; only the flood kept the Mexicans from crossing the river to secure the ford and pursue the Rangers.

In the midst of a hurried retreat, Smithwick noticed that they had left behind their sentry, old Jimmy Curtis. Curtis had earlier received word that his son-in-law had been killed at the Alamo, and he'd been drowning his grief with whiskey. Smithwick rode back to find Curtis sitting beneath a tree with his bottle, quite unconcerned about the danger of his situation. Smithwick later reported their conversation:

"Hello, Uncle Jimmy," I cried, "mount and ride for your life. The Mexicans are on the other side of the river and all our men are gone."

"The hell they are! Light and take a drink."

"There's no time for drinking. Come—mount and let's be off. The Mexicans may swim the river and be after us any moment."

"Let's drink to their confusion," he persisted, and thinking it was the quickest way to start him I drank with him and we struck out. "Well, we can say one thing—we were the last men to leave," said he, not in the least disturbed.

So ended one of the earliest confrontations between Mexican soldiers and the Texas Rangers. Future meetings wouldn't end so comically, or without bloodshed.

A Flight to Victory

The Colorado was in full flood stage by the time Houston's small army, escorting a staggering mass of civilian refugees, arrived at the western banks of the river at Burnham's Crossing. He managed to get the civilians across first, then followed with his troops to set up a camp at Beason's Ford. More volunteers joined him at that camp, bringing his forces up to a strength of about seven hundred men.

The Ranger company had lost two horses in the retreat from the river crossing, and others had gone

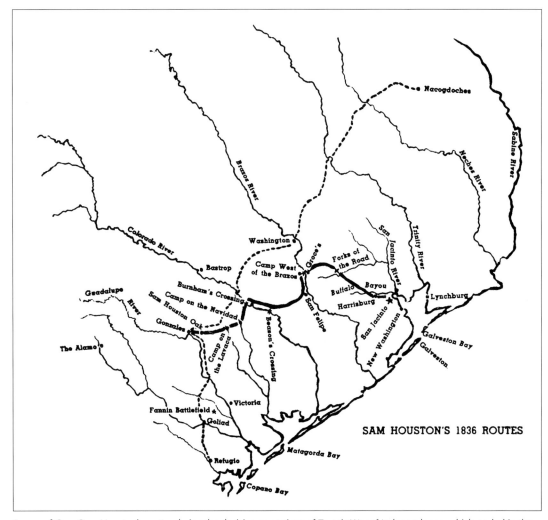

A map of Gen. Sam Houston's routes during the decisive campaigns of Texas's War of Independence, which ended in the Battle of San Jacinto.
UT Institute of Texan Cultures at San Antonio

lame in negotiating the muddy trail. Leaving command to Lt. George M. Petty, Williamson took two men and rode ahead in an attempt to locate the army or the refugees.

Following him through a landscape of deserted villages and churned muddy roads, the rest of the company finally began to run into groups of fleeing settlers. At Cole's Settlement, they found a note from Williamson waiting for them with shocking news of the massacre of Col. James Fannin and the four hundred Texan prisoners from Goliad, executed on May 27 by the direct order of Santa Anna. As they approached Washington-on-the-Brazos, the Rangers

sent out scouts who, unnerved by their earlier surprise encounter with Gaona's division, mistakenly identified a herd of cattle as possible Mexican troops. When the company left the road to find a safer ford over the Brazos River, they contacted elements of the Texas Army's scouts. The groups combined forces to make the river crossing and struck out to find Houston's army.

On the afternoon of April 20, the combined group of Rangers and scouts heard the sound of gunfire from the direction of the San Jacinto Plain. What they heard was the Battle of San Jacinto. Sam Houston had lured Santa Anna into a trap, isolating him between

Buffalo Bayou, the San Jacinto River, and the coastal marshes.

On the morning of April 20, Houston's army had crossed Buffalo Bayou, secured Lynch's Ferry, and set up their artillery in the tree line along the bayou. Santa Anna's troops were surprised to find the Texans waiting for them, but after a short artillery duel and some exchanges of musketry and rifle fire, the Mexicans settled in to wait for the Texans to come out into the open. Houston refused to oblige them, so Santa Anna set his men to setting up camp in preparation to spending a night on the field.

Ranging company scout Deaf Smith rode in to report that General Cós had crossed Vince's Bridge with reinforcements from Fort Bend, but that the 500 additional troops were weary from having marched all night. Houston sent Smith to burn the bridge, ensuring that there would be no escape for either army. It would be victory or death. By midafternoon, the Mexican troops had settled in to rest and Santa Anna was dreaming over his opium pipe. Smith returned with the news that he'd destroyed the bridge, and Houston assembled his men, the 800 ragged, vengeful volunteers he'd lead against 1,250 regular troops.

Although they weren't assembled as a group, the men of the Texas Rangers came to the fight at San Jacinto as experienced veterans and leaders. They stood side-by-side with the other Texans, officers joining in at whatever rank was available to them. The rest of Tumlinson's company was still some distance away, but Major Williamson, First Ranger Company Capt. John J. Tumlinson, his brother Joe, and his cousins, John and David, had caught up with Houston's army and joined up as privates. Deaf Smith returned after burning Vince's Bridge to do his part in the fighting. Former *Alamo de Parras* flying company members Pedro Herrera, Nepomuceno Navarro, and Manuel Tarín had followed Capt. Juan Seguín, now a colonel in the Texas Army, to fulfill the oath he'd made at the Alamo.

Third Ranger Company Capt. Isaac Burton had joined up as a private in a company commanded by ranging company leader and frontier scout Henry Wax Karnes. Quick-triggered Conrad Rohrer had left Tumlinson's company earlier to enlist with Houston. Benjamin and Henry McCulloch, who would later lead Texas Ranger companies through the days of the Republic, the Mexican War, statehood, and the Civil

A portrait of Erastus "Deaf" Smith, the famous scout and ranging company leader of colonial Texas and the Texas Revolution, is depicted on the right-hand side of this five-dollar note. Issued by the Republic of Texas, this currency was referred to as the "Redback" for the color of ink used on the reverse side.
Prints and Photographs Collection, Center for American History, University of Texas at Austin

War, had joined up for their first big fight. One of Houston's companies was commanded by Gen. Edward Burleson, who had commanded at the Battle of Béxar and who would in future days serve with the Rangers.

At 4:30 in the afternoon, Houston gave the command. The Texans surged forward and began to gather momentum. At the first shot, a shout went up: "Remember the Alamo! Remember Goliad!" The few musicians in the group struck up the popular tune of the day, "Come to the Bower," a somewhat ribald tune for such a grim business.

Taken completely by surprise by the determined, deadly assault, many of the Mexicans began to flee. The vengeful Texans continued to shoot them down even as they ran. Sgt. Moses Bryan, the nephew of Stephen F. Austin, said later, "The most awful slaughter I ever saw was when the Texans pursued the retreating Mexicans, killing on all sides, even the wounded." The battle lasted only eighteen minutes, but the Texans, who suffered only nine men killed and twenty-six wounded, killed over six hundred Mexican troops and took most of the rest of the force prisoner. Houston had two horses shot from under him and took a severe wound in his right leg, but the next day he managed to sit up to confront the captured Napoleon of the West, Santa Anna, and force him to order all Mexican troops to leave Texas.

The war for independence, finally won on the battlefield at San Jacinto, was a new beginning for Texas, but still only a beginning. Independence would itself be a struggle for the Lone Star. To stand on her own, Texas would still require defenders upon whom she could call at a moment's notice.

In the Wake of the Storm

After San Jacinto, Isaac Burton's company returned to its assignment of watching the coastal areas. In June 1836, they served in a unique action that put a coda to the revolution and added to the Texas Ranger reputation for a willingness to employ unorthodox

methods. While on patrol near Copano Bay, a detachment of Burton's Rangers noticed a strange ship not far from shore, at anchor by Copano Reef. The reef extended far out into the bay; low tide revealed the reef, but at high tide, it was a foot to eighteen inches under water.

The folklore of the *corridas*, the Mexican-style heroic ballads, claims that the Rangers actually rode their horses across the water to take the ship. Some recorded accounts say that they used a signal fire to decoy a boat out from the ship and used the boat to take their prize. Knowledgeable residents of the Texas coast say that the mythic tale of water-striding horses came about because the Rangers rode out onto the reef at high tide, their horses splashing hock-deep through the bay over the sunken reef. Whatever the means they actually used, when Burton's Rangers boarded the ship they found that it was carrying supplies for Mexican troops. They loaded their horses aboard and forced the captain to turn his vessel toward the port at Velasco.

Along the way, despite weather that at times threatened to becalm them or sink them, the Rangers used the captured ship, the *Watchman*, to lure in two other gunrunner vessels, the *Comanche* and the *Fanny Butler*. When they signaled the other ships' crews to send over a boat, each time the crew complied. They captured the boat crew, then tricked the crews into letting them board each ship. They sailed the captured ships into Velasco harbor, where they turned contraband worth over $25,000 to the regular Texas military. They never had to fire a single shot in this action, the only known instance where Texas Rangers actually operated against enemy forces on the high seas. After that, the Rangers of Burton's company carried the highly irregular distinction of being known as the "horse marines" of Texas.

Smithwick, Tumlinson's company, and the volunteer scouts who rode late onto the San Jacinto battlefield felt, as Smithwick wrote, "mean and ashamed" that they had missed the battle. They weren't the only ones to arrive late; soon after the battle, Houston had an army several times larger than the one with which he'd started. Many of the Rangers were assigned to escort the Mexican troops out of Texas, but then rumors of Comanche raids in the abandoned settlements drew them back to Ranger service on the frontier.

Newspapers from Louisiana to Tennessee carried accounts of the battles at the Alamo and San Jacinto, and of the massacre at Goliad. The New Orleans *Picayune* noted the exploits of the Texas Rangers in the revolution, particularly the story of Burton's horse marines. This news from Texas drew the attention of the American public to the frontier, to the new Republic that had won such an unlikely victory over impossible odds, and to the men known as Texas Rangers.

The victorious revolution was only the beginning for the Texas Rangers.

3

RANGERS OF THE REPUBLIC

THE TEXANS TOOK THEIR VENGEANCE AND WON THEIR INDEPENDENCE in eighteen hellish minutes of slaughter at San Jacinto, but it was only the beginning of their struggle. The Texan leaders remained divided on vital issues: providing for a standing army and a frontier defense force; a standard policy in relations with the Indian nations; defining the legal provenance of land titles; and the question of annexation by the United States.

The balance of the Texas treasury, such as it was, lay deep in the red ink of her war debts to the American supporters of the Revolution. The only asset she had to meet those debts lay in the land grants she could offer. The four civilized Indian tribes held much of that land, and the nomadic Comanche, Kiowa, and Apache rode at will through the rest. The government's practice of trading land for debts, for military, and for Ranger service, also brought the *Tejanos* and the original colonists into conflict with the newcomers who flooded into the new Republic.

Many of the immigrants made no distinction between antagonistic Mexicans and patriotic *Tejanos*, between settled, peaceful Cherokees and Comanche raiders. To the less scrupulous land speculators, improved farm and ranch land abandoned during the Runaway Scrape looked like a better bet than unsettled lands held by hostile Indians. When the original

owners returned to reclaim their homes, whether they had run from the Mexican Army or had fought to defeat it, they often found themselves forced to deal with the freebooters and squatters. In their absence, newcomers had filed claims recognized by the government of the Republic. They resorted to the typical, self-reliant frontier method of dealing with such disagreements. Violent confrontations became the standard method of settling disputes.

Mexico and Texas both claimed the territory that lay between the Nueces River and the Rio Grande. Because of this dispute the "Nueces Strip" became a no-man's land in which Texas and Mexico fought an undeclared war. Santa Anna had given his parole to Sam Houston, had promised to end the war, and never to trouble Texas again, but he was not one to give up easily or to forget a grudge. After his release he retreated to his estate in Vera Cruz, a safe place from

49

ered the Texian colonists as possible trading partners and allies against the Mexicans, their depredations against the colonies had remained relatively isolated and minor affairs.

As the Comanche and the westering Texans came into contact more and more frequently, deadly moonlight raids and vengeful ambushes became the rule rather than the exception. Buffalo skin lodges and farmhouses would burn under the light of the full moon, fresh scalps would hang from lances and gun belts, and the blood of both races would darken the prairie.

The opening of the frontier to the east brought the best and the worst of the world to Texas. Farmers and artists, scholars and soldiers, entrepreneurs and explorers came to answer her challenge; she also drew the dregs of the outlaw populations of the United States and unscrupulous speculators from Europe. To badmen from the Natchez Trace and feuding gunmen

"Austin Colony Rangers," a watercolor painting by Bruce Marshall of colonial-era ranging company riders, the original Rangers who helped forge the Republic of Texas.
Bruce Marshall Collection

which he could plan his eventual return to power. Within a year, he would rise once again to rule Mexico and to turn his attention toward punishing the people who had humiliated him.

As long as the Napoleon of the West had any influence left, Mexico would remain a threat to Texas. His legacy would be an enduring mistrust and animosity between the Lone Star and her former mother country. The southern border would remain a source of strife, banditry, and guerrilla warfare long after Santa Anna became dust.

To the west and the north, the Comanche, Apache, and Kiowa began to see the continued Texan encroachment into their hunting and raiding territory as a challenge to their mastery of the plains. Prior to Texas gaining her independence, the Comanche raided mostly to the south of San Antonio de Béxar, down into Mexico. Because they'd originally consid-

The first official flag of the Republic of Texas, designed by Lorenzo de Zavala. It was blue with a single gold star, the letters T-E-X-A-S between the star's points.
UT Institute of Texan Cultures at San Antonio/Barker Texas History Center, University of Texas

from Missouri and Tennessee, "gone to Texas" became an easy answer to their troubles with the law and their enemies. They didn't change their ways when they came to the new land, but brought their feuds

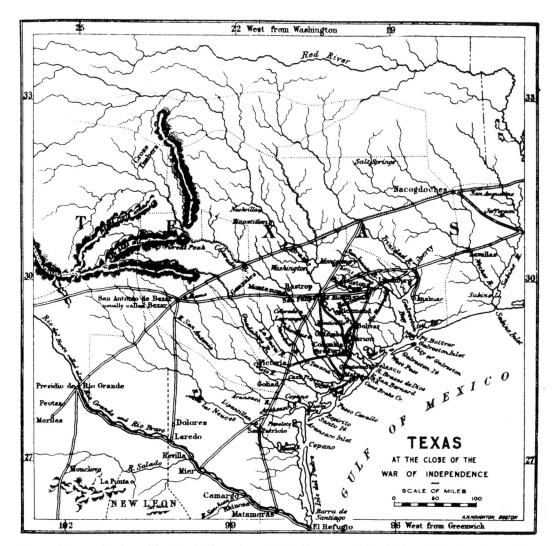

A map of Texas at the close of the War of Independence, 1836. This appears in Alfred Williams's *Sam Houston and the War of Independence*.
UT Institute of Texan Cultures at San Antonio

and their recklessness with them to the frontier in hopes that law wouldn't follow.

The victorious declaration of independence and the successful creation of the Ranger companies were only the first gleams of light from the Lone Star of the new Republic. The Texans balanced their fragile frontier society between borders of darkness, threatened by enemies from within and without. For the most part, the Herculean burden of defending the borders, of pushing back the darkness, would fall squarely on the shoulders of the few brave men of the Texas Rangers.

Comanche Moon

According to Tom Morgan, who was born in Coleman County and grew up to join the Texas Rangers near the end of the nineteenth century, his mother often told her children that, "...the Indians at first were not feared. They came on moonlight nights and stole the horses but did not kill until they realized they were being run out of their own country, then they began to kill, burn, and pillage."

The Comanche preferred the light of the full moon for staging their raids. They particularly favored raiding in the fall months, after they had completed their big buffalo hunts and set aside their supplies for the winter. The full moon gave them plenty of light by which they could target horse herds, light by which they could track and fight and flee. Once the moon went down, they could camp until morning or use the darkness to avoid pursuit. Every child born in Texas, even up into the twentieth century, grew up hearing bloodcurdling tales of Comanche raiders riding through the plains under the full light of an October moon. (See "A Texas Family Saga.")

The Comanche looked with natural envy upon the large, strong horses and the far-shooting rifles of the Texans. Their early raids against Texans followed the usual customs of the Plains Indians, not intent on fighting but on counting coup, on acquiring fine stock, and making a grand adventure of it all. Raiding, riding, and fighting were the staff of life to them, and if theirs was an often savage and sanguine sport, sport was how they thought of it. War the way Europeans and Americans fought it was far too serious a concept for the Comanche way of dealing with one's enemies. "Play" might be a more fitting description of the Comanche outlook, no matter if that play ended in torture and death for the Comanche warrior or for his enemies.

All was fair in war to the Comanche. They would ruthlessly exploit every weakness, take any advantage, and indulge in any brutality they deemed necessary to win. They expected no less from their opponents. To most Texans the Comanche way appeared base and treacherous, but a Comanche warrior's honor meant more to him than his life. An invited guest in a Comanche camp could depend on the warriors to defend his life with their own, while that same man could expect nothing but death if he later met those same warriors in combat. It was all part of the game of life as the Comanche understood it.

The Comanche view of war as sport began to change as they noticed the bite of the plow into the soil of the prairie, their *comancheria*. They quickly discerned the meaning of the surveyor's transit and the boundary stakes he left behind him in the earth. Noah Smithwick wrote: "They had learned the import of surveying and never lost an opportunity of manifesting their hostility toward it." Survey parties drew a considerable measure of their wrath; more than one surveyor's scalp ended up decorating a Comanche lance or shield. In turn, more than one surveyor also served with distinction in the Texas Rangers, fighting to protect his colleagues and others against the Comanche. Surveyors learned to navigate the wild country before anyone else, so they made some of the best scouts and Indian fighters.

The Comanche could see the threat posed by the Texans who settled on the land and did not move with the seasons or follow the buffalo. No longer content to raid just for horses and goods, they began to attack isolated farmhouses and bands of travelers, brutally killing some, taking others captive. The usually independent Comanche bands also began to join up for raids, even gathering in strength to attack settlements, forts, and towns.

Their hostility would grow slowly but certainly, until warfare with the Texans would become a sport no longer, but serious business to the Comanche. Under the Comanche moon, they would strike to kill, to drive the white man from the *comancheria*.

The Rangers Return

Once they'd finished escorting Mexican troops out of Texas, the members of Tumlinson's old company got new orders from the War Department. They were to return to Bastrop to reestablish their Ranger post and to serve out their terms of enlistment. Col. Robert M. Coleman took command of the Ranger companies after the war. Captain Tumlinson and Lieutenant Rogers hadn't returned to service, but Noah Smithwick found several of his old comrades waiting at Bastrop. In the fall of 1836, the Rangers built a log stockade fortress near Walnut Creek, six miles south of present-day Austin, and they named it for their new commander.

A TEXAS FAMILY SAGA

The May 19, 1836, attack on the settlement at Parker's Fort, the most famous Comanche raid in Texas history, took place not by moonlight on the plains but in broad daylight in the oak-forested hills of East Central Texas. It sparked a hatred between the Comanche and the Texans that influenced the entire course of their history and began one of the most enduring family sagas in Texas history, one that would unite Texan and Comanche in ties of blood and honor and tragic destiny.

Eight-year-old Cynthia Ann Parker, taken captive along with her six-year-old brother, John, was the link in that destiny. Taken to eastern Colorado, they were adopted by Peta Nacona, chief of the Naconi (Wanderers). John grew up to become a warrior, and he eventually made his way back into white society. Cynthia Ann grew up to marry Nacona. Atypically, their relationship went far beyond that of captor and captive. Not only did Cynthia Ann refuse to be parted from him when she had the opportunity in 1840, but Nacona went very much against Comanche custom by refusing to take other wives. Their first son, Quanah, was born in 1847, and they had two more children, a son named Pecos and a daughter named Topsannah (Flower).

Cynthia Ann Parker was abducted in childhood by the Comanche. When she was rescued twenty-four years later, she asked to be returned to her Comanche family.
The Texas Collection, Baylor University, Waco, Texas

Cynthia Ann's world turned askew once again on December 17, 1860. While Nacona was away hunting with his sons and some of his warriors, Capt. Lawrence Sullivan Ross led a mixed force of Texas Rangers, 2nd U.S. Cavalry, civilian volunteers, and Tonkawa scouts in a raid against the Naconi camp on the Pease River, near the present-day site of Quanah, Texas. In the no-quarter warfare between Rangers and Comanche, Indian women were targets; indeed, some of the women took up weapons to defend the camp. Future cattle baron Charlie Goodnight, riding as a Ranger scout, held his fire when he caught a flash of the greased blond hair and blue eyes hidden under one warrior woman's blanket.

Although the woman known as Naduah could speak no English, she recognized her own English name when the Rangers took her to Isaac Parker. She became excited, pointed to herself and shouted, "Cynthia Ann, Cynthia Ann!" The news of her rescue after a quarter of a century among the Comanche electrified the Southwestern frontier. The Parkers welcomed their lost child and her little daughter, Flower.

But far from feeling rescued, Naduah saw her return as a second kidnapping. Her white family turned down her repeated requests that she be allowed to return to her Comanche husband and children. The Parkers put her under guard to keep her from escaping. When her little Flower died of a civilized disease, Naduah grieved Comanche-style, with wailing prayers and self-mutilation. Eventually, she starved herself to death.

Peta Nacona lived for several years afterwards, but never took another wife. He threw himself recklessly into every battle until he found his own death by neglecting an infected scalp wound. Pecos fell ill and died as well, but Quanah, whom white men began to call "Quanah Parker," grew into a tall, strong man with bold features and startling, blue-gray eyes. He became a splendid rider, a matchless warrior and leader. He rose in the war councils to become the last great chief of the Quahadie Comanche band.

When he learned of his mother's death, Quanah swore vengeance on the whites who had robbed him of his family, particularly on the Texas Rangers. He fought the Rangers and the U.S. Army until the Comanche horse herd was slaughtered at the final battle at Palo Duro Canyon in 1874. By a strange twist of fate, during the last years of the free Comanche, Quanah forged a friendship with John R. Hughes, a trader who would later become one of the greatest captains of the Texas Rangers. He also became friends with Charlie Goodnight, who assisted Quanah in protecting and marketing the grazing rights to the Comanche reservation, thus giving him the political and economic power he needed to protect his people's rights in the white world.

When Quanah obtained leave from the Washita River reservation to visit his mother's grave in East Texas, his great uncle, Silas Parker, accepted him with open arms. So did many other Texans who had once hated him; they had always looked upon him as one of their own, a fierce frontier warrior to whom they owed at least a grudging respect.

Quanah had always been a political negotiator as a war chief, and in his new role he became an accomplished lobbyist. He spoke out against injustices and treaty violations, all the while using the white man's law as the basis for his arguments. He even invested in a railroad and served as a deputy sheriff, a school district president, and a judge. He rode on hunts with President Theodore Roosevelt, and perhaps did something to ease the great conservationist's prejudice against Indians. Most important of all, he won full American citizenship for all of his people.

In the person of Quanah Parker, an extraordinary man in whom the blood of two strong peoples flowed, the Lone Star and the Comanche Moon at last found common ground.

Photo of Quanah Parker, rancher and political leader of Comanche tribal affairs.
UT Institute of Texan Cultures at San Antonio, Courtesy of Gibbs Memorial Library

In the confusion at the end of the Revolution the Indians had begun raiding the settlements more frequently. In typical laconic Ranger fashion, Noah Smithwick remembered, "The return of the rangers, however, checked hostile incursions for a time." As men of fighting age returned to Bastrop and the other western frontier settlements, the people who had been forced to take refuge in forts and at other strong points reclaimed their fields and farms.

In much the same way as Spanish and *Tejano* society had coalesced around the *presidios*, so did the frontier Texas settlements grow up around the military forts and the Texas Ranger stations. The Rangers of the Republic participated directly in their frontier society, valued for more than just their skills as trackers and fighters. Like many other Rangers on the frontier, Smithwick wore more than one hat, contributing not only his fighting skills but his other talents to building the new civilization of the Republic. At Coleman's Fort, he once again set up his blacksmith's shop; when not on patrol, he forged new tools and implements and repaired old ones, not only for his fellow Rangers but for the local citizens. Any blacksmith provided a vital service to frontier settlements, but as a gunsmith Smithwick had no peer. Everyone, from the settlers to the friendly Indians, congregated around Smithwick's forge.

Despite the cold weather, frequent delays in pay, and infrequent supply deliveries, Smithwick signed on again in 1837 to serve out another term of enlistment in place of a man who wished to leave the service. The Rangers took hardships and shortages in stride. They even managed to find some humor in the shipment they received of surplus U.S. Army uniforms, most of which were of such a small size that they produced a comical effect when paired with the large-framed Rangers.

Colonel Coleman proved an ineffective commander for the Ranger companies, and because he allowed his men "too much license in the way of foraging," he became unpopular with the settlers as well. The lieutenant who commanded Smithwick's company, a man named Robel, was a rumored deserter from the U.S. Army. Robel often abused his authority in disciplining the free-spirited Rangers, who didn't take kindly to military-style order. Then he went too far in punishing a local recruit for being drunk on duty by tying the man to a post overnight. When the drunken man passed out and inadvertently hanged himself, Robel skipped out just ahead of the angry locals, leaving Coleman to face the consequences

alone. The War Department recalled Coleman, but he drowned in a boating accident before he could be brought to trial for the charges against him.

The company made its first foray under its new captain, Micah Andrews, early in 1837. While they sat around their campfire at the fort, telling tales and playing music, the Rangers spotted a large fire on a hill on the opposite side of the Colorado River. Settlers wouldn't risk such a big fire in Indian territory, so the Rangers figured that a raiding party must be responsible. The Indians evidently weren't aware that the Rangers could see their fire from the fort. Andrews surmised that the Comanche had just set up camp in the light of the waning moon, probably to rest after a raid.

Captain Andrews was reluctant to order his men into a night action, but Smithwick suggested that he ask for volunteers. The whole company stepped forward. Fifteen Rangers led by Lt. Nicholas Wren and Smithwick scouted ahead. They found the raiders' own *remuda* and their stolen horses, stampeded them, and then moved on to meet up with the second group for the attack on the camp. In the dark, the Rangers missed their rendezvous. It was close to dawn when they stumbled onto the camp. The Indians awakened and traded shots with the Rangers; the Rangers wounded one Comanche, but Ranger Philip Martin

A sketch by N. Donaldson of Fort Coleman, the first station of the Texas Rangers of the Republic. The view is from the northwest with the Colorado River to the right and Walnut Creek to the left. This drawing comes from Noah Smithwick's *The Evolution of a State.*
UT Institute of Texan Cultures at San Antonio

took a bullet in the head. The Rangers recovered the stolen horses and goods, but they felt it was a poor trade for the life of a Ranger. Adding insult to injury, the Comanche avenged their honor by returning later to run off some of the horses.

The fight taught the Rangers something the Comanche already knew, that the perils of a night attack most often outweighed the benefit of surprise. As with many of the other hard lessons they would learn on the battlefield, it carried a steep price. Another Texas Ranger had fallen in the service of the Lone Star. As Smithwick related, "Poor Philip Martin was one of the best men in camp; a genial, warm-hearted son of old Erin. We carried him back and buried him with the honors of war outside the fort on the north side, beside the victim of Robel's cruelty."

A Missed Opportunity

A party of Comanche led by Quinaseico and Puestia rode under a truce flag to Coleman's Fort in the summer of 1837; there they proposed a conference that might lead to a peace treaty. Because Smithwick spoke fluent Spanish, the common language the Indians used to communicate among tribes, he volunteered to accompany them back to their camp, there to speak with their leader, Muguara. Captain Andrews granted him leave to do so, but many of the other Rangers believed that it was the last time they'd see their comrade alive.

Instead, Smithwick lived among the Comanche for three months. (See "Noah Smithwick's Adventure among the Comanche.") His recollections of his adventures with the horse lords provide the modern reader with some of the finest recorded insights into the lives and character of the Comanche people. The Ranger came to admire the warriors who would become the fiercest enemies of the Texans, much as the Comanche came to admire him. By the end of his stay, he'd worked out a treaty with them that called for the establishment of a trading post at Bastrop and a basic set of agreements for peaceful relations.

Unfortunately, other than his preservation of the image of a unique culture as it existed at its height, Smithwick's friendship and negotiations with the Comanches went for nothing in the end. He took the Comanche proposals to President Sam Houston, who had once been adopted by the Cherokee and had always actively pursued cordial relations with the different Indian tribes. Even as the revolution against Mexico concluded, Houston had written letters to the Comanche suggesting alliance and trade between them and the Texans. But the treaty Houston and Smithwick negotiated with the Comanche fell through as more radical minds in the Texas government began to take hold and more settlers flooded into the newly opened territory.

By the time Smithwick got back to permanent station at Coleman's Fort, Capt. William M. Eastland, a strict disciplinarian, had replaced Captain Andrews as commander. More than a bit disappointed with the situation, the veteran Ranger decided not to reenlist when his term expired. Smithwick recognized that the last chance for peace between the Comanche and the Texans had expired along with his Ranger service and the failure of his mission. Perhaps he didn't wish to meet his Comanche friends again when they were both "under shield," ready for war, or he might have been reluctant to use what he'd learned about them against them.

If so, his hope was in vain. He later wrote: "Assuming that I would remain with them indefinitely, the Indians instructed me in various signs which I afterward treacherously turned to account." Riding as a scout with the Rangers in subsequent actions against the Comanche, Smithwick used his familiarity with the individual Comanche war leaders and his knowledge of their combat tactics, war paint, hand signals and sign language, whistles, and animal calls against his former friends. Even as he'd shared the campfire with the Comanche, Noah Smithwick had figured that in the future the Lone Star and the Comanche moon would not meet in friendship, but in blood and fire.

NOAH SMITHWICK'S ADVENTURE AMONG THE COMANCHE

In *The Evolution of a State*, Noah Smithwick's reminiscence of his 1837 sojourn among the Comanche gives us a fascinating alternative look into the life of the Plains Indians when they were at the apex of their culture. It's also the stuff of a boy's adventure tale or a Western movie, a dream of living with "wild Red Indians." The Comanche gave Smithwick an honored warrior's name, "Wahqua," and invited him to ride with them on the hunt. He joined them in their races and wrestling matches, and he sat and smoked with them at their council fires:

> I had many long, earnest talks with those old Comanche chiefs, and I could not but admit the justice of their contention. The country they considered theirs by the right of inheritance; the game had been placed there for their food.

Most Texans knew the Comanche only for their brutal raids, for their unparalleled ferocity in war; the frontiersmen thought of them as a savage force of nature, as an obstacle to be overcome, as vermin to be destroyed. Although he never lost sight of them as his deadliest enemies, Smithwick came to know and admire the Comanche as individuals and as a people.

Noah Smithwick, Texas Ranger of the Republic, at age 66.
Prints and Photographs Collection, Center for American History, University of Texas at Austin

On the warpath, the Comanche usually showed no mercy or compassion, no regard for the age or sex of their enemies or their captives. In camp, Smithwick found that they displayed a surprising gentleness and even sentimentality toward their own children and the young captives they'd adopted. The adults didn't fight among themselves, and although the women did all of the hard labor, Smithwick never saw a woman or a child abused as he sometimes had in his own society. He came to think of the Comanche camp as the most peaceable community in which he'd ever lived.

Muguara, the leader of the several bands camped at Brushy Creek, had welcomed Smithwick, "...with every mark of friendship, conducting me to his lodge, where I was made the recipient of every attention known to their code of hospitality." The chief and his head wife, whom Smithwick called "Madame Muguara," became so fond of him that they called him "son."

The Comanche lived by their own draconian code of honor. One point of that honor ensured that a guest was safe in a Comanche camp, even if he was an enemy otherwise. When a war party of Huacos who had raided the settlements visited the camp to trade their stolen horses, they demanded that the Comanche turn the Ranger over to them so they could take vengeance on him for the members of their band the Texans had killed in the raid. Lance in hand, Muguara promised to kill every one of them if they so insulted him as to harm even a single hair on his honored guest's head. The Huacos, not being fools, immediately made tracks in the opposite direction.

Using the Spanish they had in common, Smithwick studied the Comanche language and attempted to set some of it down in print. He said:

> I use the Spanish alphabet in spelling these Indian names, it seeming better adapted to the soft sound
> of the Comanche tongue. I tried to get some knowledge of the latter language, succeeding fairly
> well with the nouns and adjectives, but when it came to the conjugation of the Comanche verb I
> gave it up.

This is a list of Comanche names and words, as recorded by Smithwick, with pronunciations and translations:

Names

Mugua-ra
Quin-a-se-i-co (eagle)
Pote-se-na-qua-hip (buffalo hump)
Ca-ta-ni-a-pa
Pa-ha-u-co
E-sa-nap
Juaqua or Wah-qua
Un-ar-o-caddy

Nouns

tuhaya (horse)
ait (bow)

pock (arrow)
wood-ah (bear)
quasack (coat)
    (possibly from Spanish)
beesone (buffalo)
    (Spanish pronunciation of "bison")
wah-ho-lo-te" (turkey) (possibly Aztec)

Numbers

mammiwassett (seven)
semimammiwassett (eight)
seminot (nine)
samot (ten)

Smithwick also recorded his impressions of Comanche daily life, of their customs and religion, details about their clothing and weapons and their individual personalities. One image stands out in particular, that of his description of the Comanche greeting to the dawning sun:

> Although it was customary for the first fellow who woke in the morning to announce the fact in
> song, the act seemed rather a spontaneous outpouring akin to that of the feathered songsters than
> a religious rite; the song itself resembling the lay of the birds in that it was wordless save for the syl-
> lables, *ha ah ha*, which furnished the vehicle on which the carol rode forth to the world; the perfor-
> mance ending in a keen yell.

Much of the Comanche culture and language disappeared when the horse lords lost their battle for dominance in Texas, but Smithwick's observations provide us with a tantalizing glimpse of what it must have been like. His adventure among the Comanche also remained one of his fondest memories of his time as a Texas Ranger:

> I still retain some vivid recollections of the kindness and friendship evinced toward me by the
> Comanches, especially the old chiefs, while I was with them. What their course toward me would
> have been had I met them "under shield," I never had an opportunity of testing; but, some way, I
> always thought that if I had fallen into their hands by accident they would have remembered
> Wahqua.

New Trails and Hard Lessons

Capt. Thomas H. Barron's company was one of the renewed groups of Rangers added to Colonel Coleman's command in the reorganization under the act passed by the Texas Congress on December 5, 1836. Along with Colonel Coleman and a few members of his escort, they cleared a road from Coleman's Fort on Walnut Creek to a new site on the Brazos River, near the Falls. There, provided with only the barest of essential supplies and tools, they established a new outpost and built shelters.

George Bernard Erath, an Austrian immigrant and a surveyor, fought with the Texas Army at San Jacinto and against Indians with Capt. W. M. Robertson's frontier volunteers before he joined Barron's company in October 1836. Erath wrote in his memoirs that the Rangers found the country around the Falls still mostly deserted by the settlers who had fled in the Runaway Scrape. Some cornfields planted before the war had survived to ripen even without tending, so the Rangers had plenty of cornmeal. They also found cooking utensils and other items they needed cached in the woods. They never had enough coffee; they supplemented their other meager supplies by hunting deer, bear, turkey, and wild honey.

Erath and the company at the Falls didn't get to enjoy their winter quarters for long before they went into action. Commanded by Lieutenant Curtis, in January 1837 the company rode forth under orders to intercept a group of suspected Indian raiders. A ten-man scout party led by Erath and Sergeant McLochlan caught up with the raiders and ambushed them in their camp at daylight. The Rangers' first shots killed some of the warriors and caused them to scatter, but as the Texans reloaded their rifles, the Indians began to advance on their position. The Rangers' fire stopped a charge by the Indians; Erath's shot dropped one man practically at his feet. Erath split his group into two squads, hopscotching them back, one covering as the other reloaded. As they were gravely outnumbered, this strategy probably saved all of their lives.

Although they did manage to kill several of the

George B. Erath, surveyor, Texas Ranger captain in the days of the Republic of Texas, and major in the Frontier Organization during the Civil War.
Texas State Library & Archives Commission

enemy in the fight, the Rangers suffered their own casualties. The Indians found the mortally wounded David Clark and civilian scout Frank Childress and finished them off. Unable to come to his aid, the Rangers had to listen to Clark's screams as the Indians killed him. They never saw Childress again, and subsequent scouting parties failed to recover the bodies or to pick up the tracks of the raiders. After this fight, Erath resigned from the service and returned to surveying. Four years later he would return as a captain to lead the Milam County Rangers and Minute Men against the Indians in the Brazos River country.

Other Ranger companies and volunteer forces in the north and west experienced similar battles and losses, a kind of on-the-job training in frontier warfare for both veterans and new recruits. A. J. Sowell's *Rangers and Pioneers of Texas* notes a battle that took place in October 1837 in the vicinity of "Fort Prairie," probably a sobriquet for Coleman's Fort. Eighteen Rangers of Smithwick's former company engaged a much superior force of Indians in a fight that ended with ten Rangers killed, three wounded. In this case, the casualty count could be exaggerated or could include civilian volunteers or militia who had joined forces with the Rangers. Indeed, many accounts of "Ranger" battles with Indians may actually refer to militia campaigns or forays by mounted volunteers. To those who remembered and recounted stories of colonial days and the early Republic, any force of mounted irregulars were a Ranger company.

Henry Wax Karnes, a confidant of Houston and veteran scout of Deaf Smith's ranging company formed one such company in 1838. After the Revolution, Karnes had been taken prisoner by the Mexican Army while he was in Matamoros attempting to conduct a prisoner exchange. He'd escaped, only to be taken prisoner by a band of Comanche. In much the same fashion as they had accepted Smithwick, they eventually accepted Karnes as a friend. Even as did Smithwick, Karnes learned much about the Comanche character and their methods of warfare, lessons he'd later turn to his advantage in battle against them.

In the summer of 1838, Karnes's company began to run patrols in the Hill Country to the northwest of San Antonio de Béxar. Near Arroyo Seco in the Medina River country, his scouting party of twenty-two men ran into a superior Comanche force and engaged in a running battle with them. Karnes got to field test what he'd learned from the Comanche, and he used that knowledge to exploit the strengths of his weapons and his men while minimizing their vulnerabilities. Withdrawing to a secure, protected position in the arroyo, he commanded his men to dismount. From the top of the bank he directed them to take careful aim and fire in relay volleys. This allowed one squad to reload as the other fired, thus never leaving all of the rifles empty against a Comanche rush.

After losing twenty warriors to the concerted, measured rifle fire, the Comanche withdrew from the field. Of the men in his company, Karnes took the only serious wound, an arrow that lodged in his shoulder while he stood exposed to spot targets for his men. He subsequently recovered to fight again and to train other leaders in his successful methods of defeating the Comanche.

Texans who allowed the Indians to catch them with their guns empty or to split them up into small groups couldn't expect such success. In January 1839 a group of volunteer settlers under Benjamin Bryant attacked a Caddo war party that had been raiding the settlements and farms near the Falls of the Brazos River. The Texians' first volley scattered the Caddo and wounded the Indian chief, José María, but the Indians counterattacked when the settlers fired all at once and stopped to reload. The war party cut the volunteers to pieces. Eli Chandler emerged a hero for riding back into the fight to save a wounded man. When he later made his mark as a Texas Ranger, he would remember the hard lesson of Bryant's defeat.

Chandler wasn't alone. As the bloody school of racial conflict unfolded, the Texans took to heart its hard lessons about life and death on the frontier.

Spies, Allies, and Political Ambitions

In May of 1839, a company of Rangers patrolling with Capt. Micah Andrews cut a strange trail near the Colorado River. The tracks of shod horses and more than a hundred pack mules lay mixed in with the hoofprints of Indian ponies. Andrews sent Lt. James O. Rice and seventeen scouts to intercept the party; riding at top speed, Rice and his men caught up with them at the San Gabriel River south of Austin. What they encountered was a mixed force of Mexicans and Indians escorting a large pack train of munitions. This same group had earlier murdered four members of a survey party near Seguin.

Even though vastly outnumbered, Rice and his men attacked, killed three men in the first assault, scattered the rest, and captured most of the supplies. One of the dead Mexicans, Manuel Flores, carried papers

Mirabeau B. Lamar served as the second president of the Republic of Texas. Later, he led a Ranger company during the Mexican War.
Texas State Library & Archives Commission

that indicated he was an agent for the Mexican Army. The papers detailed a plot to incite the Indians of the civilized tribes, the Cherokee in particular, to rise against the Texans.

When another company of Rangers attacked a large war party near the Red River in August of that year, the results gave further proof to the rumors that the Mexican government had sent agents provocateurs among the tribes. Among the dead Indians lay the body of Pedro Julian Miracle. In his saddlebags the Rangers found a meticulously kept journal of his efforts to foment uprisings among all of the tribes, friendly and hostile, from the Rio Grande River into Arkansas. Under orders from the commander-in-chief of the Mexican Army, Vicente Filisola, Miracle had visited with the Indian leaders. He had distributed munitions and other gifts to them in an effort to persuade them to cooperate with the Mexican plan.

The four "civilized" tribes, the Shawnee, Choctaw, Delaware, and Cherokee, had migrated to Texas from the United States at about the same time as the Anglo colonists. Although they had settled out on the borders north and west, they had far more in common with the Texans than with the Comanche, Kiowa, and Apache. They farmed and ranched and raised fine horses; they built houses and towns and businesses. They also had good rifles, and they didn't hesitate to use them against the Comanche and other raiders. In a few instances some adventurers from these tribes participated in raids on Texan settlements, but for the most part they served as allies and as a vital buffer between the Texas settlements and the "wild" Indians.

Cherokee leader John Bowles and other leaders of the civilized tribes had received Miracle and his gifts warmly enough, and some of them had even traveled to Matamoros to hear what the Mexicans had to say. Still, it's unlikely that the Cherokee and other civilized tribes never intended to act against the Texans — many of them considered themselves to *be* Texans. Unfortunately, the mere possibility of such treachery was enough to give the new President of the Republic, Mirabeau B. Lamar, the excuse he'd been looking for to alter the Republic's policy toward the Indians.

Lamar, an elegant, erudite Georgian, had served in the Revolution, had stood by Sam Houston at San Jacinto, and had served as Houston's Vice President. Despite this, Lamar didn't share Houston's partisanship for the Indians or respect for the *Tejano* population of Texas. As the head of a group of radicals within the government, he advocated the complete removal of all Indians from Texas, as well as measures that would secure land rights for Anglos alone. He had come not only to oppose President Houston for his liberal political and social views but to hold a great personal animosity toward him. While he couldn't directly affect Houston, he could turn his anger toward Houston's beloved Cherokees.

He found others who agreed with him, especially those land speculators who looked with envy upon the lands the Cherokee and other civilized tribes had cultivated so well. Lamar and his supporters maintained that the Indians had no title to Texas lands under the Republic, and so should be expelled from their holdings.

"Muster Roll of Capt. Lewis Sanches' Company of Mounted Gunmen, 1839." This company roll includes several Anglo names; the captain also notes that "each man furnished his own horse."
Texas State Library & Archives Commission

Upon his inauguration to the presidency of the Republic in December 1838, Lamar shifted military policy to the offensive. The lack of funds in the treasury hampered his efforts, but he eventually pushed through the Texas Congress several acts intended to increase the size of both the Ranger force and the regular Texas Army. The congressional act of December 10, 1838, subordinated the Ranger command officer to the first brigade commander of the Texas Army and to the Secretary of War, thus giving the Rangers a more military role. This act authorized new Ranger companies to operate in Gonzales, Bastrop, Robertson, and Milam Counties, but unlike the Rangers of the previously established companies, their service didn't earn them land certificates. Few muster rolls and payroll records survive for these companies, but one of them probably served under Henry Wax Karnes on the frontier in 1839.

Some records do exist for the defense forces formed in 1839 for the frontier counties. The captains of these groups included some familiar names from previous Ranger units: George B. Erath at Milam, Micah Andrews at LaGrange, William Eastland at Coleman, and Noah Smithwick at Bastrop. These new companies formed around the core of experienced veterans from the earlier companies, thereby benefiting from their experience in frontier combat.

Other military expansions planned in the congressional acts of December 1838 never took place, mainly because funding failed to materialize. A further funding reduction passed in January 1839 forced President Lamar to disband much of the regular army, other than the northern frontier forces under Col. Edward Burleson and the Ordinance Department. As the Texas Congress authorized additional Ranger companies to defend Goliad, Refugio, and San Patricio, it became more apparent to Lamar that most Texans preferred to rely on the Rangers and other irregulars rather than to maintain a large standing army.

This attitude prevailed in Texas for almost a century, the entire history of the frontier period. Most of the male population of Texas would show up to fight invaders from Mexico, and local militia groups would gladly take the field to pursue a band of Indian raiders, but this volunteer spirit extended only to emergency situations. Because volunteers often rode with Ranger units, and because many of the muster rolls and records from the Republic period have not survived, it's sometimes difficult to distinguish informal ranging companies from actual Texas Ranger companies. (See "Spies, Mounted Gunmen, and Rangers.")

Without an organized militia or a standing army, Texas based her frontier defense on the few men who were willing to sign up for service in Texas Rangers. Even though they became the first line of defense and proved themselves effective time and again, the Rangers often found themselves subject to the political whims of the Texas Legislature and the public. Under the Republic and then the State of Texas, funding and support for the Rangers often rated as a low priority. Only dedicated, determined men could operate under such conditions.

Also, and not for the last time, the question of just who determined the structure and mission of the Texas Ranger service became a political issue. The President of the Republic, the War Department, the Texas Congress and local protection committees all claimed authority to create "ranger" units. They issued conflicting decrees and ordinances, interfering for personal and political reasons in the appointment of officers and commanders.

Determined to drive the Indians out of Texas, President Lamar did his best to turn the Texas Rangers into the instrument of his policies. In the end, Lamar failed in that effort. Most of the Ranger companies remained on patrol elsewhere, fighting the Comanche, when Lamar opened his military campaign against the Cherokee in July of 1839.

The forces President Lamar gathered under the command of Col. Edward Burleson and Col. Thomas J. Rusk to send against the Cherokee were regular

SPIES, MOUNTED GUNMEN, AND RANGERS

From the earliest days of the colonial ranging companies, the mounted men called "rangers" had served as scouts and spies, as a cavalry screen for militia infantry and other troops, and as a rapid-deployment force to protect civilians. Even before the final battle at San Jacinto, Sam Houston had recognized the value of ranger units in military and peacekeeping operations. In an April 6, 1836, letter to Henry Wax Karnes, Houston so referred to the company of scouts Karnes had raised at Goliad: "I wish that a company of Spies would range as suggested by you."

The Texas Rangers continued to serve the same basic function as the ranging companies; even in official documents the Rangers were often referred to as "spies" or "scouts" or "ranging companies." The frontier custom was to refer to any force of mounted irregulars — men who provided their own weapons and mounts and didn't wear a regular uniform — as "rangers." Texas Rangers generally served a set term of service and remained on duty even when not active in the field, whereas militia groups and other volunteers served only as needed. This has led to much confusion by scholars, historians, and folklorists about which of these men were actually Texas Rangers. The few records and muster rolls of the period that have survived in the Ranger Papers (Texas State Archives) give a researcher only a tantalizing glimpse of the whole truth.

Records from the companies mustered in from 1839 to 1873 use several different designations: spies, scouts, mounted gunmen, volunteers, minutemen, rangers. The commanders used these terms interchangeably, sometimes describing a company by one name, sometimes by another. They used the rank of "scout" for some members of their companies but also defined associated or auxiliary companies as "scout" or "spy" companies. Members of different companies often transferred among them, formally or informally. Many of the younger men who joined up were foot-loose characters, always ready to move on to a new adventure. Sometimes a private in a "Ranger" company would show up weeks or months later as a lieutenant in a "company of Mounted Gunmen" or a scout in a "spy company" attached to a militia brigade. Terms of enlistment in these companies varied from a few weeks to a year.

Other mounted units served directly with militia or army units, or as local emergency protection forces, but used the same spectrum of terms to define themselves — including "ranger." These companies drew volunteers from the local populations they were meant to protect, so service in them wasn't by any means limited to Anglos. Some units consisted primarily of *Tejanos* right up to the time of annexation and the Mexican War.

A company of mounted scouts led by Capt. Antonio J. Manchaca, originally part of Col. Juan Seguín's command at San Jacinto, performed basic ranger duty in the San Antonio area after the Texas Revolution. The company served until they were mustered out, along with most of the revolutionary army, in 1837, but Manchaca continued to serve with other Ranger companies and volunteer forces. Capt. Lewis Sanches commanded a company of "Mounted Gunmen" attached to the Third Militia Brigade in 1839, and several Anglo names appear in his company's muster roll alongside the mostly Spanish names of the forty men under his command.

Another *Tejano* commander, Capt. Antonio Perez, recruited a Ranger force of fifteen men from San Antonio de Béxar in 1841. His official enlistment roll includes the names of Antonio Coy and John O. Trueheart, both of whom served on other occasions under Capt. John Coffee "Jack" Hays.

"Muster Roll of a 'Spy Company' commanded by Capt. Antonio Perez, 1841." This muster roll includes Antonio Coy, Antonio Sanches, and John O. Trueheart.
Texas State Library & Archives Commission

During this enlistment period, Hays and Perez joined their companies at San Antonio to protect the trade routes from Agaton's freebooters and a band of brigands led by Ignacio Cortez.

The men who served in frontier defense units didn't see much distinction among the definitions under which they served. It also evidently didn't matter to them if their comrades happened to have Spanish or Indian names, or English, German, or French, as long as they could ride and shoot and endure the hardships of the frontier. It's absolutely true, as some people say, that not a single "Mexican or Indian" ever served as a Texas Ranger in the nineteenth century. It's true because the Rangers were all Texans, no matter what their racial background. The Texas Rangers of the Republic had names like Hays or Smithwick, Chevallie or Erath, but they also had names like Galvan or Flacco or Perez, Coy or Spy Ruck or Red Wing.

The racial bitterness stirred up by the Mexican War (1846-1848) and the Mexican government's successful campaign to discredit and isolate *Tejano* leaders like Antonio Perez and Juan Seguin put an end to *Tejano*-led Ranger companies. Even so, some *Tejanos* continued to serve with Anglo-led companies. As late as the early twentieth century, Spanish names like Martin Trejo and Juan Gonzales appeared in the enlistment papers of the State Rangers of Texas. Manuel "Lone Wolf" Gonzaullas, one of the premiere Texas Ranger captains in the 1940s, is often called the "first Hispanic Texas Ranger," but one of the long line of *Tejanos* who served before him must certainly claim that honor.

Allied Indian units sometimes carried the designation of "scouts," but they mustered in under similar conditions of service. An official 1837 roll for "Captain Panther's company of Shawnee

Indians" lists the colorful names of a group of Cherokee, Delaware, Choctaw, and Shawnee who served as "ranger scouts" for a militia brigade. Two notable Indian units of "scouts and rangers" joined up from among the Lipan Apache, a Southwest Texas tribe traditionally engaged in continual warfare with the Comanche. Chief Castro mustered a company of Lipan Apache scouts for service with other Ranger units in President Lamar's general buildup of 1839; they fought beside the Rangers in several engagements against the Comanche. When young Flacco, son of old Chief Flacco, volunteered his party of ten Lipan Apache warriors to scout for Captain Jack Hays in 1841, it was his first step toward his enduring comradeship with Hays and command of his own unit of Texas Rangers.

Of those men who rode for the Lone Star in the nineteenth century, who was and who wasn't a "real" Texas Ranger? The distinction seems much more important to modern-day scholars than it was to the men themselves. The Rangers of the Republic served at times with regular army units, militia groups, and local volunteers, as well as with their Ranger companies. The determination of just which individual was a Texas Ranger remains more a matter of individual opinion than historical import.

Until the State of Texas mustered in the six companies of the Frontier Battalion in 1874, the official division between Texas Rangers and associated volunteers remained unclear. Even then, a marked difference existed between the Frontier Battalion, which served under the authority of the Adjutant General against Indians and outlaws in the west, and special units created by the governor, such as Leander H. McNelly's company, which operated against bandits on the Mexican border.

From the earliest days of the Republic until the time the Frontier Battalion gave way to the State Rangers of the twentieth century, official and formal definitions didn't amount to much more than paperwork. At the time, if a man rode in a company of mounted irregulars, if he fought side by side with his comrades against the common enemy and risked his life to protect his fellow's back, most people considered him worthy of the name Texas Ranger

military, militia, and volunteers, although some of them had no doubt served with ranging companies. Actual Ranger companies under Capt. James Carter, Capt. Lewis Sanches and others did serve as scouts and spies for the expedition; their experience and endurance proved invaluable. The Cherokee were well-armed and determined not to give in, even though they were scattered and outmatched by the five-hundred-man force Colonel Burleson had mustered. After the first attack against the central Cherokee settlement on the Neches River, the scout companies remained in the forefront of the running fight. Not content to just maintain contact with the opposition and direct the main forces, they were the first to ride each battle. Even in a less-than-honorable conflict, the Rangers served with honor.

The campaign took only a few days to accomplish its objective. The Cherokee, the Delaware, and the Shawnee scattered to Indian Territory and Mexico. Chief Bowles, the adopted father of Sam Houston, had refused to retreat. He said, "I am an old man. I die here." So he fell, still clutching in his dead hand the sword Sam Houston had given him years before.

Except for the Alamo, it was perhaps the most costly victory Texas ever experienced, and the wounds ran even deeper than lives lost in the pointless fight. Lamar's treasury inflation rendered the Republic's currency almost worthless; the hatred between his followers and Houston's threatened to break into open warfare. Without the Cherokee and other friendly tribes as a buffer, the borders stood open to the Comanche and to Mexican agents, leaving only the Texas Rangers to stand between Texas and her enemies.

Learning on the Battlefield

Noah Smithwick noted that the real Indian troubles began in 1838, when:

> The land office was opened and speculators began flocking into the country, accompanied by surveyors, who at once began an aggressive movement upon the hunting grounds of the wild tribes, thereby provoking them to a more determined resistance to the encroachments of the settlers. Then, too, the Mexican government egged them on, furnishing them with arms and ammunition. True, the Indian mode of indiscriminate warfare was barbarous, but there were not wanting white men to follow their example. Extermination was the motto on both sides. That was President Lamar's avowed policy.

President Lamar's policy and the political battles in the Texas Congress over military funding left the Rangers as the only effective defense between the settlers and the increasing Comanche threat. Led by experienced captains who had served well in prior engagements, the Rangers had begun to grow to fit that role. In particular, two 1839 engagements against the Comanche proved that the Rangers had the will to fight as frontier warriors; they also proved that the Rangers still had much to learn and much to lose.

John Henry Moore took command of the Bastrop and LaGrange companies in January of that year. He'd fought well at Gonzales during the Revolution, and he'd fought other Indians, but he'd never before faced enemies like the Comanche. His company captains, Noah Smithwick and Thomas Eastland, did know the Comanche well, as did Juan Castro, the Lipan Apache chief in command of the attached scout company. Young Flacco, Castro's lieutenant Juan Seis, and Castro's son, Juan, also signed up with the scouts.

Soon after, Castro's scouts discovered a large raiding party of Comanche camped on the San Gabriel River with a stolen horse herd. The Comanche also held a white captive, young Matilda Lockhart, daughter of a local colonel of militia. Colonel Moore put together a force to intercept the raiders. Smithwick and Eastland each took thirty men; Castro's sixteen Lipan scouts joined them. The expedition immediately ran into bad weather and other mishaps, including an accident in which a rifle fell from where its owner (one of the scouts) had propped it. The shot hit one of Captain Eastland's men. The unfortunate Ranger died later as two others tried to ferry him back down the Colorado River to the settlements.

The Rangers and the scouts tracked Comanche through snow and ice for several days, finally catching sight of smoke from their fire near the mouth of the San Saba River. Castro's Lipans managed to slip in and steal the horse herd from where the Comanche had it hidden. Even though the scouts reported that the war party was far larger than they'd originally estimated, the Rangers attacked the camp just at daylight on a mid-February morning. Eastland's company flanked

This woodcut first appeared in J. W. Wilbarger's 1889 book, *Indian Depredations in Texas*, to depict the incident in which the Comanche burned the soles of Matilda Lockhart's feet to prevent her from escaping. The name of the engraver of this image, T. J. Owen, was actually another pseudonym for the author William Sydney Porter, better known as O. Henry.
UT Institute of Texan Cultures at San Antonio

the camp on the right to block escape into the woods, Smithwick's company made the frontal assault and Castro's scouts took the left.

The first rush took the Comanche by surprise. The Rangers killed many Comanche who were still wrapped in their sleeping robes, but the attack fell apart as the Rangers stopped to reload or scattered to pursue the fleeing enemy. "At this juncture," Smithwick later wrote, "for some unexplainable reason, Col. Moore ordered a retreat, which threw our men into confusion. Quick to grasp and take advantage of the situation, the Indians rallied and drove us back to the cover of a ravine, our only casualty being an arrow cut on the nose sustained by Captain Eastland." If the Rangers had held together and pressed the attack, they might have emerged victorious. Instead, they were forced to withdraw from the camp and take up a defensive position.

The Rangers were able to stop the Comanche counterattack, but two of the company received severe wounds in doing so. The Indians, who had suffered heavy casualties, called for a parlay. When they saw that the Lipans had killed the Comanche prisoners, they withdrew from the field. Castro, angered by Moore's order to retreat, took his command and the captured horses and left.

To make matters worse, Colonel Moore had made the mistake of leaving the Rangers' horses unguarded. The Rangers returned to the camp to find that the Comanche had stolen them. They had to cover the hundred miles back to their station on foot, carrying their wounded. Joseph Martin, who had taken a bullet in the spine, lived through the ordeal but died several weeks later. Smithwick notes that the Lockhart girl remained captive until her rescue some time later, and that he lost a fine horse in the "worst swap" he'd ever made. In his report, Colonel Moore gave much credit to his men for their courage, and he estimated that they'd killed or wounded as many as a hundred of the enemy. He also neglected to mention the rather humiliating loss of his company's *remuda*.

Late in May of that year, Capt. John Bird of the Fort Bend detachment responded to civilian reports of Comanche raids along the Brazos River. At Fort Milam, an army post not far from the Falls on the Brazos, he rendezvoused with a smaller volunteer company recruited in Houston by Lt. W. G. Evans. They traveled to Fort Smith on the Little River and set up a base camp from which they could run patrols.

On patrol on May 26, Captain Bird and thirty-five of his men cut a fresh trail and caught sight of a small party of Comanche. A chase ensued, but the warriors easily outdistanced the Rangers. The captain called a rest halt and had his men dismount to walk their exhausted horses back the way they'd come.

It was an old but usually very successful Comanche tactic: a few scouts lure the enemy into a chase to wear them out, then the main strength of the war party closes in to spring the trap. Perhaps Captain Bird had actually figured out what the Indians were trying to do, or perhaps he'd only called off the chase because his horses had given out. In any case, the Comanche ruse almost worked.

A force of forty or more Comanche rushed from ambush, giving tongue to their fierce war cry and filling the air with arrows. The Rangers managed to break through and reach a defensive position in an arroyo just barely in time. A vastly superior number of Comanche and other Indians joined their fellows to surround the Rangers. Unlike the Comanche, the Kickapoo warriors carried trade rifles.

A Comanche arrow had taken Captain Bird's life in the first few minutes of the fight, leaving Lt. Nathan Brookshire in command. As the Indians made repeated attacks from all directions, Brookshire coolly ordered his men to pick their targets, then to fire and reload in relays so that they never lacked loaded weapons with which to repulse a charge. As it had at Erath's battle in the Falls country and Moore's fight at the San Saba, this tactic proved to be the Rangers' salvation. The Indians sustained heavy losses in their attacks — Brookshire estimated thirty or more killed and as many wounded. They withdrew

"THE TEXAS RANGER"

A letter from a Ranger to his faithless sweetheart in Colorado contains the earliest surviving written version of the song, "The Texas Ranger." The song itself was handed down as a traditional folk ballad for decades before this example; the original tune and mood is derived from a sixteenth century Irish ballad lamenting a lost battle. Recycling a tune was a common practice for the Texans descended from the old Scots-Irish borderers.

The location of the fight and the number of Rangers killed in the battle vary to fit the preferences of the bard who sings it. In any case, traditional songs tend to mix myth with reality and to confuse and combine separate events. The song may refer to the Battle of Bird Creek in May 1839, in which Capt. John H. Bird and four of his men were killed. It may also include circumstances from the Battle of Walker Creek in June 1844, although Capt. Jack Hays emerged unscathed and the Rangers lost only one man, Pvt. Peter Fohr. Several Rangers, including the future captain Sam Walker, were so severely wounded in the Walker Creek fight that the Rangers had to camp at the site for several days until the casualties recovered enough to be moved; inaccurate rumors and newspaper reports at the time listed the wounded as killed. Capt. A. C. Cage, cousin to Jack Hays, died along with eight of his men in an 1838 fight with the Comanche, and even though his was a volunteer militia company, the song may derive some of its substance from his death.

The actual circumstances matter little. Whether or not the anonymous author was a young ranger scout, as the song suggests, or if it confuses facts and combines events, the song certainly elicits the emotions the author intended. It comes closer than any other bit of verse to serving as an anthem for the Texas Rangers.

The Texas Ranger

Come all ye Texas Rangers, wherever you may be;

I'll tell you of some troubles that happened unto me;

My name is nothing extra; to you I will not tell:

But here's to all good Rangers, I'm sure I wish you well.

It was at the age of sixteen I joined a Ranger band;

We marched from San Antonio down to the Rio Grande;

And there our Captain told us — perhaps he thought it right —

"Before we reach the river, boys, I'm sure we'll have a fight."

And before we reached the river, our Captain gave command,

"To arms, to arms," he shouted, "and by your pony stand!"

I saw the smoke ascending, it seemed to reach the sky,

And then, the thought it struck me — my time had come to die.

I saw the Indians coming, I heard them give a yell;
My feelings at that moment, no mortal tongue can tell;
I saw their glittering lances, their arrows 'round me hailed;
My heart, it sank within me; my courage almost failed.

I thought of my old mother, who in tears to me did say,
"To you they are all strangers, with me you'd better stay."
I thought her weak and childish, and that she did not know;
For I was bent on roaming, and I was bound to go.

We fought for nine full hours before the strife was o'er;
The likes of dead and dying, I'd never seen before;
And when the sun had risen, the Comanche, they had fled;
We loaded up our rifles and counted up our dead.

And all of us were wounded, our noble Captain slain,
As the sun shone down so brightly upon the bloody plain.
Sixteen as brave a Rangers as ever rode the West
Were buried by their comrades, with arrows in their chests.

Perhaps you have a mother, likewise a sister too;
Perhaps you have a sweetheart who'll weep and mourn for you;
If this should be your portion, and you are bound to roam,
I advise you from experience, you'd better stay at home.

to pick up their casualties and to snipe at the Rangers' position, but at dusk they gave up on the fight and rode away.

It was a victory for the Rangers in that they'd survived a battle against such mismatched odds. They'd used their weapons to deadly effect, and they'd proven that they could develop the right tactics to fit their strengths. Until technological advances gave them an advantage in firepower, they'd rely on staggered volleys of fire to prevent being overwhelmed by the superior forces they faced.

It is possible that this engagement, the only recorded fight with the Comanche in which a Texas Ranger captain lost his life, was the inspiration for the anonymous song, "The Texas Ranger" (see "The Texas Ranger"). If so, the song's doleful lyrics certainly suit the emotions the Rangers of Bird's company must have felt after the battle ended. It wasn't an easy victory. The Ranger casualty list included five men killed: their captain, John Bird, 1st Sgt. William H. Weaver, Pvt. Thomas Gay, Pvt. H. M. C. Hall and Pvt. Jesse E. Nash. Two other Rangers received severe wounds. Lieutenant Brookshire directed his men to bury their dead in the soft earth of the ravine near where they'd fallen. Alternately walking and riding their tired horses, the Rangers retreated through the night to Fort Smith.

Moore and Brookshire were only two among a growing cadre of experienced Texas Ranger leaders, men toughened by their own sacrifices and by those of their comrades. Such experience didn't come cheap, but the Rangers learned from their mistakes as well as from their successes. In that sense, Andrews's and Smithwick's night attack at the Colorado River, Erath and McLochlan's deadly fight at the Falls of the Brazos, and Moore's premature retreat at the San Saba fight weren't failures, even though those actions cost some Rangers their lives. Bryant's disastrous fight against the Caddo at the Brazos Falls taught Eli Chandler the importance of maintaining battlefield discipline, a principle he would apply to great effect as a captain of Rangers. Moore would remember the mistakes he had made at San Saba, and he would use what he'd learned to win his next battle against the Comanche.

The Rangers of the early Republic era proved their willingness to take the fight to the enemy. Although they were usually outnumbered, even when they lost a battle they inflicted higher casualties on the enemy than they sustained themselves. Sometimes, they won. At Arroyo Seco, Karnes used his knowledge of Comanche tactics against his enemies even as he made the best possible use of volleyed rifle fire from a defensive position. Brookshire won an even more important victory at Bird Creek by maintaining his men's discipline and morale after they'd lost their captain and sustained several casualties. These hard-won victories provided the Texans with the much-needed hope that they could prevail in their struggle to defend the frontier.

The frontier offered no bloodless, academic military school classes in Indian fighting. The Texas Rangers had only the battlefield as a schoolroom, the enemy as their only instructor. By 1840, they had joined together in a brotherhood of experienced fighting men, a force destined to surpass the Comanche as the ultimate warriors of the Wild West. From within their ranks would emerge a captain who would lead them to that destiny, a man who would outshine them all in the science of frontier warfare. His name was John Coffee Hays.

4

DEFENDERS OF THE LONE STAR

B Y 1840, THE TEXAS RANGERS COULD CALL UPON ALMOST TWO decades of tradition and experience. In defeat as well as in victory, the Rangers had proved themselves as worthy foes to the Comanche and the Mexicans, as frontier warriors in their own right. All they needed to excel at their calling was a rallying point, a captain who could lead the defenders of the Lone Star to their destiny.

John Coffee Hays came up through the Ranger ranks, elected from among the brotherhood of warriors. More than any other captain in their long history, his influence would shape their destiny, would define the term "Texas Ranger." His friends called him Jack, and the men who served with him in the Texas Rangers called him "Captain Jack," but his Comanche enemies gave him the nickname that became feared, respected, and hated by the enemies of Texas all across the Southwest: "Devil Jack."

In February 1840, two new companies of Rangers mustered in to protect South Central Texas around San Antonio and the South Texas coastal area around Victoria. John T. Price was elected to command the Victoria company; the San Antonio company chose as its leader twenty-three-year-old Jack Hays.

In his time as a surveyor for the Béxar district, Hays had come to know every trail and waterhole in the country. He'd fought Indians and bandits in companies under the command of Juan Seguín and Henry Wax Karnes, and he'd learned well the hard lessons of frontier survival. He was, without a doubt, the best choice the Texans could have made for the captain of the San Antonio unit. In his first company Hays enlisted such men as Michael Chevallie, Christopher "Kit" Acklin, and R. A. "Ad" Gillespie, who would later ride with him during the Mexican War. The famous frontiersman, Bigfoot Wallace, volunteered as a scout.

Hays suspected that Laredo, on the Rio Grande, was being used by the Mexican military and irregular forces as a staging ground for scouts into Texas and for espionage missions to incite the Indians. His famed ability to bluff, outwit, and defeat much larger forces came to the fore when he and thirteen of his company,

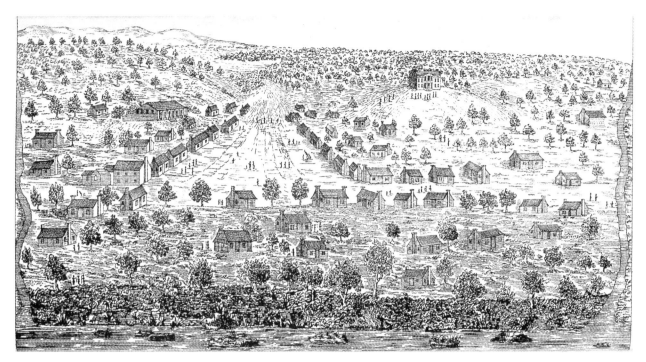

A view of the city of Austin in the 1840s, looking north across the Colorado River. President Mirabeau Lamar's house is on the right at the top of the hill, the temporary capitol is the large building at the top left. This served as the frontispiece illustration for *A History of Texas or the Emigrant's Guide to the New Republic by a Resident Emigrant* by William Allen.
Texas State Library & Archives Commission

Photo of John Coffee Hays, "Captain Jack" of the Texas Rangers.
UT Institute of Texan Cultures at San Antonio/Library of Congress, Prints and Photographs Division

while on scout near Laredo, ran into a Mexican cavalry company. This company, led by the Laredo *alcalde*, outnumbered the Rangers more than three to one. Hays set his men into a defensible position, then rode out to parley with the *alcalde*, who demanded that the Rangers surrender to his superior force. Instead, Hays gave the order to fire; his aide shot the Mexican leader out of his saddle.

The Mexican cavalry charged, only to be repulsed by the massed fire of the dismounted Rangers' rifles. Both the Rangers and the Mexicans used standard frontier tactics; they rode forward, then dismounted to fire their muskets, then retreated a bit to reload, always holding some charged weapons in reserve. Hays saw an opportunity in this. In a bold move, he ordered his men to reserve their fire, then to empty their rifles and charge into the Mexican formation as the enemy dismounted to fire and reload. With single-shot

William "Big Foot" Wallace.
UT Institute of Texan Cultures at San Antonio, Courtesy of the Gonzales Historical Museum

pistols and clubbed rifles, the Rangers killed the senior officer and eight others, completely routing the Mexican force and taking many of them prisoner.

When Gen. Rafael Vásquez learned of this action, he set up a plan to lure the Rangers into a trap using spies and a false request for help from a trader. Informed of the ruse by a *Tejano* friend at San Antonio, Hays took forty Rangers and followed the Mexican spy back to his camp. They surprised the ambush force, which was ten times their number, while the Mexicans were still in camp. So confidently did the Rangers charge that the Mexicans assumed that they were only the vanguard of a larger force and fled back across the Rio Grande. When the truth of the encounter came out, General Vásquez never quite lived down the blow to his pride.

Armed with an uncanny ability to develop and implement innovative strategies even in the heat of battle, Hays defeated vastly superior forces time and again. He was not above using his reputation to strike terror into the hearts of his enemies; indeed, it was just one more tactic that Hays and the other Texas Rangers learned on the battlefield.

War of Moon and Star

It was inevitable that the Comanche and the Texans would fight to the end, despite the best efforts made by both sides to reach an understanding between them. The two cultures were too radically different and too dominant to exist in the same country. The Texans would continue to move west, and the Comanche would never willingly withdraw from the *comancheria* or give up their warrior way of life. Either the Comanche moon or the Lone Star would hold sway in Texas. Nothing could stop the battle between them.

The deaths of twelve Comanche leaders at the Council House fight that erupted at a peace conference in San Antonio on March 19, 1840, brought the constant, low-level conflict between the Comanche and the Texans into the full flame of war. For a short time,

Comanche raids almost ceased. The Texans allowed most of their official and volunteer ranger units to finish out their enlistments but didn't muster in any replacements. They may have thought that the deaths of the twelve chiefs had taken some of the starch out of the Indians, but Comanche leadership depended on ability, not heredity. The Comanche bided their time, chose new leaders, and distributed weapons and munitions they'd received from Mexican agents.

Early in August 1840, the Comanche launched what would become known as the Great Raid. A party of six hundred to a thousand warriors slipped down from the plains through sparsely populated country to the coast. They hit some isolated outposts along the way but avoided the scattered settlements to reach their main objectives on the coast. On August 6, they attacked the South Texas city of Victoria, one of the major settlements and an important trade and shipping center. Unaccustomed to street fighting, they didn't close in to torch the town, but they fought off the Texan defenders and looted the outskirts of goods and a huge herd of horses.

The raiders moved on to sack the port village of Linnville, a less defended settlement. Although most of the inhabitants managed to escape into the bay in boats, they watched in horror as the Comanche butchered several stragglers. The Comanche took even more horses, loaded them up with goods looted from the warehouses, then set fire to the town. They also took a number of captives, mostly women and children. Honor satisfied, they decided that the raid was a success and turned north for home.

Unfortunately for them, the wide trail they'd left through the prairie had been spotted. Throughout the Texan settlements, volunteer forces hastened to take up the trail, to rescue the captives, and to seek vengeance for the raid. Ben McCulloch led a company of twenty-four volunteers from Gonzales to join up with Capt. John J. Tumlinson's force of one hundred militia. Companies mustered by Adam Zumwalt and Clark Owen also joined in. They caught up with the raiders on August 9 and attacked the vastly superior

Comanche force at the Casa Blanca River crossing. One Texan lost his life in the short, desperate fight; despite McCulloch's objections, Tumlinson decided to withdraw until reinforcements arrived.

Col. Edward Burleson's militia, aided by Chief Placido's Tonkawa scouts, moved in from the north. Burleson decided to hit the Comanche at Plum Creek, south of Austin. Placido's men traveled on foot, running the entire thirty-mile distance beside the militia's horses. At Plum Creek they found Capt. Matthew Caldwell and Capt. James Bird from Gonzales already waiting with 117 men who were willing to fight the Comanche and hold them despite the bitter odds. Caldwell reportedly told his own command before Bird joined him, "Boys, the Indians number about one thousand. They have our women and children captives. We are only eighty-seven, but I believe we can whip hell out of them!"

Lafayette Ward brought in twenty-two men from Port Lavaca and the surrounding settlements on the coast, and McCulloch's men and the other companies came in from the south. Jack Hays brought in a company from Béxar with Mike Chevallie and Bigfoot Wallace. Probably the largest force the Texans had gathered in one place since the end of the Revolution, the two hundred volunteers were men from all walks of life — professional men, farmers, preachers — as well as almost all of the experienced Rangers, Indian fighters, and Indian auxiliaries. One famous captain was absent, though not of his own accord: Henry Wax Karnes, only thirty-eight years of age and perhaps the most experienced of the Ranger leaders at the time, was dying of yellow fever.

Gen. Felix Huston took command and reorganized the Texans into three companies under Bird, Caldwell, and Ward. No relation to Sam Houston, Felix Huston was an adventurer from Kentucky who had no real battlefield experience but who had managed to win command of the Texas militia by using his political connections with the radical elements in the Texas Congress.

On August 12, as the unconcerned and unwitting

A woodcut of Placido, Chief of the Tonkawa, from *A Pictorial History of Texas*.
Texas State Library & Archives Commission

Comanche approached in a long, strung-out line toward Plum Creek, mounted Texan scouts hit the rear of the column from the south. The Comanche rode north into the trap to find themselves facing a long line of vengeful Texans. Huston was reluctant to allow his men to break lines, but as the main body of the Comanche moved off with their outriders covering their retreat, Ben McCulloch rode up and shouted, "That's not the way to fight Indians!" The Texans answered him with a charge; the Comanche outriders rode to meet them, repeatedly firing showers of arrows and wheeling away.

In the best Comanche tradition, one fearless warrior rode in the forefront of the screening force. He'd

This woodcut depicting the Battle of Plum Creek against the Comanche in 1840 first appeared in J. W. Wilbarger's 1889 book, *Indian Depredations in Texas*.
UT Institute of Texan Cultures at San Antonio

decked himself and his horse out in his looted finery — streaming ribbons, a tall silk hat, a long coat with brass buttons, and a fine silk umbrella. His war chants rang out even above the roar of the Texans' rifles. He seemed impervious to their shots, even though bullets carried away his hat and his umbrella. Only a few of the Comanche outriders fell to the Texas rifles, and most of those because their horses were hit. Even the grim frontiersmen found themselves impressed by this show of bravery, astonished by the way the Comanche ducked and dodged their bullets.

Jack Hays saw it first — the Comanche were angling their shields, stout frames of wood covered by tough buffalo hide, just enough so that the rifle balls glanced off of them. He had his men hold their fire until the outriders fired their arrows and turned away. At the next volley, the brave Comanche leader and many of his followers fell from their mounts. The Texans mounted up and charged into the main Comanche formation, turning their retreat into a rout. The running battle spread out for miles across the prairie as the Comanche broke up into small groups to escape; Burleson's men chased one band almost to the San Marcos River.

In the end, the Texans killed an estimated eighty-seven of the enemy to their one dead, seven wounded. The Comanche also lost most of the goods and horses they'd captured. McCulloch's call to charge established his reputation as a bold leader; stories of Jack Hays's battlefield insight added to his legend. In Huston's report he noted the many Mexican trade goods found among the captured material. The Texans took this as a clear indication that the plan for the Great Raid had originated with Mexican agents in Matamoros.

This defeat may have convinced the Comanche that large raids weren't profitable, but that didn't stop them from launching a campaign of smaller lightning raids all along the frontier, from Gonzales to the northern settlements. Ben McCulloch emerged as the leader of the company mustered at Gonzales to fight these raiders; Jack Hays and his Rangers found themselves living in the saddle to defend Béxar.

In the fall after the Great Raid, ninety Fayette County volunteers moved north from LaGrange to strike at the Comanche in their own territory. Capt. John Henry Moore, who had learned from his previous errors at the Battle of the San Saba River in 1839, took command. He also enlisted the aid of Castro and his Lipan scouts. On October 14, Moore and Castro attacked a large Comanche village on the far northern waters of the Colorado River.

The surprised Comanche put up a fight, then broke for the opposite bank of the river. The Texans pursued them across the prairie in a running battle. Unlike Moore's first campaign, this was a complete victory for the Texans. They killed forty-eight Comanche, took thirty-four prisoners, and captured many horses; only two of the company were wounded.

The War of the Moon and the Star would go on for decades, but Moore's company returned to Austin with a new hope that the Texans would emerge as the victors.

Men to Count On

In the aftermath of the Great Raid and Moore's campaign, sentiment intensified for more extensive military operations against the Comanche. The debate raged between those who wanted to establish a standing army and those who preferred the militia system, but the sad state of the Republic's treasury remained the deciding factor. In any case, most Texans wouldn't support a military draft or taxation to support an army. During the latter part of 1840, as Texans argued about how to pay for frontier defense, only a few volunteers and unpaid Rangers rode the borders. Meanwhile, the Comanche and other enemies of Texas continued to carry out depredations against isolated settlers and traders.

Trouble moved north from the contested Nueces Strip in the form of bandits and military adventurers, not all of them from Mexico. The Nueces attracted all kinds of lawless men, freebooters who didn't discriminate but robbed and killed Mexicans, Texans, and Indians alike. Centralist Mexican agents continued to arm and incite the Indians against the Texans even as they waged a rumor campaign to discredit loyal *Tejanos*. In particular they targeted Ranger Capt. Antonio Perez and Col. Juan Seguín, the two outstanding *Tejano* representatives of the Lone Star in the San Antonio community. At the same time, bandits sponsored by Mexican agents raided caravans and trading posts and isolated ranches all across South Texas, not sparing Juan Seguín's *rancho* south of San Antonio.

The government turned back to the Rangers as their most effective weapon, to Jack Hays in particular. Although Hays was a protégé of Houston's, President Lamar trusted him because he got results. When Lamar's government mustered in three fifteen-man Ranger companies for six months of service early in 1841, he appointed Hays, John T. Price, and Antonio Perez to command them. Hays and Perez stationed their companies in San Antonio, a central point from which they could act against threats from the south and the north, from the Mexicans or the Comanche.

THE MYSTERIOUS DEATH OF CAPTAIN FLACCO

Although they were the traditional enemies of the more numerous Comanche, unlike the other Apache tribes of the Southwest the Lipan Apache fought on horseback with lance and shield in much the same way as did the Comanche. Flacco, the young war chief of the Lipan Apache, saw the Texans as strong allies against his old enemies, and from the first battle he fought beside them he remained a loyal defender of the Lone Star.

After he gained experience with Castro's scouts in earlier fights alongside Ranger companies, Flacco recruited his own mixed company of Lipans and other Indians. Eventually, his company expanded to include some *Tejanos* and Texans. President Sam Houston commissioned him as a captain of Texas Rangers and listed Flacco's scout company on the official muster rolls; he also granted Flacco the rank of a full colonel in the Texas militia.

According to Jack Hays's biographer James Kimmins Greer, in appearance Flacco combined the fierce attributes of the hawk with the lean strength of the panther. He was a brilliant tactician who had few equals in the mental and physical science of frontier warfare. His friendship with Jack Hays provided the great captain and his men with valuable insights into that science. Side by side, Hays and Flacco faced death together many times in the service of the Lone Star. If there was ever any living model from which Hollywood should have drawn the fictional Tonto, the Lone Ranger's *compadre*, it should have been Flacco.

It's one of those tragic ironies of frontier history that the brave Flacco didn't die in combat as a Texas Ranger beside his old comrades. He died alone, except for one of his scouts, murdered by treacherous thieves. According to Noah Smithwick, even Flacco's friends conspired to obscure the true nature of his death to prevent a war between the Lipan Apache and their Texan allies.

Late in 1842, when Jack Hays and Gen. Alexander Somervell decided to abort the ill-advised Texan invasion of Mexico at Guererro and return to Texas soil, Hays continued on to Mier to run escort for those men who refused to break off the advance. He ordered Flacco to scout for Somervell's retreating force and to round up fresh horses for them. For his own escort, Flacco took only a deaf mute Lipan scout, an elderly man blessed with extremely keen eyesight in compensation for his hearing loss.

The Rangers, whose regular pay could best be described as paltry to nonexistent, often took their payment Indian style in horses, weapons, and other goods gathered from their conquered enemies. Flacco and his company had done so well in the campaign against the Mexicans that their share loaded down a considerable pack train. With these goods and about forty horses he'd liberated for Somervell's men, Flacco and his companion set out to meet Somervell on the trail to Laredo. After the rendezvous the company divided and Flacco and some others headed for San Antonio. When his mute companion fell ill, Flacco camped at the Medina River to allow him to rest.

On December 24, Jack Hays found the bodies of his murdered comrade and his mute scout lying on the trail, their horses, mules, and goods stolen. In San Antonio, Hays heard that Flacco had hired two Mexicans to help him drive the pack train; these two drovers turned out to be bandits who had murdered the chief and his companion and taken his goods. Hays and the men of his company promised to avenge Flacco's murder, as well as to protect the members of his tribe as a tribute to his memory. Indeed, Hays did his best to protect Flacco's people until he left the Ranger service and moved to California after the Mexican War.

Herein lies the mystery: Hays wasn't the kind of man to go back on his word, but of his vengeance for the murders no report survives. Also, Flacco was an excellent judge of men, so it was unlikely that he'd have hired untrustworthy drovers or would have turned his back on them if he didn't know them well. It would have been difficult, if not impossible, for anyone to catch Flacco off guard. How could two Mexican drovers have succeeded where the whole Comanche nation and the Mexican Army had failed? Why did Hays never keep his promise to bring the killers to justice?

Noah Smithwick provides a possible answer. By his account, the morning after Flacco camped at the Medina two members of the returning militia company, Tom Thernon and another man, turned up missing. Smithwick heard rumors that two men fitting their description were spotted in Seguin some days after the murder. According to the report, these men had a large herd of horses and packs of Mexican trade goods that they'd tried to sell. Thernon and his partner were never caught with solid evidence of their guilt, but Smithwick believed that these two men, not Mexican bandits, had murdered Flacco for his horses.

President Houston and other members of the government knew that Old Flacco, the murdered Ranger's father, would declare war on the Texans if it became known that white men he'd fought beside had so treacherously killed and robbed him. When Old Flacco went to his friend Smithwick for answers about his son's death, Smithwick wrote to Gen. Edward Burleson, Antonio Navarro, and President Houston. All of the Texas dignitaries replied with the same answer, that Flacco had been murdered by Mexican bandits. They also instructed Smithwick to leave Old Flacco in no doubt about the veracity of the story.

This duty Smithwick found distasteful in the extreme, but he carried out his orders, in part because revealing the truth would have led to a war in which all of Flacco's people would have perished:

There was but a small remnant of the band at that time, about sixty warriors, but, had they known how young Flacco died, they would have declared war to the death against the whites, and, as often has been the case, the crime of one miserable wretch would have caused the death of hundreds of innocent people.

When he read the letters to the old chief, the entire camp shook with an outpouring of grief of a magnitude that Smithwick had never before seen among Indians:

I had heard the loud lamentations with which they were wont to bewail their dead, but here was a sorrow too strong to be repressed, too genuine for noisy demonstration. Tears rained down the old man's face while sobs fairly shook his frame. I felt how useless words were in such a crisis. I could only express my sympathy by the tears that welled up to my own eyes.

No doubt Hays felt the same grief at the loss of the brave Lipan Apache comrade who had more than once saved his life. It may be that President Houston also felt that it was best not to inform Hays and his Rangers of his suspicions about the true nature of Flacco's fate. It's even possible that he ordered Hays to remain silent about the rumors. Even if Hays knew, he probably wouldn't have told Old Flacco for the same reason Smithwick kept the secret, to prevent bloodshed. If Hays did know or find out about the truth, however, there would have been no force on earth that could have kept him from seeking justice.

In any case, it wasn't until years later, after Hays left Texas for California, that the rumors about the murders leaked out to the Lipans. At that time, the last of them broke with the Texans and declared war on their former allies. Thernon and his companion vanished, perhaps to New Mexico, but more likely to a more final destination. Whether in the end justice spun from the muzzle of a Ranger's Colt or sprang from an Apache bow, the odds are that somewhere in the West, by some lonely trail or in some hidden canyon, two murderers lie in unmarked graves. For the death of Captain Flacco, they deserved no lesser sentence.

Texas State Library & Archives Commission

Probably the most famous and accurate description of Jack Hays comes from his closest comrade, the Lipan Apache chief Flacco, who was himself commissioned as a Captain of Texas Ranger scouts by President Sam Houston. In search of a Comanche war band with whom he'd had an earlier battle in the summer of 1841, Captain Hays led his company into the rugged country along the Frio River. His twenty-five regular Rangers, fifteen *Tejanos* from the Gonzales company, and Flacco's dozen Apache and Tonkawa scouts ran into a party of Comanche hunters and pursued them along the river.

The Rangers chased the hunting party for more than eight miles before reaching the Comanche encampment, only to find themselves facing more than one hundred warriors. The Comanche engaged the Rangers in a running fight, further tiring the Rangers' already winded horses. In preparing a counterattack, Hays selected the men whose mounts appeared up to the task. He borrowed one of the less winded horses from a volunteer and rode out in front of his men, Flacco at his side, to fire his pistol at the advancing line of Comanche warriors. The borrowed horse bolted, took the bit between its teeth, and carried Hays straight into the middle of the enemy formation.

Unable to stop the maddened horse, Hays drew his pistols and readied himself for battle. Flacco, unwilling to be left behind, whipped his mount up to speed to overtake his friend. As they hit the Comanches almost together, Hays fired right and left, then Flacco did the same, only a beat behind. The Comanche quickly overcame their shock and shouted war cries as they closed in around the pair. Hays managed to wheel his horse back toward the Rangers, and with Flacco again just behind him, they shot their way out through the encircling warriors and outdistanced their pursuers.

After a fight that had left their horses exhausted and ten or more warriors dead, both sides decided that they'd had enough for one day.

Later, when the men of the company asked Flacco to explain why he'd made that suicidal charge with Hays, he replied that he'd be damned if he were ever to be left behind on any charge that Captain Jack led, no matter how it ended. Even so, Flacco was obviously glad that the affair ended so fortuitously. "Me and Red Wing," he said, talking of his scout lieutenant, "we're not afraid to go to Hell together. Captain Jack, he's too *mucho bravo*—he's not afraid to go to Hell all by himself."

This woodcut of Hays and Flacco charging the Comanche comes from J. W. Wilbarger's *Indian Depredations in Texas.*

Price's company patrolled out of Victoria, often fighting against bandits and Mexican military incursions in the Nueces Strip.

Traders on the southern routes often suffered from the deadly attentions of the Nueces Strip outlaws, in particular from Agaton's group of freebooters and Ignacio Cortez's bandits. In an effort to hunt down these bandits, Hays's Rangers began patrolling the trade routes. While on one of their earliest joint patrols north of Laredo, Hays and Perez met and soundly defeated a large force of Federal Mexican cavalry that had joined with Cortez's bandits. The Rangers again used their pistols in their charge, killing three Mexicans, capturing twenty-five, and sending the remainder of the enemy into a hasty retreat. The tales the cavalrymen told of the Rangers' ferocity caused a panic in Laredo, set civilians fleeing south, and prompted the *alcalde* to ride forth under a white flag to beg the Rangers to spare his town. Hays and Perez replied that they'd simply intended to ensure that the bandits leave the traders alone. They then turned and rode for home.

It was at about this time that the younger Flacco, a Lipan Apache war leader, met Jack Hays and offered him the services of his ten-man company of Indian scouts. Flacco and Hays formed a friendship that would last until Flacco's tragic death (see "The Mysterious Death of Captain Flacco") at the hands of outlaws. The men of Flacco's company, unlike most of the Indian auxiliaries listed as scouts, participated so fully in the fighting and patrol duty that they eventually gained their own place in the official muster rolls of the Texas Rangers. Their young chief achieved the singular honor of becoming the only Apache to ever be commissioned as a Captain of Texas Rangers.

Although muster rolls indicate that the Republic formally recognized and funded only the South Texas companies during this period, they weren't the only ranger-type units operating in Texas. Ben McCulloch and James H. Callahan led a volunteer ranging company from Gonzales against Comanche horse raiders, while Eli Chandler and George B. Erath commanded companies of scouts from East Texas on forays into the Brazos River and Cross Timbers country. A volunteer force of Texans and Lipans commanded by Mark B. Lewis protected Austin, fighting against Comanche raiders and bandits on the San Saba and Nueces Rivers. "Minute Men" from San Patricio and Refugio and Fannin Counties patrolled the southwestern and southern frontier.

Most of the informal volunteer companies were actually better supplied and far superior in number to the Ranger companies led by Hays, Perez, Flacco, and Price. The Republic couldn't have expected the small regular Ranger companies to serve except as scouts, a kind of early warning system to detect and report trouble. Hays didn't always see it that way, even when he didn't have a full complement of fifteen men on his company's muster roll. Using his knowledge of the land and his battlefield genius to shock and surprise the enemy, Hays often led his company to victory over forces superior in numbers, if not tactics. When one of his spy patrols detected a major threat, he'd combine forces with Perez, Flacco, and other Ranger or militia units. He'd also call for volunteers from the local community, including Juan Seguín and some members of his old ranging company. Using his experienced corps of Rangers as a rallying point, he was able to muster a rapid, effective response to any threat.

Captain Hays didn't hold overall command of the Rangers until his promotion to major in 1842. By virtue of his abilities and his devotion to duty, he emerged as their leader in spirit long before that. From 1841 to 1846, even during those periods between formal six-month enlistments, Hays seldom left the field. His company and those of Perez, Price, and Flacco often continued to patrol even when there was no pay or formal muster roll.

A wound Hays received in a fight with a Comanche band near San Antonio in March of 1841 didn't slow him down. After the fight, he returned to San Antonio to rest, take on supplies, and seek medical attention for his wounded men. Almost immediately, he took to the field again, his own understrength

THE LEGEND OF ENCHANTED ROCK

Enchanted Rock is a focus of Texas legend, so it's only natural that one of the many stories told about it involves Jack Hays in a fight to the death with Comanche warriors. A bronze plaque placed at the site reads, "From its summit in the fall of 1841, Capt. John C. Hays while surrounded by Comanche Indians who cut him off from his ranging company, repulsed the whole band and inflicted upon them such heavy losses that they fled."

The massive dome of granite called Enchanted Rock rises more than 400 feet high to dominate the surrounding Texas Hill Country north of present-day Fredricksburg. Surrounded by lesser formations, twisted stone pillars and tumbled boulders, the rock is the remaining core of a weathered batholith, a bubble of molten stone formed millions of years ago. Geologists say that natural forces cause the eerie noises that emanate from the rock and the lights that dance across its surface on moonlit nights. The stone surface creaks and moans as it cools from the day's heat; moonlight reflects from condensed moisture or rainwater trapped in small indentations, or from chips of mica and feldspar embedded in the granite.

To the Indians, Enchanted Rock was a haunted place, home to demons and elemental spirits that danced over the rock like shards of ball lightning. The Comanche said that the voices of the dead spoke to them there, sang to them, and cursed at them, especially on nights when the moon was full.

The legend says that Texas Ranger Jack Hays, whom the Comanche called "Devil Jack," decided to leave his party of surveyors camped at a tributary of the Pedernales River while he rode out alone to scan the countryside from the top of Enchanted Rock. Armed with two Colt Paterson revolvers, his rifle — with only the loads in them — and his Bowie knife, Hays climbed to the crater at the top of the rock. When, after taking in the view, Hays turned to climb back down to his horse, he almost ran into a "score" of Comanche warriors who were climbing up after him. Cut off from escape, he sprinted back to the meager cover offered by the shallow crater in the top of the rock.

At first, the Comanche tried to trick the Ranger into wasting his shots or coming out into the open. They taunted him with their war cries, shouting "Devil Jack" to let him know that they knew him for their hated enemy. Hays emptied one pistol, killing or wounding at least two of his opponents and holding the Indians off for two hours. When they finally tired of this sport, the warriors rushed the crater. Hays cocked his remaining loaded revolver and prepared to sell his life dearly. He killed one warrior, then another, clubbed down two others, and drew his knife to make his final stand.

Just as the Comanche closed in for the kill, shots rang out from the base of the rock. The warriors dropped back, then suddenly retreated. Henry McCulloch and the rest of the survey party had heard the shots and had arrived just in the nick of time.

The Comanche later said that "Devil Jack" had called the spirits of the rock to his aid. To many amateur historians and folklorists who have visited Enchanted Rock, this must seem a more likely explanation than the standard story one hears. The depression at the top of the rock is too shallow to provide cover for a jackrabbit, much less a full-grown Texas Ranger. If Hays had tried to hide in it, the Indians would have filled him full of arrows.

Enchanted Rock, the site of the legendary battle between Jack Hays and the Comanche. The monoliths and tumbled boulders scattered on and around the main slope of the Rock make it a natural fortress.
Photo by Tom Knowles

Hays himself never confirmed or denied accounts of his Samsonlike stand at Enchanted Rock, and no direct written evidence of it exists today. There's no hard evidence that Hays was armed with Paterson pistols in 1841, three years before the Ordinance Department issued them to the Rangers. The story first gained wide circulation among the soldiers who served in the Texas units commanded by Hays and other Rangers during the Mexican War. It was exactly the kind of campfire adventure tale veterans would exaggerate in order to astonish and amaze inexperienced recruits. The details of the story shift around, depending on the storyteller.

And yet, the legend persists, and when one looks closely enough at any legend or myth one often finds a kernel of fact. Hays never denied the incident, although he was most reticent when it came to taking credit for his own achievements and most outspoken when it came to setting the record straight. If there had not been some truth to the story, Hays would have made a point of saying so.

Hays was a surveyor, and surveyors in the old days used major landmarks as benchmarks, points of established location and elevation. As the surveyor for the Béxar district, he ran most of the original land surveys in South Texas. He would have selected Enchanted Rock as a perfect landmark for location and as a natural benchmark to establish elevation. If a surveyor or scout of the time said he'd been "at Enchanted Rock" or "on Enchanted Rock," he wouldn't necessarily mean he'd been out on the exposed surface of the main rock. In recalling an event, he'd naturally cite the major landmark in the area to give his listener a sense of location.

Think of Hays being "at" Enchanted Rock instead of "on" it. The crater at the top is an exposed position, but Hays could have held off a good-sized war party from the protection of any one of several niches or small caves that break the surrounding rock formations. If Hays found a wall to guard his back, a fallen boulder to protect him while he fired, or a cave to prevent the Comanche from arcing arrows down into him, the story would make perfect sense. When the story tells of how the Comanche taunted Hays and ran around to draw his fire, it fits other accounts of Comanche tactics. The Comanche exalted courage, but they also believed in living to fight another day. Despite their eagerness to come to grips with "Devil Jack," they would have done their best to lure him out of a defensible position.

Hays's own account, an unpublished letter or report, may lie hidden in a dusty chest or locker, awaiting future discovery. Maybe the pistol bullets Hays fired rest in the gravel of the nearby stream bed, carried there years ago by the rain that washes the face of Enchanted Rock. Perhaps, on certain moonlit nights when the blue ghost lights dance across the granite hillside, the spirit voices of Comanche warriors still whisper the name, "Devil Jack," and cry out for vengeance. Proof of the legend isn't as important as the legend itself, especially when one stands in the shadow of Enchanted Rock and imagines what it must have been like to ride with a Texas Ranger like Jack Hays.

company reinforced by Flacco's scouts and a number of volunteers. Hays's Rangers attacked the main Comanche camp and drove the Indians north, away from San Antonio. It was after this fight, during which Hays charged directly into a line of a hundred Comanche warriors, that Flacco characterized his friend as, "too *mucho bravo*." This incident, as much as Hays's famed lone battle against overwhelming Comanche odds at Enchanted Rock (see "The Legend of Enchanted Rock"), created a cult of personality about Hays. The modest captain found his public reputation an onerous burden, but the Rangers who served with him considered it his due.

His fame did serve a separate purpose. His reputation attracted fighting men to service and convinced Texans that the Rangers were worth supporting.

Indeed, without Hays to lead by example, the Texas Rangers might not have survived as a discrete force. In battle after battle with bandits, Mexican cavalry, and the Comanche, Hays led his men to victory, keeping the Rangers in the field, operative and effective for the last five years of the Republic. His accomplishments established the reputation of the Rangers in the public mind, firmly convincing the Texans that the Rangers were a necessary instrument of frontier defense. Jack Hays forged the Texas Rangers into a weapon, a vital force that would continue to have an impact on the most important aspects of Texas culture and tradition.

When the volunteer groups, militia, and even regular army units faltered and disbanded, Hays's Rangers stayed in the saddle. They would ride without pay, without support, without sanction. It was said of his Rangers that they would ride into hell itself in the service of the Lone Star, just as long as Captain Jack gave the order. When Jack Hays took command, the Texas Rangers became the kind of men Texas could count on.

War Clouds on the Border

Despite treaties and agreements signed at the end of the Texas Revolution and after, there was little love lost between the Lone Star Republic and Mexico. Texans and Mexicans barely coexisted in a low-level, undeclared state of war, especially in the disputed southern territory of the Nueces Strip between the Nueces and Rio Grande rivers. Fortunately for the Texans, the Centralist versus Federalist feud occupied most of Mexico's attention, holding the Mexicans at the sharp edge of balance between uneasy peace and civil war.

While their internal distractions did keep the Mexicans from mounting a full-scale invasion into Texas, the political strife in Mexico gave free reign to military adventurers, bandits, and opportunistic "revolutionaries" who saw a profit in raiding Texas. Also, some Texans weren't immune to adventurous ideas; more than one freebooter or military leader dreamed of carving out a piece of Mexican territory and adding it to the Lone Star. The growing enmity between Texas and Mexico also began to spill over into relations between Anglo Texans and *Tejanos*.

While the *Tejano* population didn't substantially increase after the Texas Revolution, between 1836 and 1846 the overall population of Texas grew from 35,000 to about 130,000. Except for the small number of immigrants from European nations (Germany in particular), the majority of the new immigrants came to the Republic from the Southern U.S. This put the *Tejanos* at a disadvantage, socially and politically.

The rumor campaign against Juan Seguín, which included hints that he was cooperating with Mexican plans for an invasion of South Texas, eventually achieved its goal. A mob forced the *Tejano* leader to flee for his life to Mexico, where the Mexican government arrested and imprisoned him. Had Seguín not been so treated, he would have been in place to alert his fellow Texans about the designs Mexican military had on San Antonio and to do something about it himself. Unfortunately for Texas, the Mexican plan to remove Seguín had succeeded.

In March 1842, a large Mexican force commanded by Gen. Rafael Vásquez left Laredo to march on San Antonio. Vásquez brought five hundred regular soldiers and some *vaqueros* and Indians — not exactly a full invasion force. He held no grandiose intent to conquer Texas. The general just intended to raid San Antonio, to get a little of his own back for the humiliating defeat Jack Hays had inflicted on him.

Jack Hays, newly appointed as the commanding major of the Rangers, wasn't taken by surprise. He'd been listening to local reports and rumors of an invasion for quite a while. He had his Ranger companies and volunteers ready, about one hundred men. When he received reports of the Vásquez expedition, he sent Ben McCulloch and others of his company to scout out the enemy force and determine its strength. The Mexicans captured Rangers Michael Chevallie, Antonio Coy, and James Dunn; McCulloch, believing that Vásquez must be only the vanguard of a larger force, scouted deeper into Mexico. By the time McCulloch got back, the invasion was over and Vásquez had withdrawn to Laredo.

In an uncharacteristic move, Hays had followed the wishes of the people of San Antonio and his own volunteers to avoid a fight, had acceded to Vásquez's demands and withdrawn from the city. Before the evacuation, the citizens had stripped the town of almost everything of worth and had destroyed their stores of gunpowder. If Vásquez was looking for loot, he was out of luck; he held the city for only two days before he withdrew to Mexico. Perhaps this short, victorious raid had satisfied his sense of honor, for Vásquez released his three Ranger prisoners unharmed.

In any case, Vásquez must have taken great satisfaction in hearing that his raid had almost set off another Runaway Scrape. When Edward Burleson, the Republic's Vice President, rode with a company of volunteers to defend Austin, he found that the Texas government and much of the capital city's population had evacuated in fear of a full-scale invasion.

Sam Houston, who had not long before won the presidency back from Lamar, knew that he'd have to authorize some serious action against Mexico in retaliation for the Vásquez raid. He sent appeals for volunteers to newspapers in the United States, put the militia under Brig. Gen. Alexander Somervell on alert and directed Somervell to assemble at least a marginal force. Although Somervell sent letters seeking assistance from several recognized Ranger leaders, including Eli Chandler and Ben McCulloch, he met with very limited success. Some American volunteer groups from Southern states did come to Texas to join, and some Ranger units responded. Their presence along the border, easily detected and reported by Mexican spies, fed the fears of local Mexican authorities that a Texan invasion of Northern Mexico was imminent.

In June, Mexican irregular leader Gen. Antonio Canales put together a two-hundred-man force of bandits, *rancheros*, and regular troops and made a pre-emptive strike against the American volunteer forces commanded by acting Adj. Gen. James Davis and Capt. Ewan Cameron's mounted gunmen at Corpus Christi. Both sides reported a victory, but the main result of the action was to confirm the worst fears of each. Despite this, Davis allowed the volunteers to muster out and disperse, leaving Hays's Rangers as the Republic's only line of defense.

The Second Campaign Against Texas

Hays in the meantime once again found himself paying out of his own pocket, dipping into his surveyor's salary to secure the supplies and ammunition necessary to keep the Rangers in the field. The Texas Congress attempted to fill the breach by authorizing in a July resolution the formation of several new Ranger companies. They specifically ordered Jack Hays and Antonio Manchaca to muster in new companies of 150 men each. Because of the lack of funds, Manchaca couldn't find enough volunteers to fill even one small spy company. Hays had to struggle to keep his own small company in the field. When rumors surfaced late in August that Gen. Adrian Woll intended to invade Texas, Hays had to send Bigfoot Wallace to Austin to purchase munitions with private funds.

Leaving Manchaca in charge of the San Antonio defenses, Hays took a small company of spies out to scout the southern route for any sign of Woll's forces. Woll, a highly competent European mercenary officer who had served with Santa Anna during the Texas Revolution, managed to accomplish what no other Mexican commander ever had or would ever do again — he slipped past Jack Hays's scouts. To avoid detection, Woll led his force away from the main road, then headed west to approach San Antonio from the north. On September 11, the Mexican force of 1,300 cavalry and artillery took San Antonio after a short fight. Woll took most of the *Tejano* loyalists prisoner, but he released some of them on parole to carry forth his proclamation: "The second campaign against Texas has been opened."

When Hays learned of the situation, he began gathering Texas forces at Seguín, some thirty miles to the east of San Antonio. Bigfoot Wallace, Matthew Caldwell, and Henry McCulloch joined him there. The call went out by messenger and through the newspapers for volunteers to repel Woll and any force that might be following to reinforce him. Caldwell's company came in from Gonzales, followed by James Bird and his company. Ewan Cameron, who had managed to hold his company together after his June fight with the irregulars under Antonio Canales at Corpus Christi, rode in from Victoria with forty South Texas *vaqueros* and cowboys. Daniel Friar brought in thirty-five men from Cuero, and Captain Adam Zumwalt brought in twenty-five men from Port Lavaca. The Texans at Seguin soon reached over two hundred in number, most of them experienced fighters commanded by veteran Ranger leaders.

Caldwell took overall command while Hays took command of the mounted scouts. Hays took five men to run hazardous scouts through the country around San Antonio, ducking Mexican patrols as they gathered intelligence. He fought one running battle with a cavalry unit and managed to run off some of their horses. Because he wouldn't allow them to hunt for fear of giving away their position to the Mexican cavalry patrols, Hays's men came close to starving. They were greatly relieved when Henry McCulloch joined them with reinforcements and supplies.

The intelligence Hays had gathered was anything but reassuring. Early in his scout, he'd cut the trail of a large mounted force that was headed toward Gonzales. He also observed that Woll had settled in to fortifying the Alamo and had received three hundred reinforcements from Mexico. In addition, he'd recruited volunteers from among the Mexican loyalist citizens of San Antonio and hired on some Cherokee auxiliaries commanded by Vicente Cordova. He ran his cavalry patrols in a professional manner, so it was unlikely that the Texans would catch him off guard.

Even so, Hays and Caldwell knew that to leave Woll in place would only allow him time to dig in.

They decided to use the time-honored Comanche trick of luring some of Woll's cavalry into an exposed position. Hays and a company of about forty men mounted on the Texans' fastest horses would serve as bait, while the rest of the Texans lay in ambush at a point on Salado Creek not far from the city. Using his superior knowledge of the topography, Hays suggested Salado Creek as the ambush point. Its steep banks and deep water would serve as a natural firing position and would prevent the Mexican cavalry from flanking the main Texan force.

The ambush didn't work quite as well as expected, probably because Woll had trained his men well. Early in the morning after the Texans had set up their ambush, Hays rode out with his company to entice Woll's cavalry from the Alamo. He left most of his force behind on the plain, then rode almost to the gates of the old mission with only six men. Instead of a small detachment, the entire cavalry force of six hundred men poured out to chase the Texans. Hays retreated to rejoin his men, and the forty Texans soon found themselves the object of a hot pursuit. McCulloch and a few Rangers dropped back to act as rear guard, fighting a delaying action to protect those men whose tired mounts couldn't keep up with the rest. Only by pushing their horses to extreme effort did the Texans escape being cut off and killed.

The Mexican cavalry stopped far short of the ambush point, out of range of the Texas rifles. Even as the decoy party dismounted to join their comrades, Woll reinforced his cavalry with artillery and volunteer infantry. The Mexican artillery fired at the Texans with grapeshot, a cannon charge similar to that of a shotgun, containing many bullet-sized projectiles used to inflict maximum casualties on massed troops. Most of the shot ripped through the trees far over the Texans' heads or struck the riverbanks. When the Mexican infantry advanced with fixed bayonets into rifle range, the Texans fired in volleys that cut them down. A group of Rangers armed with shotguns met and destroyed a Mexican unit that attempted to flank their position. Vicente Cordova and a number of his

Cherokees attempted to infiltrate through the woods as the infantry mounted another frontal assault. Although they killed and wounded some Texans, the Texans' long rifles killed the Cherokee leader and eleven of his men.

During one lull in the battle, the Texans heard a sudden flurry of artillery and musket fire from the rear of the Mexican position. They didn't find out until later what had happened. A small force of volunteers led by Nicholas Dawson had ridden eighty miles to join Caldwell, only to run directly into Woll's artillery and cavalry. Cut off from their main force, their horses exhausted, the Texans had been cut to pieces. The Mexicans had shot most of the few survivors who had tried to surrender. A scouting party led by Henry McCulloch later found the bodies of Dawson's unfortunate company lying on the prairie. Among the dead lay Samuel Maverick's black servant, Griffin, who had fought armed only with a mesquite staff until the Mexicans shot him down

Finally, Woll broke off the assault, called for a cease-fire, and retreated toward San Antonio. The Mexicans managed to retrieve some of their casualties, but they left at least sixty dead and wounded on the battlefield. The Rangers had won a solid victory at Salado Creek, but Caldwell wisely restrained his men from following Woll's retreating forces onto the plain where they'd have been exposed to the Mexican artillery.

More men rode in during the night to join the Texan force. Samuel H. Walker, a veteran of the Seminole Wars, came in with Capt. Jesse Billingsley's hundred-man company from Bastrop. Taking the dangerous scout duty, Walker rode through the night to locate the main Texas force and lead Billingsley's company safely to them. Ben McCulloch, William Eastland, and John H. Moore brought in their companies, raising the Texan strength to nearly five hundred men. Most of them didn't have mounts; Woll still had an advantage in cavalry. The Texans had no artillery.

Even so, Woll's command had suffered at least as many as three hundred casualties, perhaps as many as six hundred. Finding himself facing a large and determined force much closer in number to his own, he decided to evacuate San Antonio and withdraw to Mexico. Burdened by prisoners, loot, and over two hundred wounded, most of whom died along the way, Woll began his retreat the very night after the fight at Salado Creek.

Caldwell sent Hays as an advance guard to scout after the Mexican retreat, then followed with the rest of his command. Hays found Woll camped at the Hondo Creek crossing of the Medina River. The general had secured the ford by placing an artillery unit and infantry support to cover it. Later that night, Hays decided to gather a little intelligence in the kind of daring scout that made him his reputation for boldness. Hays and Henry McCulloch, both of whom understood Spanish and often wore Mexican-style clothing, put on sombreros and serapes, lit Mexican-style cigarettes, and slipped into the camp. Listening to the talk around the campfires, they learned of Woll's losses and reduced strength. After accomplishing their mission, they took a guard prisoner and returned with him to Caldwell.

The Texans decided to attack. The Rangers would make a frontal assault on the Mexican position at the ford as the infantry and a few other mounted men moved to attack the enemy's flank. Hays gathered most of the mounted men and charged the Mexican position as Kit Acklin, Nicholas Wren, Bigfoot Wallace, and Henry McCulloch rode beside him. The Mexican gunners made a fateful mistake in not allowing for the elevation of the slope up from the crossing. Their grapeshot overshot the Texan charge and sang into the water of the creek. Although five Rangers fell wounded and Nicholas Wren had his horse shot from under him, Hays and his men got in close to the Mexican position. Wheeling their horses like Comanche warriors, they killed the gunners and sent the infantry fleeing for their lives.

When the Rangers looked back, they saw that the volunteer infantry had failed to move up to support them. They were forced to withdraw, a bitter moment for both Hays and Caldwell because they'd lost a perfect opportunity to overrun and defeat Woll.

The next day, Caldwell had to make a tough decision. Woll had arrayed his command in a good defensive position where his artillery would do great damage to any attack. The Texans were short on gunpowder and supplies, and many of them felt that an attack on the retreating Mexicans would be a foolish waste. Others argued that they must take revenge for Woll's destruction of Dawson's command and free the prisoners Woll had taken. In the end, too many of the Texans decided to leave. Hays shadowed Woll's retreat beyond the Nueces River, hoping for a chance to strike at him or to rescue the prisoners. He never got it, and he led his men back to San Antonio, the last of the Texan force to leave the field.

General Woll's "second campaign against Texas" ended in a Mexican defeat, but in many ways it was a defeat for the Texans as well. Caldwell blamed himself for losing control of the volunteers at the final battle on Hondo Creek, as did others. He retired to Gonzales and died not long afterward, depriving the Rangers of one of their most experienced commanders.

If, as some accounts indicate, Santa Anna masterminded Woll's invasion in order to create dissension among the Texans, his plan succeeded admirably. Rumors planted by Mexican agents that Seguín had cooperated with Woll during the invasion finally gave Seguín's enemies the excuse they needed to run him out of Texas. Antonio Perez and other formally loyal *Tejanos*, convinced by this that the Texans had turned against them, joined the Mexican cause. Even though some *Tejanos* like Manchaca and Hays's scout, Antonio Coy, continued to serve with the Rangers, much of the old feeling of brotherhood and cooperation between Texan and *Tejano* died in the aftermath of the invasion.

President Houston found himself faced with the political necessity of doing something to punish the Mexicans for Woll's actions. Even those Texans who had been against taking the war to Mexico began to cry out for revenge.

Black Beans

Brig. Gen. Alexander Somervell's force of seven hundred men poised on the Rio Grande on December 8, 1842, prepared to invade Mexico less than two months after Woll's capture of San Antonio. Ordered by President Houston to serve as scouts for the Somervell expedition, Jack Hays and his Rangers were the first men to enter Laredo. They hung the Texas flag from a church steeple and kept a sharp eye out for any opposition. Although the original town lay on the north side of the river, Laredo had always been a haven for bandits and Mexican Centralist sympathizers. Instead, the citizens greeted the Texans with cheers and friendly smiles. As Somervell brought the rest of his command into the town, the Rangers kept their hands near their guns.

They never had to draw them. Even though Somervell's command moved about northern Mexico for several days, the only opposition they met, a large force of *rancheros* under Gen. Antonio Canales, fled when they saw Hays and his Rangers. The *alcalde* of Guerrero offered money, horses, and trade goods to Somervell in exchange for not sacking the town. Even though the main force of the Texas Army never actually crossed into Mexico, by December 19, Somervell decided that his expedition had sufficiently satisfied Texas honor. He gave the order for his command to return to San Antonio.

Three hundred men refused to follow him; they elected Col. William S. Fisher to lead them on to Mier, a Mexican town about one hundred miles to the southeast of Laredo on the Rio Grande. Sam Walker and Bigfoot Wallace were among those who decided to join the Mier expedition, but Jack Hays and most of his Rangers refused to accept Fisher as their commander. Hays did agree to scout the road to Mier before he left. Before he set out, he sent Flacco back to guide Somervell's command and the convoy of captured horses and loot. The Rangers captured some boats, crossed the river, and entered Mier first, only to find the town virtually deserted.

After guiding the expedition to within striking

distance of Mier, Hays tried once more to persuade the Texans to give it up and follow him back to San Antonio. Hays had received reports that a large Mexican force under Gen. Pedro Ampuida had set out to repel the invasion. Ben McCulloch listened to Hays and returned with him, but Wallace, Walker, Ewan Cameron, and several other Rangers decided to stay. Even as Hays left and Fisher's force prepared to move on Mier, Ampuida's seven hundred regulars entered Mier to wait for them.

When the Texans marched into Mier on Christmas Day, they marched straight into a trap. Samuel Walker and Patrick Lusk, acting as forward scouts, were the first Texans captured by Ampuida's troops. The battle was over by the afternoon of the day after Christmas. The Texans surrendered and found themselves the prisoners of the very enemy they'd come to punish for Woll's invasion.

The Mexicans assigned them a guard of three hundred soldiers, the famed "Red Caps" commanded by Col. Manuel R. Barragan. They marched the prisoners for hundreds of miles, taking them on a grand parade through several Mexican towns. From Mier to Matamoros to Monterrey, then finally to Saltillo, the proud Texans trudged along in chains. After only a day's rest at Saltillo, Walker and Cameron led the Texans in a desperate escape attempt. Five Texans were killed, but the rest killed their guards and headed for Texas.

Without food and water, lost in the rough country where they'd fled to avoid the main roads, almost all of the Texans were soon recaptured. Enraged by the escape attempt, President Santa Anna ordered all of the Texans executed. The Mexican governor risked his own life in refusing the order.

Santa Anna ordered new guards to move the prisoners to San Luis Potosi, to the Rancho Salado. There, on March 25, 1843, the guards shoved the Texans into a line to hear Santa Anna's proclamation — as punishment for their escape attempt, the Texans would participate in a "Lottery of Death." Ten of them would die. The Mexican commander placed 159 white beans and ten black ones in an earthenware jar, shook them up and forced each of the Texans to take his turn in drawing one. Ewan Cameron and Sam Walker drew white beans, but the Mexicans marched those who had drawn black beans out into the prairie beyond the road and shot them. The next morning, the survivors marched out toward Santiago Prison, their final destination. Their comrades' bodies lay "stiffened and unsepulchered" in the field beside the road.

Sam Walker, like many other Texans, swore an oath of vengeance that day. When on April 25 Santa Anna singled out Ewan Cameron as the leader of the escape and had him summarily executed, Walker's hatred focused almost exclusively on one man. When he escaped several months later, he swore that he'd return to Mexico to see Santa Anna dead. Years later, as a captain of the U.S. Mounted Rifles in the Mexican War, Walker would have his chance to carry out that oath.

The Rangers Alone

Even news of the disastrous results of the Mier expedition and the murder of Flacco didn't slow Major Hays in the pursuit of his duty. Immediately on his return to San Antonio from Mier, he visited the Secretary of War to impress upon him the need to enlist new Ranger companies. A Congressional act passed on January 16, 1843, gave him the formal authorization he needed to pay a "spy company." Within a few weeks he was able to recruit a twenty-man company, secure supplies for them, and lead them on their first patrol.

Many of his recruits were old friends who had served with him before, including Ad Gillespie, Mike Chevallie, and Frank Paschal. Even though the Mexican invasion had sown much distrust between *Tejanos* and Texans, the Spanish name of M. Eschalara appears on both of his six-month muster rolls for 1843. As Hays reorganized his company later in 1843, Ben McCulloch would enlist as an official Ranger for the first time.

This engraving from Gen. Thomas J. Green's *Journal of the Texian Expedition against Mier* shows the Mexican troops executing a group of Texans from that ill-fated adventure.
UT Institute of Texan Cultures at San Antonio

Despite the recent troubles with Mexico, the Texas government funded no other militia or regular army groups. For the year that followed, Jack Hays and his company remained the only authorized military force within Texas. Other volunteer companies did occasionally take the field, but Hays's Rangers stood alone as the only official defenders of Texas against all of her many enemies.

President Houston had agreed on an armistice with Mexico, but as negotiations continued, Mexican agents once again began to negotiate with the Comanche and other Indians, inciting them to make war on the Texans. The Mexican government repudiated its former commitment to surrender the Nueces Strip to Texas. Santa Anna issued a proclamation claiming that he'd execute all "foreigners" who entered Mexican territory, including the Nueces Strip.

Houston declared martial law in the Nueces Strip. He sent Hays to patrol it and gave him full authority as the sole legal representative of Texas interests there. The Rangers caught and summarily executed several Mexican agents, brigands, and spies; they put such fear into the bandits that the trade route opened up again. It was said that whenever one of Agaton's spies rode in and began his report with the Ranger commander's name, the bandit chief would immediately saddle his horse to ride in the opposite direction. The mere mention of "Devil Jack" was enough to make his enemies blanch in terror.

When not on the trail, Hays instituted training exercises for the Rangers. Ranger James Nichols later recalled that the Rangers honed their horsemanship and shooting skills at every opportunity. Hays taught them how to fire their rifles and pistols from horseback until they could accurately hit small targets while riding at top speed. He taught them to ride like Comanches, to reach down from their horses at full gallop to pick up objects on the ground. Developing these skills gave them a clear advantage over other cavalry and dismounted troops. It would serve them well against the Comanche, who lived on horseback.

Despite their formidable reputation and their hard-won experience, or perhaps because they were the best at what they did, the Rangers got spread pretty thin. When a Comanche raiding party killed a farmer within sight of the Alamo, Hays and his company chased them for more than a hundred miles through the August heat. Upon learning that the Rangers were away, Agaton's lieutenant, Manuel Perez, decided to attack San Antonio. Even though the Rangers and their horses were completely exhausted from the long chase, they intercepted the bandits and routed them in a fire fight. The bandits started a grass fire and slipped away using the smoke as cover.

In September, Texas and Mexico agreed in principle to a treaty that would reestablish the Rio Grande as the border and allow those Texans taken prisoner by Woll and Ampuida to return home. On a patrol to the Nueces, Hays had a surprisingly cordial meeting with a unit of Mexican regulars. The Mexican commander, operating under the guidelines of the new agreement between the two nations, offered to assist the Rangers in operations against bandits in the Strip. He informed Hays that the Mexican government had discontinued its support for the bandits who masqueraded as Mexican troops or revolutionaries.

Squeezed between the Rangers and Mexican regulars, the bandit groups began to wither. When Agaton fell to a trader's bullet, the other bandits found themselves scrambling to hold on to their scalps. Reduced to outlawry after Woll's invasion failed, Antonio Perez found himself a prime target for the Rangers. He eventually sent word asking his old comrades to forgive him, but it's unlikely that any of them ever did. In a letter to the Secretary of War, Hays himself expressed his suspicion of any former residents of the Republic who had changed sides.

Even though the fires on the border had cooled down, the Comanche remained an active threat. Hays's Rangers served long past their six-month enlistment period; well before the end of the enlistment, Hays petitioned the Secretary of War to fund new companies to fight the Indians. As usual, the Texas government took its own sweet time about responding. It wasn't until the end of the year that Congress passed the joint resolution that compensated Hays and his company for their 1843 service.

In the interim, Hays spent the Thanksgiving and Christmas holidays with his friends in Seguin and San Antonio. He paid particular attention to Susan Calvert, the daughter of Judge Jeremiah H. Calvert. Hays had never had time for courtship before, but during the holidays his mind began to turn from the battlefield to the possibility of a gentler life. As did many who followed him, Hays realized that life as a Texas Ranger and the life of a family man would be difficult, if not impossible, to reconcile. In planning to marry Susan Calvert, Hays could see the end of his service as a defender of the Lone Star.

Even though he'd had a glimpse of the more peaceful future that awaited him, Jack Hays still had miles to ride and battles to fight. Challenges even greater than he could imagine awaited him.

The Beginning of the Black Road

On New Year's Day 1844 Jack Hays, Antonio Manchaca, Frank Paschal, Capt. G. T. Howard, and Congressman W. G. Cooke set out on a trip to Washington-on-the-Brazos. President Houston invited them to a meeting in which they discussed the future of the Texas defense forces and Houston's concerns about Mexican influence on the Indians. Houston asked Hays to devise plans for an expanded Ranger force to guard the frontier and promised to put those plans before Congress.

Houston also brought up the subject of new weapons that might benefit the Rangers. After the three ships of the Texas Navy were decommissioned — two of them fell apart from rot when brought into dry dock — the Ordinance Department found itself in possession of 180 Paterson revolving rifles and 180 five-shot pistols (see "The Colt Comes to Texas") purchased for the Navy in 1839. Hays and Houston both

Colt Paterson revolving pistol, #5 "Texas" model with loading lever, .36 caliber.
Photo by Tom Knowles, Texas Ranger Hall of Fame and Museum

felt that the firepower provided by these weapons would prove most effective in the hands of the Rangers.

Houston managed to persuade the Eighth Texas Congress to act on Hays's plan. Finally, after years of wrangling and debate, the intent of a Congressional action addressed the precise need for frontier defense. The January 23 act "Authorizing John C. Hays to raise a Company of Mounted Gun-men, to act as Rangers, on the Western and South-Western Frontier" designated Hays as the commanding captain of the Rangers. It also specified the enlistment rank and pay as well as the usual requirement that each man would provide his own horses and weapons. Mustered in for four-month enlistments, which the President could extend in times of emergency, the company would consist of forty privates, each paid thirty dollars a month. The privates would be allowed to elect their lieutenant, who would receive fifty dollars in pay. As captain, Hays would receive seventy-five dollars a month.

Even under these terms, it took Hays until late February 1844 to sign on enough men to make up an effective company; it wasn't until April that he recruited up to full strength. Again, many of his old comrades — Michael Chevallie, Frank Paschal, Antonio Coy, and others — returned to ride with him. Ben McCulloch signed on as lieutenant. Samuel Walker, recently returned after his escape from Santiago Prison in Mexico, joined to seek his destiny on the battlefield.

The men of Hays's 1844 company were the most effective force of Texas Rangers that had ever taken up the service of the Lone Star. When Houston made good on his promise to provide them with the Paterson revolving pistols from the Ordinance Department's stores, they became the most deadly fighting force ever to ride the Texas plains. The combination of the Texas Rangers and the Colt revolver signaled a new definition of the military value of cavalry, a revolution in frontier warfare. The weapon and the Texas Ranger became almost synonymous, until no one could think of one without the other. Armed with

THE COLT COMES TO TEXAS

(*top*) Colt Paterson revolving pistol, #5 "Texas" model with loading lever, .36 caliber; (*lower*) Colt Paterson #1 "Baby" model, .31 caliber. *Photo by Tom Knowles, Texas Ranger Hall of Fame and Museum*

"God made some men big and some men small, but Col. Sam Colt made them equal all" became a common saying in Texas, mostly because of the long association between the Colt's revolver and the Texas Rangers. Sam Colt's "Paterson five-shooter" helped to make each Ranger equal to or better than any ten other fighting men on the face of the earth. The Paterson first came to Texas, and in a roundabout way to the Rangers, in 1839.

The revolving cylinder wasn't a new idea for firearms designers, but previous attempts had been relatively crude. Most models, like the Allen percussion revolver and the English Collier flintlock revolver required that the cylinder be turned manually for each shot. Legend has it that during a sea voyage in 1830 Samuel Colt whittled out a wooden model of a revolving pistol with a multichambered cylinder, patterning its operation after that of the ship's wheel. What made Colt's model unique was that he transposed the ship's pawl and ratchet operation in miniature scale to fit his weapon's design. The pawl rotated the cylinder each time the shooter cocked back the hammer; the ratchet held the cylinder in place while the weapon fired. Instead of a flint and powder pan, his design used a superior and reliable innovation, the percussion cap, to individually set off the charge in each chamber.

It took Colt years to improve his designs and create a working model, but he finally succeeded and received his American patent on February 25, 1836. With financial backing from John Ehlers, Colt opened the Patent Arms Manufacturing Co. at Paterson, New Jersey, where he began to turn out revolving rifles, carbines, and pistols.

Colt designed the first Paterson five-shooter to fire light calibers, from .28 to .36, through a rifled barrel. It was an elegant weapon, but rather delicate in operation and appearance when compared to the heavy single-shot pistols of the day. It had no trigger guard because it was designed to be carried through a belt or in a pocket — the pistol holster wasn't in general use at the time, except for large weapons meant to be holstered on a cavalry saddle. Instead, the trigger remained in a recess in the frame until the shooter cocked the hammer, then it snapped down into place. To reload the Paterson after expending the five rounds, the shooter had to disassemble the barrel from the cylinder.

The Paterson could very accurately fire those five rounds just as fast as the shooter could work the hammer and trigger, a vast improvement in firepower and efficiency over single-shot muzzle-loaders. If the shooter carried an extra cylinder or two already loaded and capped, he carried more firepower than a regular infantry squad. Despite this, the U.S. Army Ordinance Department declined to contract for the Paterson pistols because the officers in charge of weapons procurement considered Colt's invention too fragile and too expensive for military use.

The Paterson rifles and carbines, which, depending on the model, could fire from five to eight shots of larger caliber (.36 to .58) were met with some limited enthusiasm when Colt demonstrated them to U.S. Army officers involved in the Seminole War in 1839. Colt managed to sell some rifles to individual members of the U.S. military, but not to the War Department. On later models of the rifle and the pistol he added an external loading lever, which allowed the shooter to reload without disassembling the weapon. Even this advance failed to convince the U.S. military to purchase them.

Legend has it that Texas Ranger Samuel H. Walker came to visit Colt as early as 1839 to suggest the addition of the loading lever and a longer barrel to the Paterson revolver. This is unlikely considering that in 1839 Walker hadn't yet signed on with the Texas Rangers, but it does make a good story. The 1840 Model 5 Paterson was a longer-barreled, more durable version with a factory-added loading lever; some called it the "Frontier" or "Texas" model. The name "Walker Paterson" was attached to it by folklorists well after Walker's death in the Mexican War.

Walker would eventually meet Colt to collaborate with him in developing a new revolver, but that wouldn't take place until after the Texas Rangers had already made Colt's weapons known and feared by the enemies of the Lone Star. Indeed, Colt found a fertile market in Texas, and in doing so became a major factor in creating the Texas Ranger legend. The Republic of Texas Congressional record of November 1839 shows that the Texas Navy Department made the first large military purchase from Colt's Patent Arms Manufacturing Co.:

NAVY DEPARTMENT, April 29, 1839.

SIR: — You are authorized to purchase for the use of the Navy, one hundred and eighty carbines, one hundred and eighty pistols, thirty-six levers for carbines, and one cap-primer for each pistol and carbine. The government will not be able to pay for these articles until it effects a loan, but ten per cent interest per annum will be allowed on all purchases until paid.

[Signed]M. HUNT
To: CAPT. E. W. MOORE, Baltimore.

The same passage indicates that in 1839 the War Department purchased fifty of the #2 model "ring-lever" Paterson rifles and accessories for use by the Texas Army, each modified with a loading lever. Even though the #2 model's "hammerless" mechanism tended to foul with powder residue after continued operation, it still represented a huge advance in firepower. Other records indicate additional orders in 1839 and 1840, including orders for a number of "belt pistols" and carbines.

Repair vouchers from several Texas military units show that some of these weapons saw hard field use. Mexican Gen. Adrian Woll reported the capture of several multishot rifles or carbines during his 1842 invasion of Texas, taken either from military stores in San Antonio or from members of the ill-fated Mier expedition. At least one of them was sent to Santa Anna as a trophy.

The real question is, when did Paterson Colt pistols fall into the hands of the Texas Rangers? According to legend, Jack Hays used two Paterson pistols to stand off a Comanche war party in his famed lone battle at Enchanted Rock in 1841. Other accounts from 1841 through 1843 have Hays and his company taking on vastly superior forces of Indians, bandits, and Mexican troops and emerging victorious because of the edge given to them by Paterson pistols. Hays's first recorded mention of Rangers using Paterson pistols can be found in his report of the Battle of Walker Creek in 1844; in this instance, most or all of the members of his company were definitely armed with Paterson pistols from the arsenal of the defunct Texas Navy.

Capt. Micah Andrews reported using a Paterson rifle against the Comanche in October of 1840 during a reprisal after the Great Raid. Another indication that the rifles, carbines, or pistols might have filtered into Ranger hands lies in a voucher for supplies from military stores dated April 2, 1840, signed by "D. R. Jackson, Capt. Rangers." The list includes not only staple foodstuffs and munitions, including "3 Doz. Gun flints," but also "3 Boxes P. Caps." The standard issue weapon from the War Department was the Tyson flintlock musket, which would account for the flints requisitioned. Rangers who used personal weapons also provided the materials for them, whether they were flintlock rifles or single-shot percussion weapons. If they requisitioned percussion caps, they must have been for issued weapons; the only percussion cap weapons the War Department had issued at the time were Patersons.

Colt, true to a marketing pattern he'd use to great effect in the future, reportedly sent Texas Chief of Ordinance George W. Hockley some Paterson revolvers as demonstration models. It's possible that Hockley gave a pair of the pistols to Hays as early as 1840, that over a period of several years, Paterson pistols and rifles filtered down to individual Rangers from both military and civilian sources. Some correspondence suggests that Colt may even have sent an engraved presentation set of pistols directly to Hays. Bigfoot Wallace recalled that S. M. Swenson purchased four Patersons from Colt himself during a trip to New York and presented them to Hays upon his return. Wallace recalled that Swenson felt Hays deserved to have the revolvers because he was "...the only fighter God ever made."

Whatever the actual timing of events, the Colt revolver gave the Texas Ranger an accurate repeating firearm he could use effectively from horseback, rather than being forced to dismount to fire. Its rate of fire allowed him to more than match the Comanche warrior's deadly flight of arrows, and at close combat range even its light-caliber round would penetrate the Comanche's bullet-resistant buffalo-hide shield. Against great odds, small companies of Rangers could hit the Comanche and get "in among them," dealing death at close range where the Indians couldn't effectively use their lances.

The revolvers were a great shock to the Comanche, who expected the Rangers to go into the typical defensive position of the frontier rifleman. Hays's men attacked with weapons that fired again and again without pause. Legend has it that after one such engagement, the Comanche war chief sent a message to San Antonio, saying that he was moving his people farther west. He said, "I will never again fight Jack Hays, whose men have a shot for every finger on the hand."

Ironically, the cash-strapped Texas government's slow payment on its contracts had much to do with Colt's financial troubles and eventual bankruptcy. Although the Paterson plant closed down in 1842, Colt's investor partner Ehlers continued for some time to sell weapons assembled from spare parts. Paterson Colts continued to trickle out to the frontier.

A few years later, it would be the Texas Rangers who would eventually bring Colt back into prominence, fame, and fortune with another weapon, this one named after a Texas Ranger — the Walker Colt.

This detail photograph features three Colt Patersons: a revolving carbine, .52 caliber, 1838 model, with Texas Army inspection markings; a revolving rifle, .52 caliber, 1837 model ring-lever action; and a revolving pistol, #5 "Texas" model with loading lever, .36 caliber.
Photo by Tom Knowles, Texas Ranger Hall of Fame and Museum

the five-shot Paterson revolvers the Rangers could match the Comanche bullet for arrow, charging in close among the enemy and shooting through his buffalo-hide shield.

For the men of Hays's company, their gathering signified the culmination of two decades of sacrifice and devotion to duty. Their combined experience and the sum of the lessons they'd learned from their enemies and allies on the battlefields of Texas made them unique, a cultural leap beyond their predecessors. In 1844, the Texas Rangers became the first true westerners of the Wild West.

For the Comanche horse lords, it was the beginning of their long, bloody retreat down the black road to the West and oblivion. They got their first bitter taste of the future in June 1844, when Jack Hays and a patrol of fifteen Rangers stopped to water their horses at a stream Hays later named Walker Creek, about fifty miles north of Seguin. The Ranger rearguards noticed that they were being shadowed by a few Comanche outriders and rode in to inform the captain. Hays had his men saddle up and start back down the trail.

A few warriors rode in close, attempting to get the Rangers to chase them, but these Rangers had used

the same bait-and-trap tactic themselves. Their gambit unsuccessful, the outriders vanished into the woods. Hays and his men readied themselves for battle. The enemy didn't disappoint them. As the Rangers drew near the hill they saw the full Comanche war band, sixty or seventy warriors strong, waiting for them on the high ground. Hurling war cries and insults and gesturing with their shields and lances, the Comanche challenged the Rangers.

Again, the time-honored Comanche tactic failed. These Texans didn't waste their fire on long-range shots that the tough buffalo-hide shields could deflect, nor did they retreat to a defensible position and dismount. The Texans just kept coming, a measured but relentless advance. When the Rangers reached a point on the slope where a brushy ravine temporarily hid them from view, they readied their rifles and charged toward the Comanche flank. They caught many of the enemy dismounted, ready to fire their arrows and few rifles downhill. Instead of holding some loaded weapons in reserve, the Rangers all fired their rifles at once from horseback and rode directly into the Comanche formation.

Shocked as they were, the Comanche didn't flinch. They outnumbered the Rangers more than

99

four to one, and the Texans had emptied their rifles. They wheeled their horses around to circle their enemies in a deadly ring of lances, but the Rangers formed an outward-facing circle, back to back. As the Rangers fired the last of their loaded rifles, the Indians closed in. Hays shouted, "Drop your rifles, men." The Rangers drew their Colts, two apiece, and spurred their horses to meet the Comanche charge.

Not a man came through the charge without at least a scratch from the rain of arrows and the flashing lances. But the little Colts fired again and again, piercing the buffalo-hide shields and dropping the Comanche from their saddles. The Rangers killed twenty or more of the enemy in the first pass, breaking the charge and sending the Comanche reeling back. As some of the Rangers reloaded their pistols by changing to fresh cylinders, the Comanche attacked again, cutting off Sam Walker and Ad Gillespie and lancing them through. Again, the revolvers cut the Comanche down until the survivors fled with some of the Rangers in pursuit.

Privates W. B. Lee and Andrew Erskin were wounded in the second charge; Pvt. Peter Fohr was killed outright. Walker lay seriously wounded, but although he was out of the fight he'd live to fight again. Because he'd been wounded before and had been one of the Texans captured at Mier, some of the Rangers nicknamed him "Unlucky Walker." Gillespie managed to drag himself back to his rifle, reload it, and climb back on his horse.

The Rangers had killed or seriously wounded an even greater number of the Comanche in the second charge, leaving about twenty enemy effectives to the ten Rangers still in the fight. Hays could see and hear the chief exhorting his men to charge again. When Hays asked if any of his men had a loaded rifle, the wounded Gillespie responded. Hays ordered him to "dismount and shoot that damned chief!" Gillespie got down, took careful aim, and shot the chief through the head. As the Comanche leader's lifeless body fell from his horse, the survivors of his war party fled. They'd had enough surprises for one day. As some of the victorious Rangers pursued them, the Comanche flung away their shields and lances and scattered into the woods.

As Hays wrote later in report to the Secretary of War, the Battle of Walker Creek proved the effective

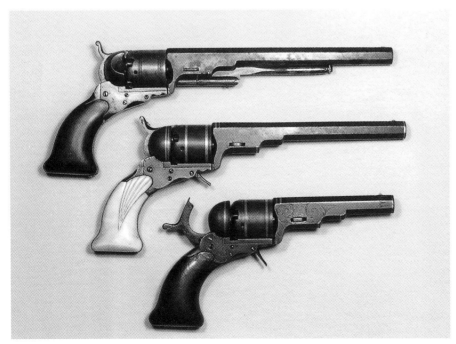

Colt Paterson .36 caliber revolvers, circa 1838–40. (*From top*) "Texas" model with loading lever, holster model with ivory grips, pocket model with nickel-silver trim and engraved cylinder.
Photo by Tom Knowles, Metzger Collection, Sam Houston Sanders Corps of Cadets Center, Texas A&M University

firepower of the Colts beyond any doubt: "Had it not been for them [the Paterson Colts], I doubt what the consequences would have been. I cannot recommend these arms too highly."

After the Walker Creek fight Hays continued to lead and train his corps of Rangers, the men who would fight for Texas long after he married his sweetheart, Susan Calvert, and settled down. At Walker Creek he'd set their future for them; he had sealed the fate of their Comanche enemies. From that day forward, when the Texas Rangers met the Comanche in battle, the Comanche would give way or die.

Soon enough, the Lone Star of the Republic would give way to the Stars and Stripes of the Union. Many Texans welcomed annexation into the United States in the belief that the defense of the frontier would become the business of the U.S. Army, that the work of the Texas Rangers was done. They were wrong. Before Jack Hays could settle down to a more peaceable private life, he'd lead the defenders of the Lone Star on one more crusade. In the war that would finally cut the ties of blood and oppression between Texas and Mexico, the Texas Rangers would lead the way.

5

THE GRAND CONSTELLATION

O N February 19, 1846, as he watched the Lone Star flag of the Republic give way to the Stars and Stripes of the United States, John S. Ford felt conflicting emotions, "... a blending of sorrow for the past, joy for the present, and radiant hope for the future." No doubt most Texans felt the same way about annexation.

Despite any feeling of regret they felt for the passing of the Republic, the Texans hoped the union would put an end to the almost constant state of war they'd endured since colonial days. They'd voted to join the United States in hopes that American investment would revitalize the Texas economy, that the U.S. Army would protect them from the Indians and secure the border with Mexico. More than thirty years after Stephen F. Austin established his first colony, the Texans felt as if they finally had a chance to secure peace without sacrificing their liberty in the process.

Their hope wasn't misplaced, but it was premature.

Former President Sam Houston, elected by the constitutional convention as one of the first U.S. senators from Texas, was too canny a politician to believe annexation would solve all of the Lone Star's problems. He knew just how hard the American opponents of annexation had fought against admitting another

slave state to the Union and against military expansion to protect the ill-defined Texas frontier. One of the opposition's main arguments was that the annexation of Texas would provoke a war with Mexico. Houston knew they were right, that Mexico would not accept the long-feared expansion of the United States to her borders. War was certain to come.

The Texans felt that their revolution against Mexico, begun in 1836 when Santa Anna sought to destroy the Texas colonies, had never actually ended. Mexico's hostility toward Texas had ebbed and flowed over the years according to the political fortunes of the dictator. Texas could never be certain of peace with Mexico, torn as she was by successive revolutions and the Federalist-Centralist power struggle. Only by forever shattering Santa Anna's influence over the Mexican political system could Texas end the cycle of bloodshed and vengeance between the two peoples.

Jack Hays must have known that the Texas Rangers

"The Republic of Texas is no more." A drawing by Norman Price of the annexation of Texas by the United States, February 19, 1846. The ceremony in Austin is presided over by Republic of Texas President Anson Jones.
UT Institute of Texan Cultures at San Antonio/Barker Texas History Center, University of Texas

would find themselves chasing bandits and fighting Indians for years to come, no matter what new hopes annexation brought to Texas. The experienced Rangers could see that it would take years of training in frontier warfare and the radically new cavalry tactics developed by the Rangers to turn the U.S. Army into frontier fighters capable of defeating the Comanche. In any case, the conventional military wasn't properly organized or funded to track down bandits and guerrillas. The Texas Rangers were the men for that job.

Instead of the hopeful future Texas sought in joining the United States, almost thirty more years of continued, bitter conflict lay ahead of them before the Union would be complete. The first step on that long,

A woodcut of Capt. Jack Hays from *Indian Depredations in Texas*.
Texas State Library & Archives Commission

bloody road was the Mexican War, which began almost before flag makers could add the Lone Star to the grand constellation of the Stars and Stripes.

In many ways, the conflict between Mexico and the United States would serve as a dress rehearsal for the American Civil War. The officers and men who served in Mexico and on the frontier after the war would emerge with more true combat experience and training than any previous generation of American soldiers. Little more than a decade after their grand adventure together in Mexico, men who had fought side by side together at Monterrey and Buena Vista and Mexico City would face each other over bayonets

and pistols, would kill each other in the wreckage of that hopeful union of 1846.

At the same time, the Mexican War served to strengthen the ties between the people of Texas and their new countrymen. The Texas Rangers and the other Texas volunteers rode out in the vanguard of the U.S. expeditions into Mexico, not just as Texans but as Americans. They fought and died on each major battlefield from Palo Alto to Mexico City, and in a dozen desperate skirmishes and lonely scouts down forgotten trails. Newspaper accounts of their exploits in the Mexican War won them national and international acclaim and

A map of Texas, Mexico, and the Southwest prior to the Mexican War. *Texas State Library & Archives Commission*

notoriety, made heroes of them in the eyes of the American public.

John S. Ford was one of many Texans who found himself riding the Ranger trail to join Jack Hays in the crusade against Mexico. Lost in his grief over his beloved wife's death, he left behind his former life as a physician and a newspaper publisher to become a warrior. Before him lay the great adventure and the terrible ordeal that was only the beginning of his long service to the Lone Star.

Many years later, despite the long and desperate trials of the Mexican War, the Civil War, and Reconstruction, Ford was still able to look back on the day of the flag ceremony as a time of undimmed hope and joy.

A Short, Victorious War

Mexico fired the first shot of the Mexican War, at least politically. In answer to the planned annexation of Texas, Mexico once again repudiated the provisions of the 1836 Treaty of Velasco that set the Rio Grande River instead of the Nueces as the Texas boundary. Mexico laid claim to the Nueces Strip and promised to punish any American or Texan force that entered it. Despite anti-war sentiment and public protests by prominent Americans, the U.S. government responded to the threat even before Texas formally joined the Union.

The U.S. 6th Infantry was stationed at Fort Jessup, Louisiana, the outpost closest to Texas. Because he was the senior officer in the area and a seasoned commander, command fell to Col. Zachary Taylor. Reinforced by elements of the 3rd and 4th Infantry division and the 2nd Dragoons (mounted infantry), Taylor was able to assemble a force of almost thirteen hundred men. At its final muster of about 3,000 men, Taylor's command was the largest organized force of American regulars to take the field since the War of 1812. In June 1845, Taylor's men began the march into Texas. By July they had set up camp in the sand grass flats of the coast near Corpus Christi. Taylor's orders

from the U.S. Adjutant General empowered him to take any action he deemed necessary to secure the border and to keep Mexican troops on the south side of the Rio Grande. He and his officers expected to lead their regular troops in a short, victorious war, to defeat the veterans and mercenaries of the vastly superior Mexican Army without the assistance of unruly Texas volunteers.

Although they would serve honorably and acquit themselves well in the coming battles, few of Taylor's regulars were prepared for the challenges they'd face in the vast, trackless Southwestern territories of Texas and Mexico. They would soon find reason to rejoice in the company of the volunteers, those "frontier ruffians." Texans, the Texas Rangers in particular, knew how to survive in the rough country, how to win in the no-quarter arena of the frontier, how to fight guerrillas and to fight as guerrillas. The Rangers were eager to fight, to take vengeance for the massacres at Goliad and the Alamo, for the Lottery of Death at Rancho Salado. They wanted payback for the Mexican invasions of San Antonio and the Mexican intrigue that had incited the Great Comanche Raid on Victoria and Linnville.

Sam Walker carried within his heart a darkness that had crept there during his imprisonment at Perote Castle and Santiago Prison; he'd sworn on his own life to see Santa Anna dead. Ben McCulloch wanted very much to meet his old comrade Juan Seguin in battle, to repay the *Tejano* leader for what the Ranger perceived as his treason against Texas. Jack Hays, who had already turned his thoughts to another way of life, found himself drawn back to the fight. Whenever and wherever his men needed him, no matter the odds, Hays would lead them.

Colonel Taylor, nicknamed "Old Rough and Ready" by some, was a far more competent and perceptive tactician than his bright young officers believed him to be. Despite his reluctance to enlist Texas volunteers, he soon realized that he'd be lost without guidance from at least a small scout or spy company of men who were familiar with the land. In September

A unique law-enforcement outfit ideally suited to frontier conditions and a symbol of the Lone Star state itself, the Texas Rangers have also taken part in every major military conflict in Texas's history. From colony to Republic and from state of the Union to state of the Confederacy, Texas has had Rangers protecting her interests. "Charge of the Texas Rangers," a watercolor painting by Bruce Marshall, depicts the Texas Rangers in combat with Mexican lancers during the Mexican War, circa 1847.
UT Institute of Texan Cultures at San Antonio, Courtesy of Bruce Marshall

During Texas's colonial period under Mexican rule, the War of Independence, and the decade of the Texas Republic, Rangers both protected settlements from Indians and bandits and rode into war. Serving for short enlistment periods and providing their own mounts and weapons, these men were highly individualistic. This painting details typical Texas Rangers of the 1830s during a charge.
UT Institute of Texan Cultures at San Antonio, Courtesy of Bruce Marshall

Following the siege of the Alamo and the massacre at Goliad, Texans regrouped at San Jacinto and won their independence from Mexico with a decisive battle under the leadership of Gen. Sam Houston. The "San Jacinto Flag," flown as the symbol of the fledgling Republic of Texas during the battle, depicted a sword-wielding Liberty holding a banner declaring "Liberty or Death." This restored version of the flag is its reverse side, rediscovered during conservation efforts.
Texas State Library & Archives Commission

Independence for Texas was won not only by Texians, the Anglo settlers, but also by Mexican *Tejanos*. Mexican culture had a significant influence on life in Texas. In adapting to the conditions of the frontier, the Rangers borrowed much from the *vaqueros*, the Mexican cowboys. This painting by Theodore Gentilz depicts a group of *vaqueros* on their way to a dance, or *fandango*.
Daughters of the Republic of Texas Library

Stephen F. Austin, "The Father of Texas," settled 300 families in 1822 in the colony established by his father, Moses Austin. After taking a petition to the Mexican government advocating independence for Texas, Austin was detained by the authorities for eighteen months. Upon his return to Texas, he was elected commander of the Texas Army and later went to the United States to appeal for aid. This portrait of Austin was probably copied from the two "Oak Tree Miniatures" painted by William Howard in Mexico City in 1833, the year Austin presented the petition for independence. It depicts him with his dog Cano, possibly near the mouth of the Brazos River.
Texas State Library & Archives Commission

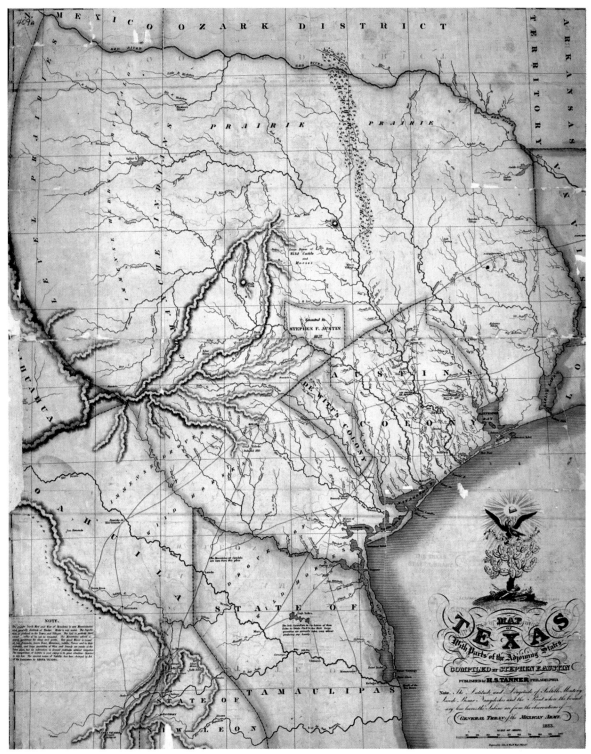

Following Texas's victory over Mexico in 1836, the former colonies formed an independent republic. Drawn in 1833 by Stephen F. Austin, this map of Texas with parts of adjoining states needed revising to reflect the new political boundaries. The land, however, remained the same. Austin's map is acknowledged as being one of the first finely-detailed and accurate maps of Texas published. It covers most of Texas and parts of the Mexican states of Tamaulipas, Nuevo Leon, and Coahuila; it shows rivers, Austin's and DeWitt's colonies, towns, missions, routes and trails—including the Old San Antonio Road, silver mines, Indian tribes and villages, and herds of wild horses and game.
Texas State Library & Archives Commission

The legend of Capt. John Coffee Hays, "Devil Jack," was built not only on his military leadership, but also on his remarkable skill and bravery. This oil painting of Jack Hays depicts his famous lone fight against the Comanche at Enchanted Rock in the fall of 1841. Enchanted Rock rises more than 400 feet high to dominate the surrounding Texas Hill Country north of present-day Fredricksburg. A bronze plaque placed at the site reads, "From its summit in the fall of 1841, Capt. John C. Hays while surrounded by Comanche Indians who cut him off from his ranging company, repulsed the whole band and inflicted upon them such heavy losses that they fled." Because Hays sat for this painting years later, while he was a prominent citizen of California, it serves as an indication that the legend of the battle was based on an actual incident.
Gift of Mrs. Roblay McMullins, Texas Ranger Hall of Fame and Museum

During their first major engagement of the Mexican War, the Battle of Monterrey, the Texas Rangers helped U.S. forces capture the Mexican city. Led by Capt. Jack Hays, they captured the Bishop's Palace above the city on Independence Hill during a sneak attack at dawn (shown here in Bruce Marshall's "Dawn at Monterrey"). Following the American victory, Gen. Zachary Taylor negotiated an armistice, but it was not to last.
Bruce Marshall Collection

During the Mexican War which followed Texas's annexation by the United States, Texas Ranger Capt. Samuel H. Walker resigned from Ranger service to take a commission as field commander of the 1st U.S. Mounted Rifles. While in Washington, D. C., Walker met with Sam Colt and collaborated with him on the development of the "Walker Colt," the six-shot revolver that became a staple of Ranger artillery. Walker was killed in a Mexican War battle at Humantla while leading a charge. In his report, Gen. Walter P. Lane recalled the captain as "one of the most chivalric, noble-hearted men that graced the profession of arms."
John N. McWilliams Collection

Although they spent much of their time on horseback or in remote campsites, the Rangers did engage in the occasional social activity. One of their favorite pastimes was the *fandango*, the traditional Spanish dance party. They enjoyed spending an evening dancing with young *señoritas*, often dressed in the same kinds of clothing worn by the *Tejanos* as seen in this painting by Theodore Gentilz.
Daughters of the Republic of Texas Library

One of the few survivors of the Alamo, Capt. Juan N. Seguín left the mission with dispatches on February 25 and was attempting to return with reinforcements when it fell to the Mexican siege. A hero of the Texas Revolution and an early ranging company leader, Seguín fought at the Battle of San Jacinto. In this painting, he is depicted in his uniform as a colonel in the Army of the Republic of Texas.
UT Institute of Texan Cultures at San Antonio

Following the famous battle that took place at the Alamo during Texas's bid for independence, the old mission stood in ruins for many years. In the years just before the Civil War, it was converted for use as a supply depot for the U.S. Army Quartermaster Corps. This painting by Theodore Gentilz shows the ruins from the period of the 1840s, before its restoration. A historical site and tourist attraction today, the Alamo is maintained by The Daughters of the Republic of Texas.
Daughters of the Republic of Texas Library

In the uneasy years between the Texas War for Independence and the Mexican War following annexation by the United States, the Rangers sought to protect Texans from bandits, Indians, and Mexican aggression. Capt. John Coffee Hays suspected that Laredo, on the Rio Grande River, was being used as a staging area for Mexican scouts sent to incite the Indians. Employing skilled men and clever tactics, Hays managed to rout the much-larger Mexican force. Here, Hays (*left*) and Capt. Antonio Perez (*right*) lead Texas Rangers and a Mexican volunteer force in an attack on the Mexican garrison at Laredo in 1841.
UT Institute of Texan Cultures at San Antonio, Courtesy of Bruce Marshall

Capt. John Coffee Hays led a distinguished company of men during his service to the Texas Rangers, as shown in this document: "Muster Roll of Capt. John C. Hays' Company of Rangers on the N. W. and S. Western frontier of the time commencing June 27th and ending August 27th 1844." This roll includes noted Ranger leaders Lt. Ben McCulloch, "Kit" Acklin, Michael Chevallie, R. A. "Ad" Gillespie, Rufus Perry, and Samuel H. Walker. It notes that Acklin and Perry were wounded in the line of duty on August 27.
Texas State Library & Archives Commission

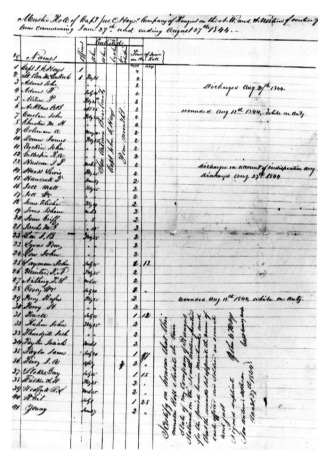

Following Gen. Winfield Scott's assumption of command of the U.S. forces in Mexico from Gen. Zachary Taylor, the Texas Rangers were once again called in to provide their unique skills in the Mexican War. Capt. Ben McCulloch's company of twenty Rangers were mustered in for a six-month enlistment in the U.S. forces and listed as "spies." After victories which gave the U.S. control of northern Mexico, General Taylor praised McCulloch's services, describing the Ranger scouting expeditions as being "of the highest importance." "The Return of Ben McCulloch," a watercolor painting by Bruce Marshall, depicts the return of McCulloch's Rangers to service in 1847.
UT Institute of Texan Cultures at San Antonio, Courtesy of Bruce Marshall

While Ranger companies took point for the U.S. forces in Mexico, Texas also had to defend her own borders. When a company of Rangers was requested to fortify the border town of Laredo, former President of the Republic Mirabeau B. Lamar became Texas Ranger Captain Lamar. Lamar proved to be an able leader, despite his earlier efforts to turn the Rangers to his own political advantage.
Texas State Library & Archives Commission

The Civil War found Texas Rangers facing troops they had fought alongside during the Mexican War. Five weeks after Robert E. Lee surrendered the Army of Virginia to Grant at Appomattox, the final battle of the Civil War took place on Texas soil. At the Battle of Palmito Ranch, Rip Ford's Cavalry of the West (Rangers) led Confederate troops to a stunning victory over a numerically superior Union force.
UT Institute of Texan Cultures at San Antonio

The name and the reputation of the Texas Rangers had become so nationally recognizable because of their service in the Mexican War that the average American tended to consider any Texas cavalryman a "ranger." The Texas Confederates did their best to live up to that reputation. Pictured is Capt. Sam Richardson of Walter P. Lane's Confederate Rangers.
UT Institute of Texan Cultures at San Antonio, Courtesy of Bruce Marshall

During the years of the Civil War, the men of the 5th Texas Cavalry were better known as the Texas Partisan Rangers. Entering Confederate service in February 1863, the Partisan Rangers served primarily in combat against Union forces in the Indian Territory, Oklahoma, and Arkansas. This watercolor painting depicts a Confederate-era Texas Partisan Ranger.
UT Institute of Texan Cultures at San Antonio, Courtesy of Bruce Marshall

Rangers carried a variety of weapons into battle during the Civil War. Pictured here are numerous artifacts of the period: U.S. Common Rifle (military rifled musket), Model 1842 Palmetto Armory U.S. Model pistol in .54 caliber; Texas military belt buckle; Texas Confederate "D-grip" bowie knife; Confederate Texas silver star worn on caps by Texas Confederate partisan volunteers, originally worn by J. T. Cyrus of Houston; fluted-cylinder Colt 1860 Army Model revolver; Texas Confederate artillery sword marked "B Co.-15."
Photo by Tom Knowles, Texas Ranger Hall of Fame and Museum

Not long after the Texas Secession Convention of 1861, Benjamin F. Terry, a prominent planter; John A. Wharton, attorney and politician; and Thomas S. Lubbock, a veteran of the Texas Revolution, decided to raise a cavalry unit for Confederate service. Not an official part of the Texas Ranger organization, the 8th Texas Cavalry, better known as Terry's Texas Rangers, proved so adept at using Ranger tactics in the great cavalry battles of the Civil War that no one questioned its use of the famous name. One Union officer who saw Terry's men in action paraphrased Rip Ford's description of the original Texas Rangers: "They ride like Arabs, shoot like archers at a mark, and fight like devils." "Breakthrough," a painting by Bruce Marshall, depicts Terry's Texas Rangers in action against Union forces.
Bruce Marshall Collection

Anson Jones was the last president of the Republic of Texas.
Texas State Library & Archives Commission

1845, he sent a request to Texas President Anson Jones asking that the Texas Rangers, Jack Hays in particular, be brought back into service to patrol the western frontier. The request was granted.

Believing that the defense of the frontier had become the responsibility of the U.S. government, the fading Republic had allowed Ranger enlistments to expire. Within a short time after Taylor sent his request to Anson Jones, the Texas government asked Hays to recruit three new companies of Rangers. He mustered in thirty men as his headquarters company; Ad Gillespie and Ben McCulloch recruited the other two companies.

In the interim before formal annexation and the outbreak of the war, the active Texas Ranger companies operated in federal service but under the direct orders of the Republic's government. They continued to serve in their roles as frontier defense forces for Texas, but they sometimes served as scouts and spies for Colonel Taylor's American forces. This service gave them an opportunity to demonstrate their capabilities to Taylor, to prove their value as a military asset.

While visiting Taylor at Corpus Christi, Hays received a report from Ranger scouts that six hundred Comanche had raided isolated settlements to the southwest of San Antonio. Hays returned to lead the chase; at its end, he fought his last major action against the Comanche at the Battle of Paint Rock (see "The Battle of Paint Rock").

In the meantime, Taylor's forces began the march to the border. On March 28, Taylor's men came into sight of their primary objective, the Mexican town of Matamoros, which lay just across the Rio Grande River.

Taylor's orders were to establish the U.S. claim to the Rio Grande as the border, to prevent Mexican forces from entering Texas in an effort to control the Nueces Strip. His own supply line stretched back to Port Isabel on the Gulf of Mexico, which left him in a dangerously exposed position. To create a secure point for resupply, field operations, and artillery support, he set his infantry to work as pioneers (construction engineers) to build a fortress on the north side of the river opposite Matamoros.

On the opposite side of the river, Gen. Mariano Arista took command of Matamoros and began gathering his forces, which included more than five thousand regular troops and Gen. Anastacio Torrejón's sixteen hundred veteran lancers. On April 24, in a rather old-fashioned and courtly gesture Arista ordered Torrejón and his lancers to cross the river and deliver the formal declaration of hostilities to Taylor.

The next day, Capt. Seth Thornton and his company of sixty dragoons set out to scout the lancers' position. The lancers found the dragoons instead and ambushed them at a deserted rancho. Their retreat to the river blocked, their captain wounded, and sixteen of their company killed, the dragoons surrendered. Unopposed, Torrejón's lancers rode freely through the countryside, scouting and harassing the American forces.

Only a few days before this incident, Taylor had accepted the services of Sam Walker's company of volunteers, the "Texas Mounted Rangers." After he'd

THE BATTLE OF PAINT ROCK

In early February 1846, while visiting Zachary Taylor at the U.S. Army's camp at Corpus Christi, Jack Hays received reports of a major raid by six hundred Comanche against settlements to the southwest of San Antonio. The largest band to strike into South Texas since the Great Raid, the Comanche war party had killed several Texans and had stolen a number of horses.

Hays led a party of forty men mounted on the best horses from their camp on the Medina River. They cut the war party's trail not far from Bandera Pass, where some time before Hays's Rangers had fought another famous battle against the Comanche. The Rangers tracked the Indians for another eighty miles north to the country near Enchanted Rock. From the direction of their trail, Hays figured that the Comanche were headed to the small lake at the base of Paint Rock, there to water their stolen horses before continuing on their way. He led the Rangers on a more direct route and pushed them along well into the night so they would arrive at the lake ahead of the raiders.

In the moonlight, the Rangers could see the length of the lake to where Paint Rock stood like a strange, twisted sentinel at the west shore. They took cover in the willows along the north side of the lake and waited through the cold night for the Comanche to come.

At dawn, the Comanche outriders rode into the ambush. The Rangers fired their rifles, knocking several Indians from their horses and sending the rest into a hasty retreat. When the warriors examined the back trail and saw how few Rangers faced them, they drew up for a charge. Their war cries filled the air as they rode back and forth, clattering their lances and bows against their shields. Then they attacked.

All during that terrible day, the warriors charged in again and again to fire their arrows. As they rode past, the Rangers cut them down with volleys of rifle fire. When the Comanche charged in for close combat with their lances, the Rangers drew their revolvers and stopped them cold. As night fell, the warriors withdrew from the field, but they didn't leave. They camped out of rifle range but kept close watch to keep the Rangers from escaping. All through the night, warriors crept through the battlefield in an attempt to retrieve the bodies of the dead. The Ranger pickets found themselves shooting at shadows.

At daylight, the Comanche renewed their attack. At one point the Comanche rush nearly rolled over the Ranger position, closing in to point-blank range. As it came down to hand-to-hand combat, the Rangers didn't have time to reload. With only the few loads left in their revolvers, the Rangers managed to hold off the Indian attack. Again, the Comanche left the field at nightfall. One of them must have recognized the Ranger leader; during the night, the Comanche shouted curses and promises of retribution directed at "Devil Jack." On the third day of the siege, the Comanche war leader directed multiple, simultaneous attacks against the Ranger position. He even sent snipers up into the rocks above the Rangers, but the Texans' long rifles sent the Comanche warriors tumbling down from the cliffs. The chief, who was so adept at using his buffalo hide shield to turn bullets that he seemed invulnerable to the Rangers' fire, directed his men from the front of each charge.

Just as he had done at the Battle of Plum Creek, Hays loaded his rifle and waited for his opportunity. Taking the split-second opening as the chief turned to deliver orders to his men, Hays fired past the shield. The chief tumbled backward from his horse, sending the Comanche charge into confusion. Hays called out a prearranged order to one of his Rangers. The brave Texan immediately jumped on his horse and rode out onto the battlefield, where he lassoed the chief's body and dragged the dead man back to the Ranger line.

The enraged warriors overcame their shock in an instant and charged in to recover their chief's body, but a withering hail of bullets forced them to turn away. After only a token attempt at another attack, the Comanche turned their horses to the northwest and retreated, leaving their stolen horses and goods behind.

The Rangers had killed at least a hundred of the raiders and wounded many more. With the hundreds of arrows the Comanche had fired, they had managed to kill one horse and to hit Emory Gibbons in the arm. Still, the battle had been a close call for the Rangers. The Comanche might have carried the fight if it hadn't been for the Rangers' Colt revolvers and the leadership skills of Jack Hays. Even so, they'd exhausted almost the last of their ammunition in stopping the final charge. Had the Comanche charged again, the Rangers wouldn't have been able to stop them.

Texas had already joined the Union by the time Hays and the Rangers fought the Comanche at the Battle of Paint Rock. Although the Comanche and the Texas Rangers would fight again, this battle marked the great captain's last official action as the commander of the Rangers of the Republic. His final meeting with another old enemy awaited him to the south, in Mexico.

finished out his enlistment with Gillespie's company, Walker had recruited more than ninety men from the Gulf Coast communities. He'd armed his men with breech-loading Hall carbines and as many Paterson revolvers as he could find before he'd headed south to join up with Taylor. On April 27, while Walker led scout detachments into the field to spy on the Mexican positions, a company of lancers attacked the fifteen men he'd left behind in camp. Six of Walker's Rangers were killed in the fight; four were taken prisoner but later exchanged.

Perhaps the capture of the dragoon scouts and the attack on the Ranger camp induced Taylor to change his mind about using more Texas volunteers. He decided to call on the governor of Louisiana for reinforcements, then wrote to ask Texas Gov. James Pinckney Henderson to raise four "regiments" of volunteers, two mounted companies and two companies of infantry. Governor Henderson could think of no better man for the job of recruiting and commanding the mounted volunteers than Jack Hays. After all, Hays was the Ranger the Texans looked to when they needed somebody to accomplish an impossible task.

James Pinckney Henderson.
Texas State Library & Archives Commission

After months of marching through chaparral and mesquite under the cruel Texas sun, after seeing that harsh sunlight flash from the ranked lances of Torrejón's disciplined cavalry, even the bright young academy officers began to think a little help from the Texans wasn't such a bad idea. Perhaps the fight with Mexico wouldn't be such a short and easy victory, after all.

The Battle of Palo Alto

By May 1846, supplies at the new fort on the Rio Grande were running low. Taylor took the major portion of his force with him to resupply at Port Isabel, leaving only the 7th Infantry to continue work on the fort and hold it against the Mexicans. Even before Taylor reached the port, the Mexicans crossed the river, lay siege to the fort and sent lancers to hold the road against his return. The Americans could hear the artillery duel from as far away as Port Isabel.

Taylor had to know if the men at the fort could hold out long enough for him to secure supplies and return. When a squadron of dragoons failed to clear away the Mexican cavalry blocking the road, Capt. Sam Walker took six of his Rangers, crept through the chaparral thickets, and swam a lake to complete the mission. Although he lost his carbine in the process, Walker brought back word that the 7th would hold out until relieved.

On March 7, the first true battle of the war took place on the road at Palo Alto as Arista deployed his forces against Taylor's return. Even though his infantry outnumbered the American forces and his cavalry could have broken their deployment, Arista allowed Taylor to set his forces in place before he prepared to attack.

The Americans attacked first, using Ringgold's flying artillery to cover their infantry as the heavier eighteen-pounders moved up to support them. The Mexican infantry withered under grapeshot and canister rounds from the mobile six-pounders. In an attempt to break through to hit the artillery, the lancers charged toward the 5th Infantry's position. The men of the 5th waited until the lancers were almost on top of them, then fired. As the lancers reeled back, then tried to form up for another charge, two light field pieces brought up by Ringgold to support the 5th fired directly into the horsemen. The entire Mexican force broke off the attack and retreated. Major Ringgold was one of the few American casualties, mortally wounded late in the battle, but he'd proven the effectiveness of his mobile artillery by winning the battle for Taylor.

Walker and the Rangers escorted a detachment of dragoons to scout ahead. They found Arista's forces set up in a strong defensive position near a ravine that led to the river. Mexican artillery with strong infantry support covered the only approach to their central strong point.

Under fire from Mexican artillery and muskets, the dragoons and the Rangers spurred their horses across the difficult, sandy ground, through tall grass that hid sinkholes and small arroyos that could kill or cripple a horse and rider. They gained the artillery position and killed the gunners, then engaged the infantry in fierce hand-to-hand combat. Slowly, the Mexican line collapsed into the center. After one brief attempt to counterattack, the lancers retreated. The Mexican infantry began to run toward the river, where the pursuing Americans shot them as they tried to swim across against the current. Many of the Mexican infantrymen drowned at the river crossing.

After the battle, Walker's Ranger company and some of the regular cavalry crossed the river to spy on Matamoros. They reported back to Taylor that Arista was preparing to withdraw from the city and had offered to negotiate a cease-fire. Taylor turned the offer down, and for the first time, U.S. troops invaded Mexico in force. By the time the Army followed Walker's scouts into Matamoros, the only Mexican soldiers in the city were the more than four hundred wounded Arista had been forced to leave behind.

The Goliad and Victoria company under Captain Price joined Taylor's command too late to participate in the battle, but they saw immediate action. Walker and Price joined forces to harass the retreating Mexicans, following them for sixty miles into the interior. The Rangers engaged in a short fight with Arista's rearguard of lancers, then returned to inform Taylor that the enemy was in full retreat.

The American victory at Palo Alto not only made Zachary Taylor a national hero but won him brevet promotion to the rank of major general. In the first skirmishes and scouts of the war, Sam Walker's company proved to Taylor and his officers that no one could outshine the Texas Rangers as advance scouts. When Hays arrived with the rest of the Rangers, the U.S. commander would learn just how valuable the Rangers would prove in serious combat.

A Gathering of Warriors

It had taken the rest of the Texans a little time to muster their forces to meet Taylor's request for volunteers, but they began arriving at Port Isabel and Matamoros soon after the battle at Palo Alto. Despite Taylor's call for infantry as well as cavalry, most of the Texans who responded formed mounted units, Ranger style; only Albert Sidney Johnston's company enlisted as an infantry unit. Following Sam Walker's example, the Texans called themselves the "Texas Mounted Rifles." The volunteers of the Mounted Rifles elected their own officers.

In an unprecedented move, Governor Henderson decided to lead the Texas volunteers himself. Adopting the rank of a major general of the militia to take command of the Texas forces, he handed control of his office over to his lieutenant governor. He recruited his senior staff from among the men who had directed Texas defenses in the past. Gen. Edward Burleson served as his aide, while former President of the Republic Mirabeau B. Lamar took the post of inspector.

Henderson planned to recruit two mounted regiments, twenty companies made up of the best fighting men in Texas. He ordered Jack Hays to bring the

Texas Ranger Captain Ben McCulloch.
UT Institute of Texan Cultures at San Antonio

Rangers to join him in Port Isabel. He'd obviously forgotten that Hays's company was still in federal service, guarding the frontier against Indians. He'd already given the designation of "A Company" to the men Ben McCulloch had brought in from Gonzales, but Henderson wanted Hays to lead the Rangers.

Hays managed to put together enough experienced Rangers whose enlistments were about to expire to muster a company of forty men in answer to Henderson's order. Other Rangers from San Antonio, commanded by R. A. Gillespie, would follow as soon as possible. On July 4, Hays's Rangers joined up as B Company of the 1st Regiment, Texas Mounted Rifles. Kit Acklin took the role of B Company commander, while Hays and Michael Chevallie enlisted as privates. They'd done this in order to get into service, after which they could stand for election as officers. Experienced Rangers and new recruits alike knew

TEXAS RANGER
(Mexican War)

"Texas Ranger, Mexican War," a watercolor painting by Bruce Marshall depicts the wild look of a Ranger during the conflict between Texas and Mexico.
Bruce Marshall Collection

who they wanted for their leader. They elected Hays as the colonel for the entire regiment, with Walker as lieutenant colonel and Chevallie as major.

With veterans like Eli Chandler, John Price, Ben McCulloch, Ad Gillespie, and J. P. Wells taking command of its companies, the 1st Regiment became a Texas Ranger affair. Mustered in the western counties along the frontier, it drew most of its officers and men from the experienced corps of Texas Rangers. The eastern counties provided the men for the 2nd Regiment, commanded by Col. George T. Wood. Although the men of the 2nd didn't have as much Indian-fighting experience as the men of the 1st, they were Texans who knew how to shoot and ride.

The Texas volunteers fought under terms of federal service, but they used Ranger tactics and thought of themselves as Texas Rangers. Hays made certain that his officers instructed the new recruits in horsemanship, marksmanship, and frontier cavalry tactics, the kind of on-the-job training he'd been using with his Rangers for years. Standard military drills were for the regulars — the Rangers spent their spare time in caring for their horses and keeping their weapons in combat condition.

Rangers wore no uniforms but dressed in comfortable, durable, and sometimes outlandish frontier clothing, using broad-brimmed hats and sombreros to shield their eyes and their faces against the sun. They carried an assortment of weapons, from shotguns and rifles to Bowie knives. Many of them had Paterson revolvers, and those who didn't carried several single-shot pistols. They wore their hair and beards and mustaches as they pleased.

Their wild, sometimes barbaric appearance and their seeming lack of military discipline often amused and bemused the regular officers of Taylor's forces. They made great copy for the journalists who followed and publicized their exploits, not only for their combat skills but also for their colorful character and appearance. To the Mexican troops who would face them in battle, they were *Los Diablos Tejanos* incarnate.

Insp. Gen. Ethan Allen Hitchcock gave a pretty fair

Gen. Zachary Taylor, commander of U.S. forces in the Mexican War and U.S. President, 1849–1850. Engraving by Alexander H. Ritchie. *Dictionary of American Portraits*

description of the Rangers in his reports from the Mexican War:

> Hay's [sic] Rangers have come, their appearance never to be forgotten. Not any sort of uniforms, but well-mounted and doubly well-armed: each man has one or two Colt's revolvers besides ordinary pistols, a sword, and every man a rifle…The Mexicans are terribly afraid of them.

The volunteer units from Texas enlisted for shorter, more irregular terms of service than did the regular troops. Whenever individual enlistment terms ran out or illness and casualties put a company drastically under strength, the company would simply reorganize and recruit replacements. Sometimes an entire company might leave service, or just a few individuals. The Ranger chain of command depended on the effectiveness of its elected officers, not on a class system of set ranks. A lieutenant whose six-month enlistment ran out in one company might reenlist in another company as a private.

Zachary Taylor often had a difficult time explaining the Ranger enlistment process to his superiors. The volunteers didn't do it the army way, but Taylor needed them and was willing to do some creative accounting to keep them.

Rangers on the Scout

Zachary Taylor exceeded his orders by invading Mexico to take Matamoros, but his superiors in Washington agreed with the results. In June 1846, the Secretary of War, William Marcy, gave Taylor unchallenged discretion in proceeding with the campaign and informed him that as many as twenty thousand reinforcements were on the way. He suggested that Taylor secure both banks of the Rio Grande in order to use it to move supplies; he also suggested that Taylor consider moving his headquarters to Monterrey.

Once the American campaign had turned into a full-fledged invasion, Monterrey became the necessary strategic point for entry into the Mexican interior. Because the Americans had little knowledge of condi-

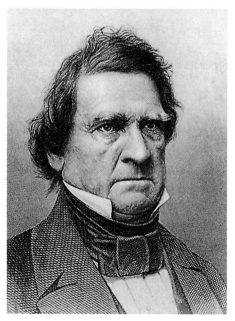

William L. Marcy served as U.S. Secretary of War during the Mexican War.
Dictionary of American Portraits

tions in Mexico, of the best routes for their advance, and the locations of the water sources they'd need, Taylor turned to the Rangers. When he sent a battalion of the 1st Infantry to take Reynosa, he sent Price's Rangers to escort them. They took Reynosa without opposition from the Mexicans.

By mid-September the expedition was ready to move out on the next step on the road to Monterrey. The Texans provided the screening force to protect the columns of infantry, artillery, and supplies. Ben McCulloch's company escorted the pioneers who went ahead to clear and repair the roads, while Ad Gillespie's company served as couriers and pickets. Hays's company scouted from China to the west, then through Cadereyta almost south to Monterrey back north to Marin, circling to intercept any attempt by the enemy to attack the flank. When both divisions of the Texas Mounted Rifles joined up for the ride to Marin, Texas Gov. Henderson, now Maj. Gen. Henderson, assumed for the first time at least nominal command of the entire force from Texas.

McCulloch was the first to sight the enemy, some of Torrejón's lancers. The lancers for the most part retreated with only a few shots fired. The Rangers brought in some prisoners, mostly civilians who had been drafted to construct fortifications at Monterrey. From the intelligence the Rangers gathered, Taylor knew that the Mexicans had put a major effort into fortifying the city with earthworks, firing pits, and artillery positions. The enemy meant to break the Americans on the rock they'd made of Monterrey.

Texas Goes Ahead

The old city of Monterrey lay on the plain at the foot of the Sierra Madre mountains, stretched out for almost two miles along the northern banks of the San Juan River. The north-to-south highway from the Rio Grande to Saltillo and Mexico City passed through the south section of the city. Spurs of the Sierra Madres that extended into the town were natural spots for artillery emplacements that could command the road.

A "Cartes de Visite" photograph of Colonel John Coffee Hays, taken by Mathew Brady in 1858 during Hays's visit to Washington, D.C.
John N. McWilliams Collection

To continue on to Mexico City, the Americans would have to take Monterrey.

General Ampuida's more than seven thousand Mexican troops stood in their way, and they'd had time to prepare for uninvited guests. Not more than a mile from the central plaza, the T-shaped ridge of Independence Hill overlooked the main road. The Mexicans had fortified it with a series of earth and stone redoubts — they called this stronghold La Libertad, or Fort Liberty — to protect a battery of artillery they'd placed there. Behind and above these redoubts, on the ridge, lay the stone fortress known as the Bishop's Palace. At the 800-foot peak of this same ridge an extensive sandbag redoubt (Fort

Independence) protected even more artillery emplacements. To the south beyond the road, artillery looked down from Federation Ridge to where the Santa Catarina River's swift current ran beside the road like a castle moat. Along with new earthworks and reinforced buildings, Fort El Soldado's artillery, two nine-pounders, covered the road from the east.

A rock indeed was Monterrey, so General Taylor sent in the sledgehammer and the blasting powder first. On September 19, Jack Hays and seventeen of the twenty companies of Texans led the advance into Monterrey, while two companies of Rangers rode rear guard and Gillespie's company again provided courier service. James K. Holland later wrote, "Texas went ahead Today — now that danger is expected old Taylor has put us in front." His sarcasm would have been lost on Taylor, who was simply using the tool best suited for the job.

At the outskirts of the city the road divided to continue into Monterrey or bypass it to the east. There the Rangers came upon the Black Fort, an ancient stone building that overlooked the west leg of the road, the path into the city. The Mexicans had piled up earth and stone barricades to reinforce the old building and to narrow access to the road.

A bugle sounded from the fortress as a regiment of Torrejón's lancers charged out to meet the Rangers. Hays formed his men up to charge, but the lancers suddenly wheeled their horses and retreated. Hays pulled his men up short. A cannon shot erupted from the stone pile that lay at the crossroads, then another. The lancers had tried to use the old Comanche trick to lead the Rangers into a trap, but Hays made a better Indian than any of them. He led the Rangers back out of range.

Hays found General Taylor and his pioneers setting up a campsite at Santo Domingo, about two miles out from Monterrey. His men, once they watered their horses and set up camp, commenced to playing Comanche games with the Black Fort's artillerymen. The Texans rode in zigzags and circles across the plain, daring the Mexican gunners to hit them. Maj. Luther

Giddings of the Ohio regulars wrote that they were like boys at play, "...these fearless horsemen, in a spirit of boastful rivalry, vied with each other in approaching the very edge of danger."

After an extensive review of the intelligence brought to him by Ranger scouts, Taylor chose his plan of attack. Gen. William J. Worth's division of two thousand regulars, supported by Hays and the 1st Texas, would circle the city to attack the western defenses from the rear. Their orders were to take Independence Hill in order to gain control of the south road. If they could cut the enemy's line of retreat and reinforcement, they might be able to defeat him in detail.

Gen. William J. Worth led troops in the Battle of Monterrey.
Dictionary of American Portraits

Taking Independence Hill was the key to Monterrey, but it was a risky plan. From the fortresses on the hills, the enemy would certainly observe the flanking attempt and move troops to meet it. Taylor would have troops ready to make diversionary attacks, but it was up to Worth's division and Hays's Rangers to take and hold Independence Hill.

The Battle of Monterrey

On Sunday morning, September 20, 1846, the Rangers moved out to escort Worth's division to stage the assault. Hays led the column in the right flanking motion, circling wide of the outer defenses. They moved through cornfields and chaparral thickets, sometimes halting while the pioneers cleared the brush for the infantry and artillery. As they neared the outer spur of Independence Hill, the enemy began moving up infantry and light artillery from the Bishop's Palace to La Libertad. Hays sent messengers back to Taylor suggesting that he commence the diversionary attacks on the northern approach.

The American forces gathered at the side road that led to the foot of Independence Hill and the Saltillo road. Hays set out forward pickets; accompanied by Walker and McCulloch, he climbed to high ground to get a better look at the situation. From the hillside they observed the diversionary movements of the American troops to the north. General Worth joined them for a moment, then rode back to join the main body. Gen. Edward Burleson, who had earlier scouted ahead with twenty men, rode back to inform Hays that he'd run into Mexican pickets. A large force of combined infantry and cavalry was moving up the road to prevent the American advance.

Hays left an observer on the hill and returned to lead the advance with a scout force of thirty-five men. General Worth accompanied him on the scout. As they neared the intersection with the Saltillo road, Mexican infantry fired at them in ambush from a cornfield. The artillery on Independence Hill began dropping in round shot and shells. When the scout force turned to retreat, the entire guard detachment of lancers charged after them. Lt. John McMullen, spying one young Ranger who'd had his horse shot out from under him, turned back and spurred his horse. Riding at a full gallop, he reached down and pulled the man up behind him. He turned to retreat, the lancers in hot pursuit.

Hays saw McMullen's predicament and turned the rest of the Rangers to charge. The Rangers drew their

FROM "THE TEXAS RANGERS IN THE CAMPAIGN IN NORTHERN MEXICO"

BY MAJ. LUTHER GIDDINGS, OHIO REGIMENT

As a mounted soldier he has no counterpart in any age or country. Neither Cavalier or Cossak, Maluke or Morstrooper are like him: and yet, in some respect he resembles them all.

Chivalrous, bold and impetuous in action, he is yet wary and calculating, always impatient of restraint, and sometimes unscrupulous and unmerciful. He is ununiformed and undrilled, and performs his active duties thoroughly, but with little regard to order or system. He is an excellent rider and a dead shot. His arms are a rifle, Colt's revolving pistols and a knife. Unaccustomed to the saber or to move in mass, the Rangers are of course unable to make a charge upon, or to receive one from, well-armed or well-disciplined troops. But when an enemy's line is broken by the rapid volleys of their rifles, they then pitch in promiscuously, and finish the work with the "five shooter," delivering their fire right and left as they dash along at full speed. And it must be confessed that for a chaparral skirmish, or an "up and down" and cross over fight upon house tops, such as the third day at Monterrey, the Rangers have few superiors. Centaurlike, they seemed to live on their horses; and, under firm and prudent leaders, were efficient soldiers, especially for scouts and advance post-service, where the necessity for uninterrupted vigilance left them no opportunity for indulging in the mad-cap revels and marauding expeditions for which they are somewhat celebrated.

pistols, gave a Texas yell, and hit the lancers head on, driving them back and scattering them. No longer protected by their cavalry, the Mexican infantrymen also retreated from their ambush positions.

As night began to fall and the Ranger companies settled into camp near some abandoned *jacales*, a large scout force of Mexican lancers rode down on them and opened fire from the hillside. One Ranger was wounded in the exchange, but the Texans replied with such a volume of rifle and pistol fire that they killed one Mexican scout and wounded several others.

The Rangers hit the saddle before dawn, taking the lead in front of Capt. C. F. Smith's light infantry. About a mile down the trail to the Saltillo road, Hays halted to wait for daylight. He moved the column to the side of the road, allowing the men to dismount to get some sleep and to care for their horses.

A force of Mexican cavalry, as many as fifteen hundred men, moved out to meet the unprepared Rangers. Sgt. Buck Barry of Eli Chandler's company later wrote, "They were good horsemen, mounted on lively steeds, and made the most beautiful spectacle of mounted men I ever expect to see." Each of the Mexican cavalrymen held a long lance, a green and red pennon fluttering from its tip. They moved expertly and almost silently into attack position, an eerie sight to greet the sleepy Rangers. As his Texans struggled to readjust their saddle girths, Hays told his captains to get the men ready for action. He deployed McCulloch's company to protect the right flank but left the rest of the company dismounted. Smith's light infantry and Lt. Col. James Duncan's artillery company came up from behind to support the Rangers.

Hays borrowed a saber from one of the American officers and rode out alone toward the lancers. He stopped halfway between the two forces and bowed to his opposite number, Lt. Col. Juan Nájera, then challenged him to a duel. Nájera accepted, removed some of his equipment from his horse and drew his saber. The two men slowly walked their horses toward each other until they were about forty yards apart, at which point the Mexican colonel suddenly spurred his horse to charge. Hays galloped forward to meet him, then dodged to the right to duck Nájera's saber cut and tossed his own blade to the ground. He drew his pistol, dropped down to hang behind his horse and fired from under the horse's neck. The impact of the bullet lifted Nájera from his saddle. Hays spurred his horse back toward his men, shouting, "Here they come, boys! Give 'em hell!"

As the Mexicans saw their gallant colonel fall to the Ranger's Comanche trick, they charged, according to Buck Barry, "like mad hornets." The dismounted Rangers fired their long rifles into the lancers, killing eighty men in the first moments of the fight. McCulloch's company drew their revolvers and took the brunt of the lancers' anger as well as some friendly fire from the infantry and artillery. When the Mexican infantry didn't come up to support the charge, the lancers fell back, still under heavy fire. In the end, Hays estimated that more than one hundred lancers died in the attack. The Texans had one man killed, seven wounded.

It was a terribly uneven victory made possible by what might have seemed an unfair or even underhanded trick, but it worked. Hays and his Rangers had learned from the Comanche that all was fair in war, as long as it worked.

As the Rangers regrouped, they heard the reports of Taylor's heavy mortars and other artillery opening up on the north side of the city. What they heard was the planned diversion intended to draw attention away from their assault on Federation Ridge. Under that artillery fire, Brig. Gen. David E. Twiggs's regulars and Capt. John A. Quitman's Mississippi Volunteers assaulted the Black Fort and other strong points in the north, suffering heavy casualties before they withdrew. Wood's 2nd Texas Mounted Rifles, the Mississippi Rifles, and the regulars attacked the heavily fortified barricades in eastern and northern sections of Monterrey, also taking many casualties.

Three hundred men made up the first wave of the assault on the first redoubts and El Soldado. Five companies of Texans under Major Chevallie, Smith's infantry, and Duncan's light artillery advanced through the chaparral under artillery fire from the hill. The artillery overshot them because they moved too fast for the Mexican gunners to find the right angle of depression. When they reached the Santa Catarina, they had to wade through its swift current while completely exposed to enemy fire. Bullets and grapeshot hissed into the water around them as they stumbled across, slipping on the stones of the riverbed.

As the Rangers crossed the river in groups, skirmishers moved down from the heights to meet them. Hays, no longer content merely to watch as his men moved forward, took another hundred men and followed. Before he could reach them, Smith and Chevallie's men swept over the Mexican infantry at the first redoubt. Hays led his men in a flanking movement to hit the hill from a different angle. Gillespie's company reached the earthworks first; Hays joined him seconds later.

As the Mexicans retreated toward El Soldado, the Rangers found an abandoned nine-pounder cannon. Duncan's artillerymen turned it onto the Mexican fortifications as the remainder of Worth's forces moved forward to support the advance. Before the retreating Mexicans could begin a defense, the Americans cut them off and took the fort. Gillespie and the 5th Infantry's color sergeant were the first men to reach it. The Texans and the regulars alike cheered as the sergeant planted his company's flag in the captured ground.

The American losses were incredibly light. McCulloch had four men wounded, while the company that had followed Hays had two killed and nine

"The Texas Rangers, 1846." This watercolor painting by Bruce Marshall presents a group of Rangers going into battle during the period of the Mexican War.
Bruce Marshall Collection

wounded. The battle, which had started at 11:00 A.M., was over in less than an hour and a half. Hays had his exhausted troops retire to camp at the junction of the Saltillo and Topo roads. They cared for their horses, ate for the first time in thirty-six hours, and then fell asleep on the ground. Even the cold rain of an evening thunderstorm failed to wake them.

After conferring with General Worth, Hays directed Sam Walker to wake 250 men and tell them to get their guns. Reinforced by 150 men from the regular units, they were to move out to storm Independence Hill. The time they set to begin the assault was 3:00 A.M.

Long before Walker began rousting the Rangers for the assault group, Hays picked out a squad of twenty men for a special assignment. Taking only their sidearms, they followed Hays to the base of Independence Hill. Slipping through the darkness, they killed or otherwise incapacitated all of the Mexican pickets and guards along the hillside.

Believing the peak of the ridge to be unassailable except via the eastern slope, Ampuida's officers had left the steep approach on the city side of the ridge unguarded. By the time Hays and his commando patrol rejoined the rest of the assault force at the foot of the hill, the guards on the other slope were no longer in place. With Hays and Colonel Childs on the left, Walker and Major Vinton on the right, the force began the climb up the almost vertical wall of the reverse slope.

Just before dawn they were within a hundred yards of the top. The sound of a regular's canteen clanking against the rock alerted the Mexican soldiers at the top. The Americans kept climbing even as the bullets whizzed past them; when the Texans got within twenty yards of the top, they started firing at the silhouetted figures of the Mexicans on the wall above them. Ad Gillespie was among the first to reach the top, followed by Hays and the others. A sniper's bullet cut Gillespie down as he stood on the sandbag walls to fire, and another ball struck Herman Thomas of McCulloch's company, but the attack sent the

Mexicans fleeing toward the Bishop's Palace. A diversionary attack by the 7th Infantry prevented the troops in the Bishop's Palace from launching a counterattack on the assault force.

The attack on the Bishop's Palace began almost immediately. The 8th Infantry and a Ranger company made another diversionary attack on the palace as the 5th crossed from Federation Ridge. The 5th brought with them a disassembled twelve-pounder, which they carried up the steep slope. With this heavy gun, once they reassembled it, they zeroed in on the Palace and began blasting the walls away. The Texans moved up to rifle range and started sniping at the defenders. The Mexican commander had no choice but to attack.

As the Mexican lancers and infantry massed to make the counterattack, the regulars moved behind an old rock fence that ran across the hill about halfway down the side. Sending Blanchard's Louisiana infantry company forward as bait, they lured the lancers into a charge. When the Mexican cavalry reached the fence, it turned into a steel thicket of bayonets. The regulars fired their muskets into the massed lancers at point-blank range. From hidden positions along the ridge, the Rangers fired their rifles and pistols. The lancers, caught in the crossfire, reeled back to trample their own infantry.

The attack sent the enemy into complete confusion, as Hays said, "so vigorously pursued by our men that they were unable to regain the Castle and continued to retreat to the town, leaving us in possession of the works with four pieces of artillery and a large quantity of ammunition." The Americans followed the remaining Mexicans into the Bishop's Palace before they could barricade the doors. They smashed all resistance, taking thirty prisoners and preventing an officer from firing the powder magazine. As the Americans brought up more artillery, their shelling of the eastern part of the city drove the Mexican forces to retreat to the outskirts.

The Rangers didn't advance without casualties of their own, however. Ad Gillespie had pretended that his wound wasn't serious and had waved his men

This Colt Paterson, the "Texas Model," has an engraved handle that identifies it as a Ranger weapon used in the Mexican War.
West Point Museum Collections, United States Military Academy

onward at the assault on the summit. He probably knew at the time that his wound was mortal. They buried young Herman Thomas atop Independence Hill, close to where he'd fallen.

On the other side of the city, the 2nd Texas Mounted Rifles and the Mississippi Rifles finally smashed through the barricades to engage the Mexican defenders in a bitter house-to-house battle. The East Texans dismounted and entered the streets, followed by other volunteers and regulars. They used axes, hammers, and gun butts to break down the doors of the houses. Once inside they cleared the rooms, then climbed to the rooftops to fire down into the retreating enemy troops. The fighting often got so close that it came down to a matter of daggers and Bowies, gun stocks and fists. As they hunted down and killed the retreating Mexicans, many of them shouted the names of men who had died long before, at Goliad, at the Alamo, and in the Lottery of Death.

At about midafternoon, Worth sent Hays with four hundred men of the 1st Texas to investigate the sounds of heavy firing they could hear coming from the east. The men of the 1st adopted the same street-

fighting tactics as had the 2nd, with one notable exception. They carried with them a number of mortar shells, which they used as overlarge grenades to clear barricades and take down entire houses. When they broke in the door of a building and came in with their Paterson Colts blazing, nothing could stand in their way. Snipers didn't last long once the Texans got on the rooftops and started sniping back. As Buck Barry wrote, "When the report of a Texas rifle was heard, it was a safe bet a bullet had been bloodied."

The Rangers weren't alone in entering the city, east or west. The artillery units, regulars, and other volunteers followed them in, some of them taking heavy casualties in the process. As the two American forces neared the famed fountain in the Plaza de Carne in the central business section, the remaining Mexican defenders pulled back into the old cathedral to make their last stand.

That final battle never took place. Even though the commanders in the combat area agreed that they were within hours, perhaps minutes, of forcing an unconditional surrender of the city, General Taylor sent out an order for all American forces to pull back. Ostensibly, this order was to allow the artillery to resume shelling the city. In actuality, it was Taylor's overture to the Mexicans to get them to agree to a cease-fire.

The Rangers at the plaza resisted the order, requesting that it be repeated. Even after they confirmed the pull-back order, Sam Walker and some of his men camped out in the city. They weren't bothered in the least by the cursory artillery bombardment. Through the night, Walker himself scouted the locations of the enemy's remaining forces. He found General Ampuida's abandoned headquarters and caught a short nap in the general's bed.

The next day, September 24, as the Rangers and the regulars moved back into the city, they found out from civilians that most of the lancers had managed to slip away during the night. From the last stronghold of the remaining Mexican forces, a bugle call rang out. An officer and a standard bearer appeared on the cathedral steps. Texan snipers who didn't care to recognize the military significance of the white flag immediately shot the envoys. Sam Walker took over from there and assured the Mexicans that they could send out another truce party.

The Rangers didn't know it yet, but the Battle of Monterrey was over, as was their first service in the Mexican War.

No Truce at All

The truce and the subsequent armistice agreement Gen. Zachary Taylor negotiated with the Mexicans after the Battle of Monterrey came as quite a surprise to the Texans. They'd just been getting started when "Old Rough and Ready" decided to quit. After the Mexicans formally surrendered Monterrey on September 25 and the Stars and Stripes replaced the Mexican flag above the city, most of the Rangers boycotted the victory party. Bugles and flag-waving ceremonies meant little to them.

The enlistment periods had expired for most of the Texas companies; enlistments for the rest would run out in a matter of days or weeks. Taylor saw no reason to keep them in service, so the Texans spent some of their time waiting for their pay and seeing the sights of the city. General Worth, who had been appointed as the military governor of Monterrey, asked that the 1st Texas assemble at his headquarters for a farewell party. Worth said to Hays, "It was the untiring, vigorous bravery, and unerring shots of your regiment that saved my division from defeat."

Sam Walker mustered out with the rest of his 1st Texas Mounted Rifles company and accepted regular federal service as a captain in the newly formed U.S. Mounted Rifles. Ordered to report to Washington to recruit men for his company, he accompanied Jack Hays on the first leg of the trip. In Galveston, Houston, and New Orleans, Hays and Walker found themselves greeted as heroes, lionized by politicians and newspaper correspondents, and overwhelmed by the American public's eagerness to learn more about the Texas Rangers. For two rather private, reticent men, it must have been a trial.

Hays had his own agenda to follow, the most important aspect of which was to return to his courtship of Susan Calvert. He exchanged farewells with his old comrade in New Orleans to make a business trip to Mississippi before returning to San Antonio. Walker continued on to Washington, where he found his notoriety had preceded him. Although he rejected most of the many social invitations he received, he did accept invitations from two individuals who would prove influential in the last year of his foreshortened life — President James K. Polk and Samuel Colt. Although Colt's firearms business had gone bankrupt, his invitation to Walker came in a letter suggesting that the Texas Rangers might want to purchase some of his "repeaters" for use on the frontier. Walker's enthusiastic response and their meeting resulted in their collaborative design for a revolutionary firearm, the "Colt Walker" six-shot revolver (see "The Two Sams, Walker and Colt").

At Taylor's request, one company of Rangers stayed in service to protect the border town of Laredo. Governor Henderson returned to reclaim his office,

THE TWO SAMS, WALKER AND COLT

It's fitting that one of the Texas Rangers who made the Colt's Paterson five-shot revolver famous played a major role in developing the first true six-shooter. Between them, Texas Ranger Sam Walker and inventor Sam Colt designed a piece of history, a weapon that would shape the cultural evolution and the mythological landscape of the American West.

Capt. Samuel H. Walker gave his support and his name to the revolver that replaced the Rangers' trusty Paterson Colt. This photo by Mathew Brady was taken around 1847, the year Walker died fighting in the Mexican War.
Library of Congress

During the armistice after the Battle of Monterrey, the enlistment period expired for most of the companies of the 1st Texas Mounted Rifles. Sam Walker, formerly a lieutenant colonel of this Texas Ranger-led regiment of volunteers, signed on with the regular army as captain of Company C, United States Mounted Rifles. Along with his friend and former commander, Col. Jack Hays, he returned to the United States in October 1846. From Houston to Galveston to New Orleans, they found adoring crowds waiting to greet them; their actions in the Mexican War had caught the attention of the public and the press.

Walker followed his orders to report to Washington, there to recruit men and purchase ordinance for his Mounted Rifle company. The Ranger's fame had preceded him to the capital city. He received invitations to many social events; President James K. Polk noted Walker's visit to the White House in his diary.

Sam Colt, alerted by the publicity surrounding the former Ranger's visit, seized his chance. He sent Walker a letter sug-

Sam Colt invented the revolver: the weapon that shaped the history of the Rangers and the West.
Dictionary of American Portraits

gesting that Walker and Jack Hays should look to Colt's Patent Arms for a new supply of "repeaters." The letter to Walker, dated November 27, was a good example of Colt's entrepreneurial spirit. Colt's Patent Arms company had virtually ceased to exist not long after his major sales of Paterson pistols and rifles to the Texas Navy in 1839. Colt had no existing factory in which he could produce the firearms but wasn't the kind of man who would allow such a minor detail to stand in his way.

Colt's letter brought an immediate reply from Walker, who wrote:

The pistols which you made for the Texas Navy have been in use by the Rangers for three years, and I can say with confidence that it is the only good improvement that I have seen. The Texans who have learned their value by practical experience, their confidence in them is unbounded, so much so that they are willing to engage four times their number....

...With improvements I think they can be rendered the most perfect weapon in the World for light mounted troops which is the only efficient troops that can be placed on our extensive Frontier to keep the various warlike tribes of Indians & marauding Mexicans in subjection. The people throughout Texas are anxious to procure your pistols & I doubt not you would find sale for a large number at this time.

Yours very respy.

S H Walker Capt. Mounted

Riflemen U S A

Colt, who had moved on to other engineering projects when Patent Arms went bankrupt, was delighted at the chance to return to designing and manufacturing weapons. Walker met with Colt in New York, where the two Sams set to work on improved designs for a new revolver. Even before their discussion produced more than a few scribbles, Colt figured out his production costs and prices for the weapon — $25 each — and the quantities in which he could produce them. Because his former partner, John Ehlers, retained possession of the assets of their defunct company, Colt didn't have a single working model of the Paterson available to use as a template. He advertised in newspapers and contacted friends in the military in an attempt to purchase one. Using the Paterson as a guide, Colt and Walker created a wooden demonstration model of the new revolver.

Armed with the model, introductions from Colt, and recommendations from influential government and business leaders (perhaps including President Polk himself), Walker took the new designs to the Secretary of War and the U.S. Ordinance Department. Skeptical at first, the War Department eventually agreed to authorize a bid from Colt:

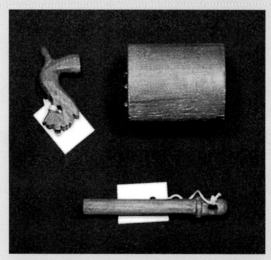

Sir:

At the insistence of Capt. Walker, the Secretary of War desires you to furnish one thousand revolving pistols — bore 50 to the pound (round ball) with elongated moulds in addition, at twenty five Dollars each, in accordance with your letter to the Captain, the whole to be delivered in three months. Please inform this Office whether or not you will engage to furnish the pistols as above.

G. Talcott

Lt. Col. Ordinance

Wooden model parts for the Colt revolver similar to those produced by Sam Walker and Sam Colt when they designed the Walker Colt.
Photo by Tom Knowles, Texas Ranger Hall of Fame and Museum

Colt had the contract offer, but he had no factory. On January 5, 1847, he persuaded Eli Whitney, manufacturer of cotton processing machinery and standard firearms, to contract with him to produce 1,000 of the new revolvers at his plant in Whitneyville, Connecticut. Secretary of War W. L. Marcy signed a contract with Colt only a few days later, authorizing production:

1000 or larger number...of said Colts patent Repeating Pistols, made to correspond with the model recently got up by said Colt and Walker...

The weapons were manufactured at Whitney's facility, but Colt personally designed the manufacturing process; some of his innovations and applications later revolutionized other manufacturing industries. He had each weapon stamped with his own mark — "Samuel Colt, New York" — as well as with a letter and number designating the particular Mounted Rifles company for which it was manufactured.

The Ordinance Department officially designated the new revolver the Colt Patent Arm, 1847, U.S.M.R., but Colt personally named it for the Ranger who had made it possible. From the moment the first model came off of the assembly line, the fearsome .44 caliber, six-shot revolver was known as the "Walker."

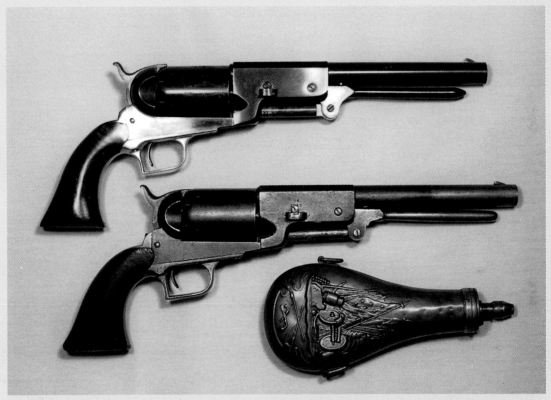

(*top*) Uberti Co. modern reproduction of the Colt Walker revolver, with visible cylinder engraving, authentic bluing, and detail. (*center*) Colt Walker revolver 1847 military model, stamped "B Co. #41," one of 100 surviving examples of the original 1,100. (*lower*) Original military issue Walker Colt powder flask.
Photo by Tom Knowles; original Walker courtesy of the Metzger Collection, Sam Houston Sanders Corps of Cadets Center, Texas A&M University; reproduction Walker courtesy of Kevin Jimmerson

In durability and performance, the huge, four-and-one-half-pound Walker Colt more than made up for the deficiencies of the light caliber, five-shot Paterson. The deep rifles in the heavy nine-inch barrel made it deadly accurate; the Rangers said that it more than matched military carbines in distance and accuracy. The powder capacity of each individual chamber was greater than that of the standard military issue Hall carbine. The improved loading lever allowed the shooter to reload the revolver without removing the cylinder; an in-production change to the design allowed the shooter to load and fire conical bullets as well as round balls.

In combat against the military muskets of conventional forces the Walker gave the Rangers an incredible firepower advantage, especially when the shooter carried an extra cylinder or two already loaded. Until the advent of the magnum cartridge in the 1930s, it was the most powerful handgun ever manufactured. It was certainly the largest and the heaviest.

Colt produced only about 1,000 standard model Walkers, but he also manufactured about 100 presentation models with engraved cylinders depicting the victory of Hays's Rangers over the Comanche at Walker Creek. Colt sent a pair of these presentation models to Jack Hays and another pair to General Taylor. The Walker Colts served as excellent advertisements for his later weapons, beginning with the sized-down Improved Holster model he produced for the U.S. military at the Whitneyville factory. The Holster Model and the Whitneyville Colt Dragoon, with minor modifications, became the standard U.S. Army sidearm. Colt sold over 200,000 units in a twenty-year period.

Although the revolver would eventually make him a wealthy man, Colt actually lost money on his contract for the Walkers. He had to fight the Ordinance Department's inspectors every step of the process. Even when he'd finished a sufficient number of Walkers to ship them, the military held them up in transit at each point on the route to Mexico. The Ordinance Department did ship 220 of the revolvers to Vera Cruz, but the local ordinance officer didn't see fit to issue them immediately. Sam Walker, who had returned to Mexico with his new recruits for the U.S. Mounted Rifles, was forced to arm his men with standard military issue single-shot flintlock pistols.

In a letter to his brother dated October 5, 1847, Walker noted:

> I have just received a pair of Colt's Pistols which he sent to me as a present, there is not an officer who has seen them but what speaks in the highest terms of them and all of the Cavalry officers are determined to get them if possible. Col. Harney says they are the best arm in the world. They are as effective as the common rifle at one hundred yards.

The package from Colt contained two engraved, presentation model Walker six-shooters, serial numbers 1020 and 1021. Just four days after he wrote the letter, Captain Walker was killed in combat at the pueblo of Humantla, the Colt revolver that bore his name clutched in his hand.

The six-shooter designed by Walker and Colt influenced the development of the frontier in ways neither man could have imagined at the time. For better or worse, the combination of Ranger and revolver defined for America and the rest of the world the image of the Texan — the deadly and skilled Western horseman who feared no man on earth.

As it made its way into other hands, the revolver would spawn a new breed of Westerner. Men like John Wesley Hardin and Clay Allison and Sam Bass, Doc Holliday and Wild Bill Hickock and Wyatt Earp would put their own mark on the legend of the gun. Some of the fast guns would choose to serve the law, while other *pistoleros* would choose to break it. The Texas Rangers, always eager for a challenge, would face off against the gunfighters, outlaws, and badmen to beat them at their own game. It was only natural that the Rangers would be the best at the six-shooter game — they were, after all, the originals.

but he empowered Mirabeau B. Lamar to reenlist eighty men from the ranks of those mustered out from other companies. Former President of the Republic Lamar became Texas Ranger Captain Lamar;

Gen. Antonio López de Santa Anna commanded Mexican forces against the United States during the Mexican War.
New-York Historical Society

his company served with distinction as it fought Indians, bandits, and guerrillas. Despite his earlier efforts to turn the Rangers to his own political advantage, Lamar proved to be an able leader, one worthy of his title.

Most of the men of the 1st and 2nd Texas Mounted Rifles dispersed and returned to their homes. They had families, farms, and businesses to protect from a new outbreak of Indian troubles on the frontier. Comanche raiders, unimpressed by the big fight down south or the annexation of Texas by the United States, had moved back into West Central Texas in force. In any case, the Texans didn't much care for the way General Taylor's armistice had broken up the party just as it was warming up. Jack Hays, Sam Walker, Ben McCulloch, Mike Chevallie, and many other Rangers from Hays's old company would return once more to fight in Mexico, but most of the Texans felt they'd already done their part.

The political maneuvering surrounding the treaty negotiations allowed an old enemy of the Texans to regain his power in the Mexican government. Ampuida enlisted the help of his old friend and mentor, Don Antonio López de Santa Anna, to bring the Centralists back into political power. Hostilities

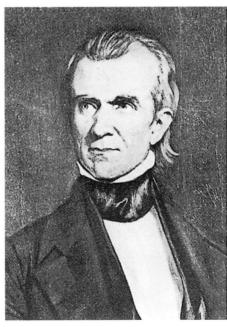

Left: Gen. Winfield Scott took charge of U.S. efforts in the Mexican War following Zachary Taylor's leadership.
Dictionary of American Portraits

Right: James Polk, U.S. President, 1845–1849. Painting by G. P. A. Healy.
Dictionary of American Portraits

resumed and Santa Anna began to recruit his own forces.

In November 1846, President Polk and Secretary of War Marcy formally handed direction of the war over to the senior U.S. commander, Gen. Winfield Scott. Using some of Taylor's own strategic conclusions, Scott recommended that U.S. forces open a new front to avoid the land route through northern Mexico. By landing at Vera Cruz and striking directly for Mexico City, Scott believed he could bring the fight to a rapid conclusion. By March 1847 he landed troops on the coast near Vera Cruz and shelled the city until the Mexican commander surrendered.

Although Scott's forces accomplished the landing and the taking of Vera Cruz with minimal American casualties, their march to Mexico City proved a far more difficult and deadly endeavor. Well-organized guerrilla forces harassed them as they marched through jungle and desert, killing stragglers and cutting the lines of communication and supply. Scott's excellent modern military tactics served him well enough in defeating the Mexican regulars, but holding captured territory against guerrillas was a separate issue. General Scott would find, as had Zachary Taylor before him, that the Texas Rangers were the masters of unconventional conflict.

Ben McCulloch Takes the Point

After Scott took most of the regulars and left for Vera Cruz, General Taylor moved his command to Agua Fria, a rancho near Saltillo. His six-thousand-man force consisted mostly of volunteers. Reports of Santa Anna's army indicated it might number as many as twenty thousand men. The guerrillas and bandits grew bolder, picking off stragglers, intercepting couriers, and raiding supply convoys. Taylor's two small cavalry units, one from Tennessee and one from Arkansas, failed to bring him accurate intelligence.

Ben McCulloch had promised Taylor that he'd return if ever the general needed him, and on

February 4, 1847, he rode into Saltillo to keep his promise. He brought with him a company of more than twenty men, including veteran Rangers William H. Kelly and Fielding Alston as his lieutenants. His men paid their own way because Taylor no longer had authorization to take on Rangers for the traditional six-month period. They'd come to fight, so they agreed to stay either as unpaid volunteers for one battle with Santa Anna or to sign up for a six-month period at regular soldier's pay. Taylor agreed to the six-month enlistment, mustered them in as "McCulloch's Company, Texas Mounted Volunteers" and listed them as "spies." As Santa Anna moved forward with his plan to destroy the American invaders, the Rangers would prove to be much more than mere spies.

Late in February 1847, Ben McCulloch set out from Taylor's headquarters at Agua Fria with most of his company and a few regulars. His mission was to scout the south road through the mountains to Encarnacion, to gather intelligence on the position and movements of Santa Anna's huge force, which was reported to be marching up from the south to attack. Riding after dark, the Rangers kept to the road. They met up with advance guard of the Mexican force, first a group of pickets who retreated at their approach, then a company of cavalry.

When the lancers fired through the darkness at the Texans, McCulloch gave forth a Comanche war cry, drew his Paterson Colt, and led his men in a charge. They hit the lancers before they could reload. Using pistols at close range, the Rangers drove the lancers into a retreat. They chased the retreating lancers almost into Encarnacion, where they rode right into the Mexican camp. McCulloch estimated that the lancer force in the encampment numbered as many as fifteen hundred men, just about the right size for the advance guard for Santa Anna's entire army. Before the surprised Mexicans could organize a counterattack, he wisely called for a retreat and returned to Taylor's headquarters with the intelligence he'd gathered.

The next night, Taylor sent McCulloch back to make another scout. With only Lieutenants Alston and Clark and four others, McCulloch slipped through the outer line of Mexican pickets to spy on the enemy camp. The Rangers picked up a Mexican deserter, sent him back to Taylor, then slipped even deeper into enemy territory. Sending Alston back with the information he'd gained up to that point, McCulloch took one man, Pvt. Billy Phillips, and rode under cover of darkness through the Mexican camp. The Rangers circled the camp to estimate the size of the force, then moved back to an observation post to wait for dawn.

From the wood smoke the morning cook fires sent up, McCulloch figured that Santa Anna had brought up his entire force to attack. McCulloch and Williams made their way back through the brush to avoid enemy pickets and returned to the road well north of them. Pushing their tired horses, they arrived at Agua Fria to find General Taylor and his staff waiting for their return as the rest of the American force retreated to the north toward Buena Vista. Again the next day McCulloch and his company rode south to scout and harass the Mexican advance guard, then returned with the intelligence they gained.

Taylor ordered Gen. John Wool to deploy his forces in a defensive position near the rancho of Buena Vista, where he could rely on a canyon to protect his forces from flanking and rear attacks and where the extremely rough, broken country would offset some of the enemy's huge advantage in numbers. Santa Anna's troops attacked early in the morning of February 23.

For part of the battle, the Rangers fought beside Col. Charles May's dragoons. Some of them acted as battlefield dispatch riders, dodging enemy cavalry patrols as they carried Taylor's orders between units. When the Rangers rode out to harass the Mexican cavalry, McCulloch wounded and captured a Mexican cavalry captain and then captured a lancer lieutenant, a German. It was neither the first nor the last time the Rangers would come up against foreign mercenaries and military advisers riding with the Mexicans. The

Gen. John Wool, Zachary Taylor's second in command, disliked the use of irregular forces like the Rangers.
Dictionary of American Portraits

presence of German officers, military advisers, and political agents in Mexico just prior to the first World War would influence the U.S. decision to enter that war on the Allied side.

The battle staggered in confusion back and forth over a large area throughout the day, from sunrise to dark. By the end, although they'd taken very heavy casualties, the American forces held the field. They'd given a lot worse than they'd taken, sending Santa Anna's battered troops reeling away in full and final retreat. His loss at Buena Vista threw Santa Anna once more into political disfavor. Taylor's forces, primarily volunteer units, had won the battle for Northern Mexico. They would have little left to do except for setting up an occupation routine and running down guerrillas. The main front now lay in the south, with General Scott.

This victory allowed Taylor to overcome the previous embarrassment of the premature truce at Monterrey, as public approval of his wartime conduct would later play a major role in his election as President of the United States. Even after his victory at

Buena Vista, he found himself explaining in writing his use of unconventional troops, especially McCulloch's Rangers. He not only defended his decision but praised McCulloch's services, describing the Ranger scouting expeditions as being "of the highest importance."

Turning Points

Jack Hays married Susan Calvert in Seguin on April 27, 1847, a ceremony that marked a turning point not only for the bride and groom but for Texas as well. Setting another tradition for future Texas Rangers, Jack Hays decided to leave the Ranger service as soon as possible after he married. Although he intended to return with the Rangers to Mexico to help finish the war, he knew that it would be his last scout as their commander.

After the wedding celebration, Major Chevallie led his four companies to join Taylor's forces in Mexico.

Taking a honeymoon of only two weeks, Colonel Hays put his affairs in order and followed Chevallie with a newly recruited regiment of Texas Mounted Rifles. In defiance of the order from the Secretary of War, General Taylor sent Hays a message in which he declined to accept the service of any new volunteer units unwilling to enlist for the duration of the war. When Hays met Taylor's messenger at the Nueces River, he returned to San Antonio and disbanded his regiment.

On July 8 Hays received another message, this time an urgent request from Secretary of War Marcy directing him to gather whatever frontier forces he could spare from fighting Indians and report to Taylor at Monterrey. McCulloch and Chevallie's companies were having a difficult time suppressing guerrilla activity and screening Taylor's forces from Santa Anna's lancers. As Hays began mustering in a new regiment, guerrillas also cut the lines of communications between Scott's advancing force and Vera Cruz. They intercepted and killed Scott's couriers, then attacked and destroyed a large supply train. Scott

An engraving of Gen. Walter P. Lane.
Texas State Library & Archives Commission

found himself burdened by his own sick and wounded; the guerrillas murdered them when he left them behind.

Weary of Taylor's waffling and occupied in fighting the Comanche along the frontier, most of the experienced Rangers refused to sign up for a year's federal service in Mexico. Hays was forced to substitute raw recruits for veterans. He gave them what training he could in a short time, and on August 12 he led them out on the road to Mier. More concerned about Scott's situation in the south than Taylor's occupation of Northern Mexico, Secretary of State Marcy changed Hays's orders and directed him to take his force instead to Vera Cruz.

From that point on, most of the action in Northern Mexico centered on cleanup operations and antiguerrilla operations. Chevallie had developed a mutual antipathy with Taylor's second in command, General Wool, a conventional officer who never hesitated to express his dislike for the irregulars. The Ranger captain was a man of quick temper, always ready to make his point with his fists. By August 1847, he decided he'd had enough of Wool's attitude. He resigned, leaving Walter Lane in command as the major of the Ranger Battalion.

Lane's battalion often rode with the dragoons in actions against the guerrillas. They fought one major battle with a large Comanche war party, and they also captured guerrilla chieftain Juan Flores, a ranchero who had long harassed the American supply lines. The bandit's favorite trick was to cut out the heart of a defeated enemy, then leave the butchered organ displayed on the corpse's torso. When the Rangers caught up with Flores, they brought him in, saw him tried before a military court, then marched him out and shot him.

A Ranger recruit from the Mexican War, John Salmon "Rip" Ford was a physician and journalist. He later became a Texas statesman and commanded of the Cavalry of the West, taking over leadership of the Texas Rangers after the departure of Jack Hays.
UT Institute of Texan Cultures at San Antonio

Hays Returns to the Fight

As General Winfield Scott marched toward Mexico City, Capt. Sam Walker and his new regiment fought to keep his supply lines open. At the two-day battle at Churubusco in mid-August, Scott's troops took heavy casualties but broke the enemy resistance. They marched into Mexico City on September 14 after a week of savage fighting. Even though Santa Anna fled the city well ahead of Scott's troops, rooftop snipers and loyalist guerrillas fired on the Americans until Scott ordered his artillery to target suspect structures. This final battle for Mexico City took place before Jack Hays could arrive with his 1st Texas, but it remained for the Rangers to smash the guerrilla threat.

Hays sent companies of the 1st Texas to Vera Cruz by available transport; the Rangers arrived separately in companies, Hays on the last ship. The first companies to arrive at the Mexican port moved inland to establish a base camp. Mike Chevallie had joined up with Hays not long after he'd resigned from his battalion in the north. Chevallie served in an unofficial capacity as a "major," even though he wasn't listed on the roll as such. Chevallie's prior experience in the field was a great asset to the new 1st Texas, which had enlisted far too few of the veteran Rangers who had served previously with Hays.

One new recruit who proved a valuable asset to the regiment was John S. Ford, who served as adjutant. Ford was a well-educated man, a physician, and a journalist. After the death of his wife, Ford had answered Hays's call for volunteers. Ford had a talent for record keeping and a keen eye for human nature. His was the sad duty of writing letters to the families of casualties, a duty that gained him his nickname, "Rip." At first he closed his letters with the salutation: "Rest In Peace." As deaths from disease and combat made this duty more frequent, Ford shortened that salutation to "R.I.P."

While he served with Hays, Ford proved to be as good a fighter as he was a manager. He devoted himself to learning every aspect of Ranger tactics and

Two Colt Walker revolvers with powder flask and eagle-headed cavalry spurs. *Photo by Tom Knowles, Texas Ranger Hall of Fame and Museum*

skills from the master himself. Although he'd come late to the life of a Ranger, Ford would do more than any other Texan to preserve the Ranger service and traditions in the years after Hays left for California.

After a few days in camp, the men of the 1st Texas were ready for a fight. Even before Hays arrived, Ford and some others went to the local senior officer of volunteers, Maj. Gen. Robert Patterson, who briefed them on the guerrilla activity in the area. They set out on a sixty-mile expedition on which they familiarized themselves with the countryside and fought skir-

mishes with guerrillas. Not long after Hays reached camp, he drew 280 of the new Walker Colt revolvers from the arms depot at Vera Cruz and issued them to the 1st Texas. Hays also signed on two Mexicans, Miguel and Vincent, as scouts and guides. Armed with the formidable new weapons and local information, the Rangers swept the guerrillas off the roads and out of the area.

In Mexico City, Scott had more than his share of troubles. He'd been forced to release a large number of his troops at the end of their enlistment. Guerrillas, rancheros, and Santanista loyalists had Scott bottled up in the city while they rode freely about the countryside. They had besieged his garrison troops at Puebla as well. After winning the battle, Scott found himself in serious danger of losing the territory. On November 2, Hays and the Rangers of the 1st Texas answered his call for reinforcements.

Such was Hays's reputation that the Rangers met little resistance on the first leg of the road to Mexico City. American troops they passed on the road at Jalapa cheered them, while the small guerrilla forces around Puebla pulled out and retreated. They made camp on the outskirts of Jalapa as Hays took two companies to Puebla to link up with Gen. Joseph Lane's volunteer infantry, a cavalry unit commanded by Maj.

A daguerreotype photo of Capt. Samuel H. Walker, Texas Ranger, in his uniform as field commander of the 1st U.S. Mounted Rifles in the Mexican War, circa 1847.
John N. McWilliams Collection

William H. Polk (President Polk's brother) and other units of dragoons, artillery, and volunteers.

The combined force moved out to pursue the enemy. At a village called Izucar de Matamoros, Vincent and Miguel led the Americans to a guerrilla stronghold. In a short fight, they drove off the guerrillas and then freed a number of American prisoners. On November 24, the guerrillas made a stand at Galaxa Pass and sent a force of two hundred lancers to strike at the advance guard. Hays led the counter charge of Rangers and regular cavalry; using the new Walker Colts to deadly effect, the Rangers broke the lancers and sent them running. When the Rangers chased the original force over a ridge, they ran almost directly into an ambush. More than a thousand Mexican cavalry awaited them.

Their Colts almost emptied, the Rangers turned to retreat. The lancers' return fire killed Ranger Lt. Henderson and one of the regular cavalrymen. Capt. Jacob Roberts fell when his horse was hit; two Rangers dropped back to pull him up. Hays, who had at least one fully loaded revolver, gave his men the order to fall back and reload. He then dropped back to face the charging lancers alone. Taking deliberate aim with his Walker, he dropped one lancer, then another. The lancers flinched from the powerful weapon. The stall worked long enough for his men to reload.

Once again, as the Rangers charged into the lancers, their pistols, their horsemanship, and their sheer audacity made the difference. The vastly superior force of lancers broke and ran.

The road to Mexico City was clear.

A Hero's End

Hays didn't get a chance to see Sam Walker again. Walker, never one to back away from a fight, had become so angry with his Colonel Wynkoop's cautious approach to battle that he openly challenged the officer's authority. In September 1847, Wynkoop charged Walker with insubordination and had him

"Rangers in Puebla, Mexico," a watercolor painting by Bruce Marshall depicting the Texas Rangers staging a celebration in Puebla, Mexico, 1847, taken from a description by Albert Brackett of the Indiana Volunteers and Lt. Col. Ebenezer Dumont.
UT Institute of Texan Cultures at San Antonio, Courtesy of Bruce Marshall

jailed at Perote Castle. This was the same fortress in which he'd been incarcerated in 1843 after his abortive escape from Santa Anna's troops at Saltillo. This was a bitter experience for Walker, one that not only reminded him of his earlier imprisonment but kept him out of the fight at Mexico City. In a letter he wrote to his brother Jonathan on October 5, he complained about his treatment at Wynkoop's hands,

noted the gift of two new six-shooters from Sam Colt, and expressed his desire to catch up with Santa Anna.

Gen. Joseph Lane, who felt that the Texan had been ill-used by Wynkoop, interceded to obtain Walker's release. On October 9, Walker resumed command of his U.S. Mounted Rifles. He took C and I companies along with the 4th Indiana volunteer infantry to join up with Lane.

In his march to attack Mexican guerrillas besieging Puebla, Lane stopped at Perote. There he learned that Santa Anna had a force of four thousand men at the town of Humantla, about twenty-five miles from Puebla. Lane wanted to catch up with Santa Anna almost as much as did Walker, but he didn't want to expose his supply column to attack from Santa Anna's lancers. He set Walker's Rifles and a force of infantry in the advance guard, instructing the Texan to remain within easy support distance.

Obsessed with the idea of capturing or killing Santa Anna, Walker outran the column. At the outskirts of the town he ordered a charge, and with their sabers flashing in their hands and a Comanche yell on their lips, his Mounted Rifles followed him. Santa Anna's lancers met them in the streets, and a Mexican artillery unit brought up two light field pieces. The infantry tried to stand against the lancers, but the cavalry swept them back.

Then, Walker's men smashed into the lancers and broke their momentum. The surviving infantry leveled their rifles and fired into the massed Mexican cavalry. Other infantrymen killed the Mexican gun crews and took the field pieces. The fight was all but over by the time Lane arrived with the rest of the American column.

Walker's charge won the day for the Americans, but it was his last charge. He'd been wounded more than once before in the service of the Lone Star, but the bullet that found him at Humantla killed him almost instantly. General Lane wrote in his report:

> This victory is saddened by the loss of one of the most chivalric, noble-hearted men that graced the profession of arms — Captain Samuel H. Walker, of the mounted riflemen. Foremost in the advance, he had routed the enemy when he fell mortally wounded. In his death, the service has met with a loss which cannot easily be repaired.

Even though he never got his chance to confront Santa Anna in person, Walker's victory at the battle at Humantla forever smashed the dictator's dreams of power. He was proud to serve in the uniform of a U.S. Army captain, but at heart he remained a Texas Ranger. Sam Walker died while leading a successful cavalry charge against the enemy — it was a fitting end for a hero.

When the Rangers Rode In

As Jack Hays led the 1st Texas Mounted Rifles into Mexico City on December 6, 1847, the people of the city lined the streets and the balconies to see them, struggling to get a look at *los Tejanos sangrientes*, the bloodthirsty Texans, in the flesh. There was no mistaking them for regular soldiers. They wore no uniforms, but dressed in civilian clothing of every kind and condition. Except for their clean-shaven captain, most of them wore long beards or mustaches. They carried their revolvers stuck through their belts beside their knives and other weapons, their long rifles balanced across their saddles.

The Rangers rode into Puebla with Comanche war whoops and horseback acrobatics; they rode into Mexico City quietly, their eyes scanning the roof line and the crowd for trouble. According to Rip Ford, the Mexican citizens stared at the Rangers with a mixture of horror and fascination. When they spoke at all, they spoke in hushed tones, as if a loud voice would shatter some barrier of reality that separated them from the nightmarish apparition of the wild Texans. Then, a young man in the crowd threw a stone at a Ranger. The Texan responded with a deadly accurate shot from his revolver. The resulting panic caused even more injuries among the crowd.

Rip Ford later wrote that even a slight misunderstanding between a Ranger and a Mexican could result in bloodshed. When Hays halted the column in the Grand Plaza, near the cathedral, one Ranger stopped to buy candy from a street peddler. The Mexican thought he was being robbed, picked up a handful of stones, and began pelting the Texan with them. The Ranger, who would have paid the vendor for the candy but would not stand to be insulted, drew his Colt and shot the peddler, killing him instantly.

In other incidents, Rangers shot street thugs and thieves who attempted to rob or molest them and other Americans. While General Scott found some satisfaction in the fright the Rangers put into the guerrillas, bandits, and assassins who had been robbing and killing his troops, officially he had to respond to civilian complaints. He ordered Jack Hays to report to him. "I require you, sir, to say whether my information is correct, and if so, you will render me a satisfactory explanation."

Hays replied in his usual quiet but direct fashion, "General, the Texas Rangers are not accustomed to being insulted without resenting it." He took full responsibility for his Rangers' actions and persuaded the general that those actions had been a justified and, for the Rangers, restrained response to provocation.

Los léperos, the thieves and muggers of Mexico City, found themselves on the receiving end of Ranger street justice. Although they robbed and killed Americans who were foolish enough to get drunk or to walk alone through the wrong part of town, most of *los léperos* learned to give the Rangers a wide berth. When a gang of muggers drew their knives to attack Rangers Pete Goss and Van Walling on a quiet side street, the two Texans drew their revolvers and killed four of them. Rangers went to cantinas where other Americans had been attacked, then pretended to get very drunk. Assassins and thieves who picked them as targets found themselves looking down the barrels of six-shooters held by sober, determined Texas Rangers.

In February 1848, a mob of thugs from the red-light district surrounded Adam Allsens, a Ranger of Captain Roberts's company. Although he spurred his horse to break through them, they slashed him nearly to pieces with their knives. Rip Ford said in his memoirs that he could see the man's heart beating through the cuts between his ribs. Allsens died within a few hours of the attack, and his Ranger comrades took prompt action against his assassins. At 10:00 that night, American officers heard the distinctive reports of six-shooters emanating from the "Cutthroat" district where Allsens had been ambushed. Scott sent his orderly to find Hays, but the Ranger commander instructed Ford, his adjutant, to say that he was "not in." American troops who heard the firing decided not to investigate.

The next morning, Mexican police entered the district to find more than eighty bodies lying in the street in front of wrecked cantinas and other establishments of ill repute. Although Scott could question their methods, he couldn't deny the results of the Rangers' street war against *los léperos*. Attacks on Americans in Mexico City, as well as most criminal activity against honest Mexican citizens, dwindled to a halt after the Rangers rode into the "Cutthroat."

The Last of the Guerrillas

The Rangers had a final mission to accomplish in Mexico, the destruction of the major guerrilla bands. On December 12, General Scott had declared a limited state of martial law, removing from guerrillas and ranchero raiders their right to civilian or military justice. In other words, he had given the Rangers a hunting license, full authority to shoot guerrillas on sight, to execute captured guerrillas without trial. By January 10, 1848, Hays had his regiment back on the trail of Gen. Mariano Paredes and Padre Celedonia de Juarata, an ex-priest who led a fanatical, well-organized guerrilla army.

Hays, Ford, and Chevallie took sixty-five Rangers on a scout down the Vera Cruz road to Otumba in search of Padre Juarata. The citizens of Otumba told them that Juarata had gone to San Juan Teotihuacan, twelve miles back toward Mexico City. They rode through the night, and by the time the Rangers reached Teotihuacan, they'd ridden over seventy miles in two days, without sleep. They took over a large stone and adobe building near the plaza, cared for and stabled their horses, then collapsed to get some rest.

"WAR SONG OF THE TEXAS RANGERS"

(attributed to James T. Lytle, a Ranger of the Texas Mounted Rifles)

Mount, mount! and away o'er the green prairie wide,
The sword is our sceptre, the fleet steed our pride.
Up! Up! with our flag — let its bright star gleam out!
Mount! Mount! and away on the wild border scout!

We care not for danger, we heed not the foe —
Where our brave steeds can bear us, right onward we go,
And never, as cowards, can we fly from the fight,
While our blades bear a blade, our star sheds its light.

Then mount and away! give the fleet steed the rein —
The Ranger's at home on the prairies again:
Spur! spur in the chase, dash on to the fight,
Cry Vengeance for Texas! and God speed the right.

The might of the foe gathers thick on our way —
They hear our wild shout as we rush to the fray;
What to us is the fear of the death-stricken plain?
We have braved it before, and will brave it again.

The death-dealing bullets around us may fall —
They may strike, they may kill, but they cannot appall;
Through the red field of carnage right onward we'll wade,
While our guns carry ball, and our hands wield the blade.

Hurrah, my brave boys! ye may fare as ye please,
No Mexican banner now flaps in the breeze!
'Tis the flag of Columbia that waves o'er each height,
While on its proud folds our star sheds its light.

Then mount and away! give the fleet steed the rein —
The Ranger's at home on the prairies again:
Spur! spur in the chase, dash on to the fight,
Cry Vengeance for Texas! and God speed the right.

Shots fired at them from the town and the surrounding countryside awakened them. Juarata's men had climbed to the housetops to snipe; seventy or more mounted men charged at the main door of their building from the plaza. Capt. E. M. Daggett and five men got to the door and fired to stop the first cavalry charge. The cavalry formed up for another charge, but Mike Chevallie shot the lead officer in the head. As other Walker Colts spoke, more lancers began to fall from their saddles.

Hays sent some of his men up onto the roof of the building; from there, the accurate fire of their long rifles swept the Mexican snipers from the rooftops and cut down the cavalry on the streets. Juarata saw that the battle was turning against him, drew his saber, and charged forward on foot in an attempt to rally his troops. The Rangers admired his bravery, but that didn't keep them from shooting him. That ended the fight; guerrillas picked up their wounded chieftain and fled.

On a later scout with General Lane, Hays came so close to capturing Santa Anna that when the Rangers entered the house where he'd been staying in Tehuacan, they found the candles still burning and the table set for dinner. Out of all of the articles Santa Anna left behind, the Rangers chose to give his jewel-inlaid cane to Hays. Hays sent it to President Polk as a gift from Texas.

The Rangers and the guerrillas met in a last, bitter battle on the morning of February 25, 1848, in the town of Sequalteplan. Taking major action against Juarata, Paredes, and other guerrillas, Scott sent forces under Gen. Joe Lane to sweep the country north of Mexico City. Lane's force included Hays and 250 Rangers, 130 men of the 3rd Dragoons under Major Polk, a company of Mexican counterguerrillas led by Capt. Manuel Dominguez, as well as other volunteers. Hays had Chevallie, Ford, Capt. Alfred M. Truett, and other old comrades with him.

The Rangers led the advance with the dragoons, the riflemen moving up to support them as they entered the outskirts of the town. Hays spurred his horse into the town gate, kicking it open before the startled guard could lock it. The Texans and the dragoons in the lead came under heavy fire from a long barracks on their right; Lane detailed one rifle company to attack this barracks.

Lancers waited for them in the main plaza, but the Texans smashed into the lancers before the Mexicans could charge. From that point on, the fight split into a series of small, intense battles, each unit commander leading his men into combat through the streets and alleyways and over the rooftops. Hays later reported, "...a running and mixed fight took place, which was continued so long as the enemy was visible...." Much of this fight resembled the street fighting in Monterrey — bloody, hand-to-hand combat with pistols and knives. The revolvers gave the Rangers a decided advantage in this kind of fight, but Polk's 3rd Dragoons and the other units did more than their share as well.

Juarata had escaped once more just before the end of the fight, but as Walker had destroyed Santa Anna at Humantla, so did the Rangers break the ex-priest's power at Sequalteplan. His lieutenant, "Padre" Martinez, and his senior officer, Colonel Montagna were killed in the fight. Of the 400 lancers and 50 infantry in Juarata's command, the Rangers killed more than 150 of the enemy and captured another 50. Several Rangers were wounded; all but one recovered. Capt. Jacob Horn died of his wounds. He was the last Ranger to be killed in an official action in the Mexican War, two weeks after the Treaty of Guadalupe Hidalgo was signed by the U.S. and Mexico to end the war.

Passing on the Torch

By April 1848, the last of the 1st Texas Mounted Rifles, less formally known as the Texas Rangers, mustered out of service. On May 20, most of the men of Hays's company attended a celebration held for them in San Antonio, a grand ball and welcome-home party.

Although he was still a young man, Jack Hays had

served the Lone Star for ten hard years. More than had any other leader before him and more than any other that followed him, Hays pioneered and defined the enduring tradition of the Texas Rangers. Under his leadership, the Rangers won their unique reputation, an unlikely alloy of ruthlessness and honor.

Jack Hays would command the Rangers no longer. He'd done his part, and he'd soon move on to California with his bride, Susan Calvert, but he'd trained his Rangers well. Rip Ford, who had learned much from Hays in Mexico, would continue as the leader of the new Texas Ranger organization. In the decade to come, Ford would prove the natural successor to Hays's leadership.

6

THE CAVALRY OF THE WEST

THE TEXAS RANGERS, WHO HAD EMERGED FROM THE TRIALS OF combat in Mexico as a stronger, more cohesive force, would need all of that strength to meet the challenges of the future. Like any new trail blazed through the wilderness, the uncertain course that lay ahead for the Texans concealed unexpected obstacles.

The high spirits and the high hopes that came in the wake of statehood and military victory masked the difficulties that lay ahead in the relationship between Texas and the United States. The Lone Star Republic was no more, but its independent spirit remained strong in the new Lone Star State. The Texans would never forget that they had once founded a nation in the wilderness and had purchased its freedom with their own blood. Despite their natural affinity with the American culture from which they'd drawn much of their traditional system of values, Texans in many ways remained a distinct people, one born of a harsh frontier reality.

Mexican bandits and adventurers continued to plague the Nueces Strip. The Comanche, Kiowa, and Apache fought back even more fiercely as American emigrants flooded into the new state, extending the frontier into the *comanchería*. The U.S. Army sent inex-

perienced troops, often dragoons and infantry units instead of cavalry, to support the state forces. Federal authorities considered Ranger service a temporary and conditional response to raiders and bandits, but they didn't come up with a more effective solution until almost a decade after the Civil War. After a Texas Ranger company cleared a region of raiders, the government considered the problem solved and disbanded the company. As soon as the Rangers left an area, the raiders returned.

The perilous and thankless nature of Ranger service stayed the same, regardless of new regulations and funding. A Ranger's pay, when he could collect it, remained pitifully low; he still had to supply his own horse and weapons. Ranger service still required him to ride long, hard miles at short rations, to be ready at the end of that ride to fight an enemy who outnumbered him five to one.

As the Texans most skilled in combat and hardened against adversity, the Rangers would continue as the first line of defense. John S. "Rip" Ford, the man who would lead the Rangers for two decades, reveled in combat and understood the nature of adversity. When Ford had joined the Rangers in the wake of a personal tragedy, he was thirty-one, an established professional man and a respected member of the community. He'd saddled up to join Jack Hays in Mexico, leaving behind him his life as a physician and a journalist to take up "the profession of arms." After the Rangers returned to Texas, a relative had reproached Ford for unnecessarily risking his life in a foreign adventure. Ford replied:

> When a man has had the bosom of destruction to pass over his domestic hearth, and feels he has little to live for, he may appear reckless; yet, if he has a proper sense of duty to restrain him he will be true to himself, and kind to his fellow men.

Like many war veterans, Ford would find it difficult to return to his former life, and what was true for Ford was true for Texas and the Rangers. They'd journeyed together into the heart of destruction; the storm of war had passed over them all, bringing about unexpected changes and delivering new challenges. The peace they'd won was only the eye of the storm, and it would pass. Even as the Lone Star joined the other stars in the American constellation, war clouds gathered in the north and to the south. The Cavalry of the West, as Rip Ford named the Texas Rangers under his command, would ride forth to meet the storm.

This daguerreotype depicts two Anglo men dressed in *vaquero* style. The man on the left wears a Colt Walker revolver circa 1848. Walker revolvers were in limited supply and were issued only to the U.S. Mounted Rifles and the Texas Rangers. Rangers often dressed as Mexicans in order to spy or to attend a *fandango*.
John N. McWilliams Collection

Passing on the Torch

On May 20, 1848, the citizens of San Antonio held a ball to honor the Texas Rangers upon their return from the Mexican War. As the guest of honor, Jack Hays was the focus of attention and speculation about his plans for the future. At the time, he was the most popular man in Texas. He could conceivably have won any political or financial reward he desired. Knowing how he shunned such public honors, his old comrades suspected he would resume command of the frontier defense forces.

A week after the celebration, he surprised everyone by announcing his plans to retire not only from the Ranger service but public life. He intended to devote his time to his family, to pursuing his original profession as a surveyor and to tending his ranch near Seguin. Hays turned command of the frontier Ranger companies over to Col. Peter H. Bell, who had commanded them while Hays had led the Texas Mounted Rifles in Mexico.

Hays had hardly settled into his new life when his friends persuaded him to lead the Chihuahua-El Paso expedition to survey a trade route leading from Central Texas through El Paso to California. He recruited a military escort, a few of his former Rangers and his friend, rancher Samuel Maverick, to

Samuel Maverick, Texas pioneer and cattleman, accompanied Jack Hays on the Chihuahua-El Paso expedition.
Texas State Library & Archives Commission

accompany him. By the time they returned to San Antonio, they had traveled more than 1,300 miles over some of the roughest, wildest country in the West.

Hays turned over his maps and reported his findings to Colonel Bell, adding his recommendation that the proposed road take the route directly west from San Antonio to the San Saba River. His excellent notes and observations would allow later surveying and road-building expeditions to avoid the difficulties he'd experienced as a pathfinder. In March 1849, during the height of the California Gold Rush, Rip Ford and Indian agent Maj. Robert S. Neighbors followed Hays's recommendations to blaze a trail from San Antonio directly to El Paso. The El Paso wagon trail remained the main land route across West Texas until the railroad replaced it.

On January 3, 1850, after a long sojourn into Apache country as the Indian agent for the Gila River region, Jack Hays resigned from his post. He realized that as long as he remained in Texas he'd never be able to leave behind his Ranger reputation. California, the country of the Gold Rush, offered him a chance to

Texas Governor Peter Hansborough Bell, who commanded the Texas Rangers in frontier defense while Jack Hays led the Texas Mounted Rifles in the Mexican War. This portrait is by William Henry Huddle.
Texas State Library & Archives Commission

find a new frontier, to build a new life for himself and his family. Hays and Susan shortly afterward boarded the steamer *Colonel Frémont*, headed to San Francisco. Although Hays would occasionally return to visit Texas, he'd left the service of the Lone Star behind him forever. As Rip Ford said, "He left a people who loved him because he served them long and well; he had never led them in defeat."

Captain Jack had left Texas, but he'd left her safe in the competent and deadly hands of the Texas Rangers he'd trained to replace him.

A Call to Arms

Civilian life soon left Rip Ford feeling restless and unfulfilled. He once more took up his pen as a journalist, but shortly afterward sold his interest in the *Texas Democrat*. He petitioned the state for funds to raise a company of Rangers to protect the northwest frontier against the Comanche, but the state government refused his request.

Above: Photograph of John Coffee Hays, taken in California years after he had retired from the Texas Ranger service.
Texas Ranger Hall of Fame and Museum

Right: 1851 Navy Colt .36 caliber revolver presented by Colt to former Texas Ranger John Coffee Hays, with rose-engraved holster, carried by Hays while he served as a peace officer in California; Hays's profile is engraved on the barrel between the loading lever screw and the barrel pin.
Photo by Tom Knowles, Texas Ranger Hall of Fame and Museum

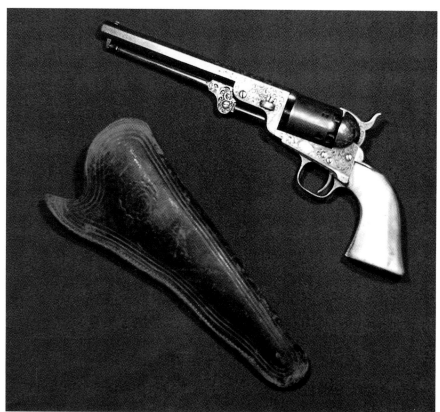

In the late 1840s, Ford's home town of Austin was still a frontier settlement. The Comanche sometimes rode into the outskirts of the capital city, stealing horses and killing any citizens they met in the process. Ford noted that he could hear "the 'check' of billiard balls, the howling of wolves, and the yelling of Indians" while he stood on Congress Avenue. Early in 1849, in answer to a series of deadly raids to the south and west, Ford gathered up a volunteer company of twenty men to chase after the Comanche. They struck the Indian trail about twenty-five miles up the Colorado River from Austin, but they lost it after two days.

Comanche depredations and bandit raids continued, particularly in the Nueces Strip. In the summer of 1849, the U.S. military commander of the Department of Texas, Gen. George M. Brooke, admitted that the small regular forces he had at his disposal were inadequate to the task of defeating these raiders. He authorized Texas Gov. George T. Wood to raise three companies of Texas Rangers for a six-month term in federal service, paid for by the U.S. government, to put an end to the raids. The Adjutant General of Texas, Col. John D. Pitts, used Brooke's authorization to allow Rip Ford to begin recruiting Rangers.

By August, Captain Ford had his command of seventy-five men organized and on the trail to Corpus Christi. Their destination was a ranch owned by Col. H. L. Kinney, the planned site of their first station. Many of the men in "Ford's Old Company," so-called because of the prevalence of veterans in its ranks, were former Ranger comrades from Hays's command, experienced fighters and frontiersmen. Ford, who didn't drink and was known to read a passage out of the Bible to start his morning, admitted that his men were a hard-drinking, hard-riding, quick-fisted lot of frontier brawlers. He also wrote that, "You might kill them but you could not conquer them."

At first armed with a motley collection of their own weapons that included a few old Paterson and Walker Colts, the men of Ford's Company later drew from supplies, pistols, military carbines, rifles, and ammunition from state and federal sources. Each man provided his own horse and other equipment. Rangers under this service drew pay at $23.50 per month. Although the original enlistment was for six months, Ford's company and the other two companies in federal service during this period reenlisted for three more terms, staying in the field for two years.

Immediately after they arrived at the Ozo ranch station, Ford sent his men out in reconnaissance parties to scout their assigned territory. Ford rode out on his own along the Rio Grande to visit with the ranchers and other civilians he'd been sent to protect. He discovered that bandit and Indian raids between Rio Grande City and Laredo had frightened away much of the area's former population. Most of the settlers and ranchers were too afraid to return to the lands they owned in the Nueces Strip.

As Ford moved his company into place and began running them through a series of training exercises similar to those pioneered by Jack Hays, the two other authorized Ranger companies mustered in for service. Capt. John J. Grumbles stationed his company about seventy-five miles away to the north on the Nueces River. Henry E. McCulloch's company took station between Corpus Christi and Goliad. Among the three companies, the Rangers could at least come close to covering the entire South Texas area.

For most of 1849, the Rangers of Ford's company practiced their shooting and followed trails without catching up to any of the raiders, Comanche or bandits. Ford expressed his frustration at this lack of combat by saying that the year "yielded nothing hoped for." His impatience was understandable, but just by recruiting men for service, by training them and taking the field with them, Ford had pulled the Texas Rangers back together and turned them once more into a formidable fighting force.

Ford had answered the call to arms, as had the men of his company. Actual combat would follow soon, fighting enough to save even the Ranger captain from boredom.

Ford's Long Scout

To allow each of the three companies to cover more territory, Ford moved his own company to a new headquarters station on the road between Rio Grande City (southeast downriver) and Laredo (northwest upriver), about seventy miles out from Laredo. The deserted *rancho* they chose, San Antonio Viejo (Old San Antonio), had a good water supply from the original wells and a stand of oak trees to shade the Rangers' tents.

When the first six-month enlistment period expired for Ford's company, virtually all of the serving Rangers signed up for another term in a "reorganization." As was their custom at such times, the men of the company elected officers. Ford remained as captain, while the men chose Andrew J. Walker as lieutenant, Malcijah J. Highsmith as second lieutenant, and David M. Level as orderly sergeant. D. C. "Doc" Sullivan, who had accompanied Ford on his survey along the El Paso trail early in 1849, joined as a private. Ford also signed up young Edward Burleson Jr., the son of the great Texas general and political leader of Republic days.

Roque Maugricio, whom Ford described as "a Mexican crossed with an Indian," joined the company as its scout. Maugricio had been captured at a young age by the Comanche and had lived among them for years. As an experienced warrior and tracker, he not only knew the country, he knew the enemy, his language, and his fighting methods. Ford came to rely on Maugricio's guidance and endurance; he described him as "indefatigable."

Most of the company's pistols had become "unserviceable" by the end of the first enlistment term, even though the Rangers hadn't been involved in combat. The weapons they'd drawn from stores in 1849 could have been anything from old single-shot muzzle-loaders to the early models of Colt Dragoons, all of which might have seen hard use in the Mexican War or by the U.S. Army in later patrols.

Early in May 1850, Ford led a patrol of forty men on an extended scout through his assigned area, north toward San Antonio, then east toward Corpus Christi, where he intended to obtain new weapons. After his men made a rendezvous at Fort McIntosh, the U.S. military post near Laredo, he turned the company to follow the Rio Grande to the west. The Rangers followed the Rio Grande for thirty miles, searching for any trace of the Comanche raiders reported to be in the area. Roque Maugricio and Sergeant Level took out smaller scout patrols, and on one occasion Maugricio found a Comanche arrow in a fresh deer carcass.

Ford split his command, sending Lieutenant Walker and half his men across country as he led the other half toward the Nueces River. At Lieutenant Walker's camp, Indians chased one of his pickets almost into the camp itself. Walker's men mounted and gave chase as the Indians fled toward the Nueces River. Even though Walker had a *remuda* of fresh horses that his men could ride in relays, the Indians managed to keep ahead of the Rangers. The lieutenant halted the chase at nightfall, knowing that it was futile and dangerous to try to pursue the Comanche in the dark.

The next morning, May 12, Ford's detachment cut the raiders' trail near the Comanche Crossing on the Nueces River. Alert for an ambush, they rode into the narrow canyon of the Nueces and cautiously approached the crossing. Ford sent a scout party across the river; when the scouts returned to report that the Indians had moved on, the rest of the men stripped their saddles from their horses. The horses swam the river on their own, while the men followed with their saddles and weapons piled on driftwood floats to keep their powder dry. Ford directed a few men to stay behind with the pack mules, to camp at a nearby water hole to wait for his return.

Ford advanced with Maugricio and Level as the other Rangers resaddled their horses. The three Rangers caught up with the Indians at the edge of the timber about eight miles from the river crossing. Ford gave a yell to call in the rest of his men, then rode to within fifty yards of the Comanche. The Comanche turned and formed up to fight as the rest of the Rangers rode up to join the captain.

The two groups of warriors were just about evenly matched in numbers, sixteen men on each side. Because few of the Rangers in the detachment had working pistols, they had to rely mainly on their Mississippi rifles. The Comanche leader rode out in front, closer to the Rangers, taunting them to draw their fire. Ford knew the tactic well from the time he'd spent with the Comanche during his survey of the El Paso route, so he cautioned his men not to allow the chief to tempt them. Sergeant Level fired his revolver, wounding the chief in the arm, but the Comanche wheeled his horse and blew notes on a whistle (probably made from an eagle-bone) to relay his command to his men. The Comanche warriors charged in, firing their arrows from behind the protection of their shields.

Ford was ready for that trick as well. He told his men to attack from the right rear angle, the vulnerable point in a shielded archer's defense. The Comanche rode at the Rangers in a square formation, but the Rangers turned on Ford's orders and hit them at the left flank. As arrows flew and guns spat fire, Ford rode in from the right rear at one warrior. When the Indian tried to turn in his saddle to shoot at the Ranger captain, his saddle girth broke and dumped him to the ground. The warrior rolled to his feet with his bow already drawn, but Ford shot him through the head before he could release the arrow.

One warrior recognized Doc Sullivan as one of the men who had spent time with the Comanche during Ford's El Paso expedition. When the warrior called out to Sullivan, "Are you going to kill your companions?" Sullivan fired his gun as his answer. As Noah Smithwick had surmised years earlier, when old friends met "under shield," no quarter would be given. Some weeks later, as he returned to the company after a furlough, some of the other Comanche who knew Sullivan returned the favor (see "A Deadly Furlough"). It was the way of the frontier.

The Comanche lost four men in the space of a few moments. The Indians, seeing that they were getting the hard end of the bargain, began to pick up their wounded and dead to withdraw into the brush. They covered their retreat by firing arrows upward, arcing them down into the Rangers. This made the arrows harder to dodge, as Ford claimed most Rangers could do when arrows flew in flat trajectories. One such ballistic shot wounded Pvt. David Steele, and another wounded Ford's horse. Ford got a scratch from an arrow across the back of his right hand; the arrowhead was poisoned with rattlesnake venom. The wound troubled him for years, partially paralyzing his arm for a time.

Ford's detachment recaptured a number of horses and picked up weapons the Comanche left on the battlefield. The next morning they found that two horses had strayed from their *remuda*, and when Maugricio returned from scouting their trail, he reported that a party of Comanche had caught the horses. Ford led his men in pursuit along the Nueces, but the Indians split up, doubled back, and managed to throw off the pursuit. By nightfall the Rangers had followed a circuitous route almost back to the river crossing at which they'd first cut the Comanche trail.

Maugricio discovered that a large war party was watching the crossing, waiting to ambush the Rangers. The Rangers were low on supplies, but they couldn't risk the river crossing, which would leave them vulnerable to attack. The Comanche circled them, looking for an advantage or an opening, and on the morning of May 14 even formed up to make a charge. The Rangers tried to draw them into a committed attack, but the Comanche held back. Ford's men managed to rejoin the rear guard they'd left behind with the mules and continued south, down the river toward Corpus Christi.

For several days the Comanche continued to shadow the Rangers as they rode down the Nueces, trying to pick off stragglers and waiting for the right opportunity to launch a devastating charge. The Rangers moved carefully, using brush and trees as cover or traveling on the high ground, never giving the

A DEADLY FURLOUGH

When Ford's Old Company reached Fort Merrill after their long scout in May 1850, Ford allowed Doc Sullivan, John Wilbarger, and Adelphus D. Neal to take a furlough to attend to a legal matter. Ford cautioned them to travel through the dangerous Nueces Strip and the Rio Grande territory only if they could link up with another party. Unfortunately, during the last leg of their return trip in August they decided not to wait for company. They set out from the Ranger camp at San Antonio Viejo to rejoin Ford at Fort Merrill, a distance of about 150 miles.

The route they traveled took them through the towns of San Patricio and Santa Gertrudis, but most of it involved riding through open, dry country that offered little cover or shelter from unfriendly eyes. When they stopped at a waterhole about twenty miles past Santa Gertrudis, not far from where Richard King would later establish the largest cattle ranch in the American West, they met up with trouble. As the Rangers saddled up to move on, they saw thirty mounted Comanche warriors waiting for them. These warriors knew Doc Sullivan. Some of them had shared a peaceful campfire with him when he'd accompanied Ford on the 1849 survey mission, but on that particular day the Rangers and the Comanche were "under shield." The men on both sides knew that no quarter would be asked and none would be given.

Their superior mounts might have allowed the Rangers to outrun the grass-fed Comanche ponies. They decided to fight instead, counting on the firepower of their revolvers to see them through. Unfortunately for the Rangers, this time the Comanche had some superior firepower of their own. One warrior was armed with a long-range rifle, possibly the same Swiss weapon with which the Comanche had wounded Sergeant Level at the Agua Dulce fight in May. As the three Rangers mounted their horses, the first bullet toppled Sullivan from his saddle. Knowing that he was mortally wounded, Sullivan pleaded with Neal and Wilbarger to go on without him. Before they could decide, another bullet hit Sullivan in the head, killing him instantly.

Sullivan's horse was still tied to the single mesquite tree that stood near the waterhole. Neal's horse bolted at the second shot and ran under the picket rope that held Sullivan's horse; the rope scraped Neal out of the saddle. Neal had tied his guns to his saddle, so the Indians captured both the runaway horse and weapons in short order.

Wilbarger tried to fight on the run, but the Comanche caught up with him. According to Ford, a later examination of the bloodstains at the site indicated that Wilbarger killed or severely wounded several of his opponents before they finished him. The Comanche had taken their revenge on Sullivan by lassoing his body and dragging it through the cactus and thorns.

Neal survived the attack at the waterhole only because he was weaponless and afoot, an easy target for the warriors. Instead of using a rifle to kill the Ranger outright, the Comanche circled him and shot him full of arrows. Ford estimated that at least three of Neal's wounds should have proved fatal. The Ranger finally blacked out from shock and blood loss. By the time he regained consciousness, the Comanche had stripped him of his clothes and boots. He played possum, waited until the Comanche rode away, then waited an extra hour to be certain they wouldn't return.

Neal broke the shafts of those arrows he couldn't pull out and began to drag himself through the prairie toward San Patricio, sixty-five miles away. Neal blistered under the unforgiving sun and scraped himself raw as he crawled and staggered through the catclaw and prickly pear. When at last he staggered into the town, his tongue had so swollen and his lips had so cracked from thirst that he couldn't speak. The citizens of the town, thinking him to be a hostile Indian, almost shot him at first sight.

The physician who came to tend him gave him little chance of survival, but Neal proved too tough a man for any flight of Comanche arrows to finish. Years later, when Ford and Neal met at the Texas Secession Convention in Brownsville, Neal handed Ford a corroded metal object. "Colonel," he said, "here is that arrow spike which has been in my lung eleven years."

To Ford, Neal's survival was just another example of how a good Ranger could call upon the essence of the superhuman, the last reserves of human strength, to survive the rigors of the frontier.

Comanche a chance to ambush them or catch them in the open. At night, only the vigilance of the Rangers on watch and the scout, Maugricio, kept the Comanche from creeping up close enough to shoot into the camp.

The Comanche might have rushed in to overwhelm the Rangers with a direct assault, but that was not the Comanche way. Almost without exception, unless he was defending his village or some other important objective, a Comanche war leader would never attack without a clear advantage — surprise, superior ground, or vastly superior numbers. He would wait and watch for the advantage, the edge, then move swiftly and ruthlessly to exploit it. Ford's Rangers were just too experienced to give the Comanche even a moment's advantage. Still, it was a tense situation. If Ford and Maugricio had made the slightest slip, the Comanche would have attacked.

At Fort Merrill, a U.S. Army post on the Nueces, the Rangers managed to restock some of their supplies. Even as the Rangers camped for the night within half a mile of the fort, the Comanche continued to track them. Early in the morning of May 26, raiders hit the Rangers' horse herd in an attempt to drive them off. The raiders got away with one mare, but just outside the camp Maugricio found a young warrior dying from the Rangers' return fire. When Ford sent Ed Burleson to the army commander, Capt. J. B. Plummer, with a message about the incident, the officer discounted the presence of Indians near his

post. He said, "I thought it was you Texians fighting among yourselves."

Not all of the U.S. Army officers on the frontier had the same attitude as Captain Plummer, but his complacency and ignorance did demonstrate the futility of using a static defense against Indians in the West. Comanches could simply avoid being seen near the fort as they moved along the many nearby trails to conduct their raids. Plummer thought that the Indians weren't there just because he hadn't seen them. The Rangers knew that the Indians you didn't see were the ones who were most likely to lift your scalp. They knew that the owl hoots that came out of the darkness at either side of a lonely camp were most likely born in Comanche throats.

Immediately after making camp at Fort Merrill, Ford sent a small party of his men to Corpus Christi to pick up ammunition and a shipment of one hundred old-fashioned, single-shot dragoon pistols. The leader of this squad, William Gillespie, was the cousin of R. A. Gillespie, the Ranger captain who had fallen at the Battle of Monterrey in the Mexican War. Ford had loaned Gillespie his own horse, the notorious and cantankerous "Old Higgins" (see "Old Higgins, the Man-Eating Horse"). Gillespie managed to avoid the Comanche on this trip, and he caught up with Ford at his second camp south of Fort Merrill. When the Rangers rode out from their camp on the morning of May 29, the captain allowed the young Ranger to continue riding Old Higgins.

That morning, the Rangers struck the Comanche war party's trail and followed it. Maugricio took the point, and he soon directed the company to the stand of mesquite trees where the Comanche had camped, about a mile from the Agua Dulce (Sweetwater) River. The Indians mounted at the first sight of the Rangers, but despite their advantage in numbers, they began to retreat toward the Agua Dulce. The Rangers charged after them, shooting them from their saddles.

Ford and Maugricio, intent on their pursuit of the fleeing Indians, were unaware that they'd left Gillespie behind them, seriously wounded. Interpreting the Comanche hand signals, the scout informed Ford that the Indians were planning to bring up hidden warriors to encircle the Rangers.

Ford ordered a charge to break through the front ranks of the Comanche before they could flank the Rangers, but he looked back to see that his men weren't following him. At first he cursed them for disobeying his order, but when he learned that they were holding up to protect the wounded Gillespie, he ordered them to ride back to where Gillespie lay. The Rangers had to fight their way through the line of warriors set to make the rear attack; when their pistols were empty, it came down to close fighting. Pvt. Robert Adams defeated one warrior in hand-to-hand combat.

On Ford's orders, Pvt. David Steele dismounted to fire at the Comanche chief, Otto Cuero, who was riding rear guard on the retreat of the forward elements of the Comanche. When the chief fell dead from Steele's shot, the remaining Comanche broke off the attack and scattered. Because the Rangers had injured men to care for, and because their horses were exhausted, they declined pursuit.

Maugricio found a wounded Comanche and talked him into surrendering. In talking with this young warrior, who bore the unfortunate name of Carne Muerto (Spanish for "Dead Meat"), he learned that the party they'd defeated on May 12 had met up with another band of seventy-five warriors after the battle. Despite their advantage in numbers, the warriors had hesitated to attack the Rangers without a clear opening. The surviving warriors' description of the battle had given the other warriors reason to respect the Rangers' marksmanship. They'd shadowed the Rangers until the nighttime fight near Fort Merrill, after which they'd decided to leave the Rangers alone. It was this combined band, led by Otto Cuero, that the Rangers had just defeated and driven away.

A Comanche armed with a good Swiss rifle had wounded Sergeant Level and killed his horse, and some of the other Rangers had taken minor wounds. A Comanche arrow had pierced Gillespie's lung, inflicting what proved to be a mortal wound. His comrades carried him away from the battlefield on a litter, but Bill Gillespie died that evening. The Rangers buried his body at the camp of Captain Grumbles's company on the Agua Dulce, setting his name beside that of his famous cousin in the muster roll of those who gave their all in the service of the Lone Star.

Siege at San Antonio Viejo

After the Agua Dulce fight, Ford's company returned to their camp at San Antonio Viejo without further incident. In June of 1850, Ford received reports that the Comanche were raiding in strength in Webb County east of Laredo. The settlers in the area had deserted the countryside for the relative safety of the town. Ford sent Lieutenant Walker with a detachment of twenty men to patrol the Rio Grande country around Laredo.

Walker found ample evidence of Comanche raiding parties in the Laredo area — burned ranches, broken lances, the tracks of stolen horses mixed in with the tracks of unshod Indian ponies. In mid-June he took the field with only a few Rangers, leaving a small company to guard his camp. Along with two volunteers who joined them, Walker's men fought and defeated a Comanche horse-raiding party at the ranch of Don Basilio Benavides, twenty miles south of Laredo.

OLD HIGGINS, THE MAN-EATING HORSE

According to Rip Ford, there never lived a more perverse, cantankerous, or evil-tempered animal than his own favorite mount, Old Higgins. The horse lived to cause trouble, and he took great delight in kicking, biting, stomping, or throwing any man who showed the slightest sign of weakness in handling him. In the space of a heartbeat, Higgins could change from a disciplined, docile-seeming mount into a fury of flashing teeth and hooves. According to Ford, Higgins could outrun just about any other animal that went on two legs or four; the horse was "noted for his extraordinary powers of endurance, his sagacity, and his rascality." Before Ford purchased him, Higgins had won a considerable amount of money for his owners in that most favored sport of the Texans, the horse race.

During the second campaign of Hays's Rangers in the Mexican War, Old Higgins endeared himself to Ford and the other Rangers when he attacked an officious watch officer aboard the ship that was conveying them to Vera Cruz. During the trip, the watchman was a general pain, continually clashing with the Rangers over their use of the drinking water and their bunk assignments. Only Ford's authority prevented the Rangers from tossing the insolent Irishman overboard. The watchman then made the mistake of abusing the Rangers' horses. As the man passed by Old Higgins, the horse stretched out his long neck, bit off his ear, chewed it up, and swallowed it.

Despite the animal's evil nature, Ford considered Old Higgins to be the best war horse he'd ever ridden on the Ranger trail. The horse was just too mean and ornery to give up or give out, no matter how difficult the trail. He feared nothing that lived, man or beast, which made him a fit mount for the Ranger who rode him. Like Ford, Higgins was born for combat.

Ford's only mistake was in allowing other Rangers to ride or handle his horse. At the Battle of Agua Dulce on May 29, 1850, young William Gillespie rode Old Higgins into the fight against the Comanche warriors led by Otto Cuero. As Gillespie passed a downed Comanche, he saw that the warrior was still alive and turned to engage him. The Indian drew his bow as Gillespie leveled his pistol. At the last moment, for some reason known only to the horse, Old Higgins decided to give his perverse nature free rein. He sidestepped, throwing off Gillespie's aim and allowing the Comanche time to fire. The arrow pierced the young Ranger's lung, inflicting a mortal wound.

If Ford hadn't been so fond of the horse, he probably would have shot Old Higgins there on the battlefield. Instead, it took another raid by the Comanche to separate the Ranger from his mount. Ford rode another horse on his next major scout, leaving Old Higgins in the care of the small garrison of Rangers at their San Antonio Viejo camp. When a large Comanche war party surrounded the Ranger camp and laid siege to it for two days, they managed to get away with only a few horses for their trouble, including Old Higgins.

Although Ford lamented the loss of his favorite mount, he took a certain satisfaction in the knowledge that the Comanche would suffer for their theft. Ford knew that if Old Higgins stayed true to his rascally character, and if the warriors didn't just shoot him and eat him, there would be many a one-eared Comanche wandering the Texas plains.

This watercolor painting by Bruce Marshall depicts a mounted Texas Ranger of the mid-1850s, the Rip Ford era of the Rangers under U.S. service. He is armed with an 1851 Colt Navy revolver and a double-barreled shotgun.
UT Institute of Texan Cultures at San Antonio, Courtesy of Bruce Marshall

Even as Walker chased the Comanche near Laredo, Ford received some disturbing news. Carne Muerto, who had proved to be an excellent source of information once he decided the Rangers weren't going to kill him, informed Ford that the Comanche planned to launch a series of retaliatory raids along the "upper line" of the frontier. This line was a series of Ranger camps and U.S. Army forts that extended from Fort Worth in the north to Fort Duncan at Eagle Pass, more than one hundred miles northwest of Laredo on the Rio Grande. According to Carne Muerto, the Comanche intended to hit the Nueces Strip hard, to drive out or kill the Rangers who were interfering with their raids into South Texas and Mexico.

Ford immediately moved to protect the southern end of the frontier line, which lay in his territory. He left Lieutenant Highsmith to hold the San Antonio Viejo camp with twenty-six men and took the remaining forty men to join Walker's detachment near Laredo. While Ford and Walker hunted for Indians seventy miles away, a large Comanche war party surrounded the Ranger camp at San Antonio Viejo.

Lieutenant Highsmith had taken Ford's advice to stock up on water and supplies, to hold his men close to camp, and to keep a sharp lookout. When the Indians rode in to attack, they found the Rangers ready for them. One Ranger's rifle knocked a warrior from his saddle, which prompted the Comanche to retreat beyond rifle range. The Comanche held the siege for two days, during which time they managed to steal several horses, including Ford's evil-tempered mount, Old Higgins. When a troop of regular U.S. Army soldiers marched in from Fort Merrill to relieve the Ranger camp, the Indians retreated.

A local civilian messenger told Ford and Walker that the Comanche had killed all the Rangers in the San Antonio Viejo camp. The entire company rode the seventy miles back to the camp "in quick time," arriving to find the Comanche gone, the men at the camp unscathed. The Rangers turned to chasing the small raiding groups that had broken off from the war party, but they had to break off the pursuit when most of the Comanche fled into Mexico.

Despite their vows of vengeance, the Comanche in the southern district patrolled by Ford's Old Company melted away like smoke when the Rangers rode after them. They'd come out the clear losers in every one of the several engagements and skirmishes they'd fought with Ford's men, and the Comanche were no fools when it came to survival. If they couldn't attack with a definite advantage, in greater numbers or by surprise, they would leave the field to Ford's Rangers.

Lieutenants Take Command

Soon after the fruitless siege at the Ranger camp, Ford's men found that the Comanche raiders had vacated the lower Nueces Strip. Ford and his company moved closer to Laredo, from which point they could better protect the trade route that ran up from Corpus Christi. They chose Los Ojuelos (Little Springs), forty miles east of Laredo, as their headquarters site. Los Ojuelos offered the Rangers a steady water supply, plenty of grass for their horses, and wood for their fires. It not only overlooked the trade route but put the Rangers in easy striking distance of the major routes the Comanche took on their raids.

On September 24, 1850, the company reorganized for another six-month enlistment period. Lieutenant Highsmith retired, leaving his position to be filled by

Edward Burleson, while Lieutenant Walker continued as Ford's second in command. When the malaria Ford had contracted during the Mexican War came back to incapacitate him, Walker and Burleson worked together to support Ford, to keep his command in the field active.

On January 19, 1851, Lieutenant Walker took his detachment of nineteen men on scout to Arroyo Gato (Cat Creek), fifty miles north of Laredo. At a spot not far from the Rio Grande crossing into Mexico, the Rangers discovered a herd of horses and mules and a cache of supplies left by a Comanche raiding party. Walker figured that the Indians had crossed into Mexico to raid, and that they intended to pick up their goods and animals when they crossed back into Texas. He picked a campsite on a high point where he could overlook the approach to the cache and stationed other lookouts along the route. He directed his men to graze their horses out of sight, on the opposite side of the slope.

For five nights, Walker and his men kept an almost fireless camp to avoid betraying their presence with smoke. On the sixth day, the lookouts spotted the Comanche advance guard, two warriors who rode ahead to check out the cache. When the main raiding party of seventeen warriors rode into the trap, driving their stolen mules and horses ahead of them, the Rangers mounted up and charged into them. The Texans' assault rolled back the warriors in front, killing one Comanche and wounding another, but the chief used a whistle to signal his men to attack. The Rangers and the Comanche charged headlong into each other, exchanging bullets, arrows, and war cries.

The chief fell, but another warrior picked up his whistle to rally the warriors. In the confusion of the battle, Walker found himself cut off from the rest of the company along with Sergeant Level, Alfred Wheeler, Wallace McNeil, and John E. Wilson. The Rangers protected one another, Wheeler shooting one Indian who was about to kill Walker with a knife. An arrow pinned Level's hand to his saddle, then another brought his horse down on top of him, pinning him to the ground. As a warrior lifted a lance to finish him, Level cried out for help. Wilson shot the Comanche, who dropped his lance and staggered away.

The rest of the company moved up to join their lieutenant, driving the Indians back. The Comanche retreated into the brush, leaving the battlefield to the Rangers. The Comanche were forced to leave four of their dead behind. The unlucky Sergeant Level was wounded; according to Rip Ford's memoirs, one other Ranger was killed, but Ford neglected to mention his name. The Rangers captured all of the stolen mules and horses and liberated a captive Mexican boy. The boy was later returned to his parents in Mexico; Walker turned the captured livestock over to U.S. authorities so they could be returned to their rightful owners.

The desperate combat between closely matched forces was the kind of stand-up battle the Comanche detested, but it was the kind of fight the Rangers relished. In ambushing the raiding party, by bringing the enemy into the fight and forcing him into direct confrontation, Walker had accomplished the Rangers' paramount objective — to carry the fight to the enemy and make him pay for his actions.

While Walker led his detachment on the scout to Arroyo Gato, Lt. Edward Burleson drew the duty of turning over the Comanche prisoner, Carne Muerto, to the U.S. military authorities at San Antonio. On January 27, as he was returning to the Ranger camp, he encountered three mounted Comanche on the road near the Nueces River. Burleson later learned that the Indians were scouting the road with the intention of ambushing a trader's caravan. He ordered his main party to continue on down the road, then took eight men to chase the Indians out into the plains. Three miles into the chase, the mounted Indians turned to face the Rangers. Eleven more Comanche stood up from where they had hidden on the ground.

What resulted was an even more intense fight than Walker's battle at Arroyo Gato. Ford notes in his memoirs that the Rangers dismounted instead of charging the Comanche line, but that Burleson wasn't responsible for that disastrous order. This time the Indians attacked, rushing in close to engage in hand-to-hand combat. The Rangers dragged their horses down and lay behind them, using them as shields because the flat, open prairie offered no cover.

Some of Burleson's men had functional revolvers. Jim Carr had a "Colt's carbine," possibly one of the few surviving Paterson revolving carbines from the 1830s Republic military purchase. Several arrows struck Carr as he tried to aim his carbine over his horse, and Baker Barton died on his feet while holding on to his saddle horn. As the battle burned to a conclusion, William Lackey, Alf Tom, Jim Wilkinson, and Jack Spencer fought on despite their wounds. An arrow cut Burleson's brow, but he returned fire and killed the Comanche who had shot him.

Suddenly, the Comanche retreated, uncharacteristically leaving the bodies of their four dead comrades behind them. Nearly every man of the Ranger party was wounded; Barton was dead and Lackey's wounds would later prove mortal. James Duncan, who rode back from the main party to check on the lieutenant, found the exhausted Rangers sitting on the ground, unable to follow the Comanche or to retreat back to the road. Duncan rode a round trip of forty miles to bring back water and supplies.

Years later, Ford wrote about this fight in an article he published in the *Brownsville Sentinel*, calling it one of the most closely contested Indian fights that ever occurred in Texas. A month after the incident, Ford paid a visit to the battlefield and found it still littered with the arrows the Comanche had fired.

The Last of the Old Company

Reports of Walker's Arroyo Gato fight reached Ford at his sickbed in Laredo several days afterward. He rode out for the Ranger camp at Los Ojuelos, where he received another false report claiming that Walker's squad had taken heavy casualties and that Burleson's men had been massacred in the fight at the

Nueces trail. This news prompted Ford to lead his remaining Rangers on a night ride back to Laredo, where he found Walker and Burleson waiting for him.

Ford was so weakened by fever and by the long ride that his men had to lift him from his saddle. This didn't stop him for long; within a month, he led the Rangers out on a patrol to visit the Nueces trail battlefield and to scout the roads and rivers for Comanche raiders. The Rangers found that the Comanche had left the territory. As Ford wrote:

> There was a cessation in the matter of Indian scouts in the region between the Nueces and the Rio Grande. This region, as has been stated previously, was a favorite resort of the Comanches. Their late visits had been unfortunate for them. They had lost some of their distinguished leaders in attempting to retain control of the territory where wild horses were plentiful. Their aim was to rob and to make war, without the loss of a man, if possible. Their measures in peace, and their efforts during hostilities, were based on these principles.

Ford's Old Company mustered in for its last term of enlistment on March 23, 1851. The battles fought by his lieutenants had put an end, for a time, to the Comanche domination of the Nueces Strip. Except for minor skirmishes and one incident in which the Rangers chased a small band of Comanche to the Mexican border, the company served its last term of enlistment without engaging in serious combat. As more settlers moved into the Nueces Strip and trade flourished between Mexico and Texas, the United States government decided to discontinue its support of the Ranger service.

Ford disagreed, maintaining as before that the frontier needed a permanent defense force, but he decided that he'd finally had enough combat to last him for a while. While he faced the dissolution of his company with great sadness, he looked forward to trying his hand at civilian pursuits once more. As his company mustered out at Laredo on September 23,

1851, he looked upon them for the last time and saw them "more like a band of brothers" than as a military unit.

Ford's Old Company was only one of the three companies formed under the original call to federal service in 1849. The companies commanded by Capt. John Grumbles and Capt. Henry E. McCulloch also saw action, if not quite so much as Ford's. Records show that McCulloch lost at least one man, Pvt. Henry J. Willis, in an Indian fight on the San Saba River on September 15, 1851, just days before the company mustered out. Ford's headquarters company saw more action because it was stationed in the right position on the frontier to intercept Comanche raiders as they entered and left the Nueces Strip. Ford's memoirs also recreate the information lost when documents were burned in fires at the capital in Austin. He naturally wrote more about his personal experiences and the actions that involved his men, so most of the surviving information deals with the Old Company's actions.

In any case, the citizens of South Texas were grateful to Ford's Old Company and the other Ranger companies for clearing the Comanche out of the Nueces-Laredo region. Because the presence and reputation of the Rangers had also discouraged Mexican outlaws and adventurers from crossing the border to raid into Texas, no one had given much thought to what would happen on that front once the Rangers left. Even as the war with the Comanche cooled down, the other major cultural conflict on the frontier would heat up.

Foreign Adventures and the Question of Human Liberty

Santa Anna had departed forever, and his power over the Southwest had dissolved, but the Centralist-Federalist feud still smoldered in Mexico. Though the Mexican War had widened the cultural gap between the two countries, many Texans harbored Federalist sympathies. Texans often became involved in efforts by the Federalists in Northern Mexico to throw off the yoke of Centralist oppression.

One such revolutionary was José María Jesús Carbajal, a Mexican citizen who had been born a *Tejano* in San Antonio. Educated in Virginia and a firm believer in the principles of Jeffersonian democracy, Carbajal formulated a plan of reforms for Mexican society. He called it *El Plan de Loba*, a blueprint for the liberation of Northern Mexico. Carbajal intended to break the oppressive social control of the wealthy, politically powerful Catholic church hierarchy of Mexico, to liberate the *peons* held in virtual slavery by Mexican custom.

Ford, who was much in favor of a liberated Northern Mexico allied with Texas, joined in Carbajal's plan. Carbajal's revolutionaries captured the Mexican town of Camargo in September of 1851, shortly before Ford's Old Company disbanded. Rip Ford, Lt. Andrew Walker and thirty of the Rangers joined Carbajal's forces in Mexico, along with a large number of other Texans, American adventurers, and international soldiers of fortune who had congregated at Brownsville.

Carbajal's army attacked Matamoros, taking Fort Paredes and the artillery there. In a difficult battle reminiscent of their house-to-house fighting during the Mexican War, the Rangers led an attack that pushed the Mexican forces under Gen. Francisco Avalos back into the city's central plaza. The next morning, as they attacked the stronghold in the center of the city, a bullet creased Ford's forehead, cutting through his hatband. Ford withdrew from command to have his wound treated, but he watched as the attack continued throughout the night. The city and the American customs house burned as the struggle moved back and forth through the streets.

When the Rangers attacked a wall held by a group of Seminole Indian mercenaries, one member of Ford's Old Company, Plas McCurly, was shot through the neck and killed instantly. The enraged Rangers attacked with such ferocity that the few Seminoles who remained among the living retreated from the fight. When the Mexicans took two Texans prisoner, the officer in charge of the prisoner detail requested that he be allowed to shoot them. General Avalos replied: "It will not do. Shoot these two Texians and a thousand will come to their funeral."

The full-scale uprising Carbajal anticipated failed to materialize. Ford couldn't fault Carbajal's intent, but he did admit that his friend's military skills weren't adequate to the task. As Ford said of the command structure of Carbajal's army: "Concert was wanting." Under pressure from his supporters in the Mexican military, Carbajal ordered his forces to withdraw to Texas.

Andrew Walker, promoted to captain in command of the Rangers after Ford was wounded, led his twenty-eight men in charge against a large Mexican force that attacked the retreating army's rear guard. Ford later wrote: "The matchless riders of the West sprang upon their horses and went as if impelled by the force of a resistless cyclone." With a fierce Texas yell, the Rangers spurred forward to hit the Mexican line at full speed. The small band of Texans broke through enemy formation and turned in mid-charge to assault the right and left flanks. The roar of their revolvers and the terrible shriek of their war cry caused the Mexican force to break up and retreat, giving the rest of Carbajal's army the opportunity to move out of range. In that one charge, the Rangers lost two men but killed more of the enemy than their own number.

It was the last battle in which the men of Ford's Old Company fought together as a group. Although Carbajal and Ford attempted to rebuild the revolutionary army after their retreat from Matamoros, the U.S. government began to take notice of their actions. Carbajal returned to Mexico with a small command, there to fight indecisive battles at Camargo and Cerralvo, but when he returned to Texas soil in 1852, the American government arrested him for violation of the neutrality laws. He was eventually acquitted, but both Carbajal and Ford were censured by fellow Texans for their "foreign adventure" and the destruction of the American customs house at Matamoros.

Like the Sommervell Expedition and other attempts to break Northern Mexico away from the mother country, *El Plan de Loba* had produced some spectacular displays of the Rangers' bravery and military skill but had come to nothing in the end. The Rangers were virtually unbeatable as a group, especially when they fought on their home territory, but even they couldn't hope to invade and conquer a foreign nation without effective support.

The Big Fight on the Canadian

In 1854, the Texas Legislature passed an act that set aside reservation areas on the northern reaches of the Brazos River and established Indian agencies on these reservations. Maj. Robert S. Neighbors, Ford's old friend from the El Paso expedition in 1849, had succeeded Jack Hays as the agent in charge of Indian affairs for the state. Most of the agency Indians were Tonkawa, Huaco, Caddo, and Shawnee, although a small number of Comanche settled at the agency located in North Central Texas, on the Clear Fork of the Brazos. The agent in charge of the lower Brazos agency was Shapley P. Ross, an influential settler who had ridden with ranging companies, militia, and the Rangers off and on since 1839. John R. Baylor, who would play a role in later Ranger activities and Indian affairs, served as agent for the Comanche agency in the north.

Most of the Comanche, as well as the Apache and Kiowa, remained hostile. Ford noted: "In the winter of 1857–1858 murders and robberies were regular occurrences on the whole line of the frontier from the Red River to El Paso and from El Paso to the mouth of the Rio Grande." In the absence of organized Ranger companies, the U.S. Army proved unable to police this frontier, a meandering line that stretched two thousand miles. As an editorial published in the January 30, 1858, issue of the *Austin State Gazette* noted: "Thus Texas, with little or no Federal patronage, is left by the

Federal Government to protect herself from the savage foe, or to heedlessly stand by and witness the daily and brutal murder of our people."

Some Texans accused the reservation Indians of joining in with hostiles on raids, claiming that nearly nude men in war paint couldn't easily be recognized when later they dressed in white man's clothes. Although Neighbors and Rip Ford argued against this claim and supported a movement to give peaceful Indians full Texas citizenship, the majority of Texans advocated the complete removal of all Indians from Texas. Despite this overwhelming public opinion, the reservation Indians at the Ross agency soon proved their willingness to fight alongside the Texans against the hostile Indians.

Hardin R. Runnels, who defeated Sam Houston in the 1857 gubernatorial election, sponsored an act in the Texas Legislature that authorized funds for a new one-hundred-man Ranger company. Runnels picked Rip Ford as senior officer, set his rank as major, and gave him the authority not only to recruit and command the Rangers but all other militia, minutemen, and volunteer companies. As the *Austin State Gazette* noted in the same editorial that deplored the conditions of the frontier defense under the U.S. Army: "It is an excellent appointment."

Ford lost no time in carrying out Runnels's orders, which were to seek out hostile Indians and "chastise" them. He recruited his veteran lieutenant, Ed Burleson, to hold that position once more, and recruited William A. Pitts as second lieutenant and paymaster. Even though Ford held his appointment from the governor, once he recruited enough men to fill his company they held an election in which they confirmed him as their commander.

Ford also took command of the state forces and volunteer groups that were already in the field, and he asked Henry McCulloch to raise a second company from among the veteran Rangers whom he knew. Ford reorganized the volunteers, promoting the officers he considered able commanders, retaining the soldiers he found worthy, and dismissing the others. By

February, the Ranger companies and the state forces were ready to move out from the capital city to the frontier. They traveled north to the Brazos River agency.

At the agency, Ford asked Shapley Ross to recruit Indian allies for the expedition. Ross convinced José Casa María, the Caddo chieftain who had defeated Benjamin Bryant at the Battle of the Falls in 1839, to join the expedition with his warriors. The old chief first insisted that he send the Creek tribe a notice that the Caddo were withdrawing from their mutual peace treaty with the Comanche. Once he did so, he gathered up his best warriors, all armed with good rifles, for the war dance. Ford described the war dance as "grand, gloomy, and peculiar." Along with the Caddo, a number of the Tonkawa and Huaco warriors also donned colorful war paint to join the war party. The other war leaders who joined in included Placido of the Tonkawa, Shot Arm of the Huaco, and Jim Linney as captain of the Delaware and Shawnee. The friendly Indians raised a full company of 113 warriors to support the Rangers.

William Ford, Rip's seventy-three-year-old father, took over for Lieutenant Burleson, who was on furlough. Shapley Ross, José Maria, and the other Indian allies met up with the 102 men of the Ranger company and the other volunteers at Cottonwood Springs on April 26, 1858. The Tonkawa, according to their custom and their legendary endurance, ran alongside the mounted troops, keeping up with them. On May 7, after a buffalo hunt and the subsequent barbecue, the expedition crossed the Red River into Indian Territory (present-day Oklahoma), and soon the scouts reported sighting Comanche hunters and scouts. Keechi, the Indian who acted as the forward scout for the company, tracked Comanche riders to the main encampment of the Tenewa band of Comanche on the Canadian River in the Texas Panhandle.

On the morning of May 12, the entire party got off to a late start, ruining Ford's plan for a dawn attack. Along the route they ran into a small camp of Comanche, two of whom escaped to warn the main camp. The Rangers and the Indian allies crossed the Canadian River in hot pursuit of the two fleeing Comanche. Ford deployed his forces so that his allies were on the right and the front, screening the Ranger force from view. By doing this, he hoped to fool the Comanche into thinking they were facing a purely Indian force. The Indian allies wore white bandannas so that the Rangers could easily identify them in the heat of battle.

As the Texans moved forward, the Tenewa Comanche chieftain rode out to meet them. His name was Po-bish-e-quash-o, "Iron Jacket" or "Iron Shirt." He was a great medicine man as well as a war leader; one major element of his war medicine was an antique long coat of scale-mail armor, no doubt taken by one of his ancestors from some unlucky conquistador. Always before in battle, Iron Jacket's armor had proven to be invulnerable to musket balls and arrows. His magnificent horse carried him in complex maneuvers before his enemies as he dared them to shoot at him. For a frozen moment, the Comanche leader rode in defiance of the Texans and the reservation Indians, the unchallenged embodiment of his people, the Lords of the Plains.

Then, six Mississippi rifles, fired by the forward group of Indian allies, broke the silence and spoke in the unmistakably final language of the future. Iron Shirt's horse jumped straight up into the air. Both man and mount fell in a dead tangle of crushed feathers and shattered steel armor. To some modern observers, it might have seemed like poor sportsmanship for the Texans to shoot down the brave chief, but to the Texans and their Indian allies, it was just proof that their medicine was the stronger.

Ford yelled for a charge, knowing that the Comanche would remain confused by the loss of their leader for only a few vital minutes. The Rangers rode directly into the line of warriors guarding the main camp; Ross and the Indian allies moved to flank them and to cut off their escape. The fight split up into dozens of small actions strung out for six miles along the river. As the Rangers slammed into the rear guard, their six-shooters cut down the warriors. The Comanche second in command rallied his men at the riverbank, charging back to engage the Indian allies. A rifle bullet fired by a Shawnee captain, Chul-le-quah, cut short the new Comanche war leader's charge and his life.

The battle lasted only a short time, leaving seventy Comanche warriors dead on the battlefield, along with some noncombatants caught in the crossfire. One Ranger was killed at this point, and two others were seriously wounded. They captured more than three hundred Comanche horses and took sixty prisoners, mostly women and children. The Tonkawa engaged in their grisly custom of severing their dead enemies' hands for a ritual feast, a custom in which they believed they could transmute some of a defeated warrior's courage to themselves.

The lead element of the Rangers pursuing the retreating Comanche met their reinforcements from another village upriver. Oliver Searcy and Robert Nickles ran directly into the advancing warriors. The Comanche lanced Nickles from his horse and killed him, but Searcy managed to shoot his way through to the river. He ran into a party of Indian allies, who drove off the Comanche charge.

As the rest of the Rangers moved up to support them, their Indian allies attempted to get the Comanche to charge. The Comanche rode back and forth, firing arrows and shouting insults in attempt to draw out the Indian allies. The two sides engaged in these maneuvers for half an hour, each seeking to gain the advantage of position and timing. Ford later wrote:

> It reminded one of the rude and chivalrous days of knight-errantry. Shields and lances and bows and head dresses, prancing steeds and many minutiae were not wanting to complete the resemblance. And when the combatants rushed at each other with defiant shouts, nothing save the piercing report of the rifle varied the affair from a battlefield of the middle ages.

The Comanche finally gave way before a concerted Ranger charge, breaking up into groups to retreat back upriver. The Rangers killed seven warriors in the pursuit; Ranger George W. Paschal was wounded and one of the Huaco allies was killed in the last of the fight. The Comanche declined their opportunity to counterattack.

The camp they had attacked was only one of many from the seven hostile bands of the Comanche. From one of the prisoners the allies learned that the camp of Buffalo Hump's larger band lay only a few miles downriver. Their horses were exhausted from chasing the Comanche; they wouldn't be up to a battle without rest. The entire allied force, Indians and Rangers alike, decided they'd done enough for one day's work. They withdrew to camp twelve miles south of the Canadian, then the next day began their trip back to the Brazos River Indian agency. The women of the villages on the reserve came out singing as the warriors and the Rangers returned, leading their captured horses and their prisoners behind them. The Rangers turned the Comanche prisoners over to Shapley Ross at the agency.

A troop of the 2nd U.S. cavalry under the command of Capt. Earl Van Dorn, along with more than one hundred Indian allies commanded by Lawrence Sullivan Ross, the twenty-one-year-old son of Shapley Ross, followed Ford's lead to strike deep into Comanche territory. Ross sent two of his scouts out to find the camp from which they suspected the Comanche had been sending out their raiding parties. The scouts found Buffalo Hump's band camped in a large village of 125 or more lodges, in the Wichita Mountains near what is present-day Rush County, Oklahoma.

Van Dorn was jealous of the reputation Ford's Rangers had for doing the job he was supposed to do, but he was also one of the few U.S. officers in Texas who had paid attention to the example set by the Rangers. In this expedition against Buffalo Hump he was ably assisted by young Lawrence Sullivan Ross, who had grown up on the frontier around Indians. On the morning of October 1, Ross sent his agency Indians to stampede the Comanche horse herd. The cavalry and the mounted Indians charged the main body of Comanche warriors, driving them back into a defensive position.

Ross, one of his Caddo allies, and two cavalry troopers caught up with a group of Comanche near the village, only to find that they were all women and children. Ross noticed that one child, a girl of eight years, was a white captive. When he ordered the Caddo to bring the child to him, she exploded into a fury, biting and scratching the Caddo. Unnoticed in the uproar caused by the girl's reaction, twenty-five Comanche warriors charged the Texans. Arrows cut down the troopers, Lt. Cornelius Van Camp and Private Alexander. Ross's rifle misfired; as he drew his pistol to defend himself, a Comanche warrior grabbed the fallen Van Camp's carbine and shot Ross through the midsection.

As the Comanche leaned over Ross and drew his scalping knife, Ross recognized him as Mohee, a sometimes war leader whom he'd met at the reservation. Before Mohee could take his trophy, a group of troopers arrived and opened fire on the Comanche, driving them back. Mohee got a bullet in the back as he tried to run. The Caddo stood up from where he

Lawrence Sullivan Ross, Governor of Texas who served as a Texas Ranger before the Civil War and led two major campaigns against the Comanche.
Texas State Library & Archives Commission

had covered the white child, protecting her with his body.

In the end, Buffalo Hump's Comanche lost more than fifty warriors in the battle. The troopers lost five men, while Captain Van Dorn and several others were severely wounded. Sul Ross made the agonizing trip back to the Brazos agency in a mule-drawn litter. Once home, he soon

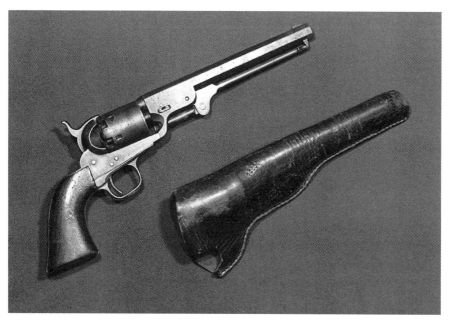

1851 Navy Colt .36 caliber revolver presented by Colt to Texas Ranger Capt. Sullivan Ross, with holster.
Photo by Tom Knowles, DeGraffenried Collection, Texas Ranger Hall of Fame and Museum

recovered enough to return for his senior year at Wesleyan College in Fort Worth. He turned the white child rescued by the Caddo warrior over to his parents, who adopted her and raised her as their own. They never found her own people, but Elizabeth (Lizzie) Ross eventually forgot her life among the Comanche to integrate fully into white society.

It was not the last time that Ross would rescue a white captive, although the results of rescue would not always prove so positive. After Ross graduated from college and returned home in 1859, the newly inaugurated governor, Sam Houston, offered him a commission as the captain of a new Texas Ranger company.

On December 17, 1860, Ross led his Ranger company, a detachment of 2nd U.S. Cavalry, the Bosque County Mounted Volunteers, and Tonkawa scouts in a raid against the Naconi Comanche camp on the Pease River, near the present-day site of Quanah, Texas. It was in this fight that scout Charles Goodnight brought the question of one captive Comanche woman's identity to the Ranger Captain's attention. She was Cynthia Ann Parker, kidnapped as a child in 1836. It was her sad fate to be kidnapped twice by the warriors of Texas, once by the Comanche and once by the Rangers, and each time separated from the two different families who loved her.

The actions of the Texas Ranger companies led by Rip Ford and Sul Ross against the Comanche from 1858 to 1860 marked a turning point. In many ways, they were equivalent in importance to Hays's first major use of revolvers at the Walker Creek fight in 1844. The big fight on the Canadian River could be considered the most important battle up to that time between the Rangers and the Comanche. Ford, in his report to Governor Runnels, praised the conduct of his Rangers and the invaluable assistance provided by their Indian allies. He also noted that the expedition had proved that Texas could launch successful attacks into the stronghold of the hostile Indian nations, if the forces she sent were tough enough to ride the warriors' trail, and if they had competent scouts and allies.

No longer could the Comanche depend on a safe haven in the north country, their formerly secure hunting grounds. The Texans had taken the fight to the enemy with a vengeance, pushing the Comanche a long way down the black road toward oblivion.

The Cortina War

On the other frontier, a leader emerged as a revolutionary firebrand to ignite the old border troubles between Texas and Mexico. Juan Nepomuceno Cortina, nicknamed "Cheno," was a man of considerable intelligence and political skill, no small military talent, and undeniable personal courage. Although other members of his family remained influential and law-abiding citizens of Texas, Cheno Cortina considered himself a Mexican national at personal odds with the Texans. He'd spent much of his early life with the wild *vaqueros* of the border country, learning their way of life, and he'd recruited a small army of *rancheros* as his personal followers. On more than one occasion he expressed his abiding hatred for the Texans, promising that he would someday drive all of the Americans out of Texas.

In 1859, Cortina used his political connections in Mexico to recruit regular Mexican troops for a foray into Texas. On the night of September 28, his army of five hundred *rancheros* and regulars crossed the border and rode into the city of Brownsville, firing their revolvers and shouting, "Death to the Gringos!" They began looting the city, and only threats and pleas from Don José M. J. Carbajal and one of Cortina's own kinsmen prevented Cortina from burning the city to the ground. Cortina withdrew his forces but camped outside the city, cutting off communications between Brownsville and the rest of Texas. Militia Capt. Miflin Kennedy and Francisco Ytúrria took command of the city's volunteers to stand off another attack.

Texas units and regular army units began moving to engage Cortina's forces and relieve the besieged city. Cortina's troops defeated a local militia unit, the

A photo of General Juan Nepomuceno Cortina, taken by DePlanque in Brownsville, Texas, circa 1866. The leader of the "Cortina War" and the sworn enemy of Rip Ford and the Texas Rangers, he continued to influence South Texas affairs well into the 1870s.
UT Institute of Texan Cultures at San Antonio/Texas Southmost College Library

"Brownsville Tigers," inflicting heavy casualties on the Texans. Cortina also defeated a regular army unit commanded by a Captain Thompson, capturing the unit's artillery pieces in the process. More men arrived from Mexico to join him at his camp on the Ebonal Ranch.

Rip Ford had seen little action since the Canadian River Campaign. After he'd disbanded his last company in 1859, he'd remained at home in Austin, trying to fight off another bout of malaria. Upon receiving the report of Cortina's invasion, Governor Runnels immediately called on Ford to muster in a new Ranger force and to take command of the state forces on the Rio Grande to deal with Cortina. Ford, appointed to the rank of lieutenant colonel, called on his old Rangers to come to his aid. With fifty-three men mustered into this company, Ford rode out for the border.

Ford's Rangers arrived in Brownsville on December 14, just as a combined force of U.S. regulars under Maj. Samuel P. Heintzelman and some local Rangers under Capt. W. G. Tobin succeeded in breaking through Cortina's defenses at Ebonal Ranch. Following up the victory, the combined regular and Ranger forces pursued Cortina's army upriver to Rio Grande City. Ford noted that Cortina had laid waste to the countryside all along the path of his retreat, destroying fences and burning buildings, raiding livestock, and sending the local citizens fleeing for their lives.

During the night of December 26, Ford took

An ambrotype photograph of Texas Ranger leader John Salmon "Rip" Ford, taken circa 1858. Ford is wearing a mismatched pair of Colt revolvers, the pistol at left appears to be a Walker, the one on the right a Dragoon model.
John N. McWilliams Collection

ninety men from the Ranger companies and scouted into the outskirts of Rio Grande City. They found Cortina's forces set up at a ranch about a mile south of the old Ringgold Barracks; the Rangers waited in position until they could hear the rumble of Major Heintzelman's artillery carriages approaching. After he reported the enemy's location to the major, Ford took command of the entire Ranger contingent and moved them to attack Cortina's position at the left flank. Just before dawn, the Rangers charged in, smashing through Cortina's pickets and sweeping forward to the old barracks.

Ford's men shot their way through the troops at the barracks and rode onto a hilltop from which they sighted the main encampment. Splitting his command, Ford sent Tobin to hit the left wing of the enemy at the old cemetery while Ford moved straight into the center. Ford believed that Heintzelman's artillery would support him, but the major had gotten the information from Ford's earlier report confused. To make matters worse, a heavy fog rolled in, obscuring visibility needed for long-range artillery.

The Rangers charged into the Mexican artillery at the corner of the cemetery overlooking the Roma road. Ford narrowly missed being decapitated by a charge of grapeshot; as the shell and shot landed all around them, the Rangers backed up a bit to find cover. They dismounted, took careful aim, and began to pour accurate rifle fire into the artillery positions. A company of riflemen under Lt. James H. Fry moved forward behind a stone wall and opened fire, repulsing an enemy attempt to advance against the Ranger position. Under heavy fire, Ford saw at least sixteen of his men fall wounded in just a few minutes.

When Fry's riflemen silenced the artillery by killing the gun crews, the Mexican infantry withdrew to fire from a distance. As the Rangers prepared to advance, Ford heard a bugle call that he knew all too well from his service in the Mexican War. It was the call to charge for the Mexican lancers. Ford had his own men lead their horses back to safety in the chaparral thicket, then move forward to wait for the cavalry charge with their rifles ready. The Rangers' fire emptied most of the Mexican saddles and broke the charge. The Mexican infantry and the remaining artillerymen began to retreat. Ford ordered his men to mount up to pursue them.

As the Rangers charged after the Mexicans fleeing down the Roma road, U.S. infantry armed with Sharp's rifles, engaged and destroyed three companies of Mexican infantry along the river. Cortina stopped to make a stand where the road crossed a ravine a few miles upriver from the city, but the Rangers jumped their horses across the ravine to capture the Mexican artillery. When the Rangers turned one of the loaded cannon to fire into the enemy, the Mexican resistance melted away. The Texans rode into Roma to prevent Cortina from taking the town, but the Mexican leader retreated away from the river road with his remaining forces. He eventually crossed back into Mexico at Guerrero.

According to official reports, the Rangers alone killed at least sixty of the enemy in the battle on the Roma road. A prisoner estimated the total killed in the battle much higher, closer to two hundred killed or seriously wounded. Cortina lost most of his artillery and his supplies, and many of his horses. It was a complete Ranger victory, one of Ford's greatest military achievements as a commander.

Despite the defeats inflicted on him at Ebonal Ranch and Rio Grande City, Cortina didn't stay in Mexico any longer than it took him to recruit replacements and resupply. Ford figured that Cortina would hit Brownsville once again, so he moved his command accordingly. The Ranger was correct; early in February of 1860, Cortina moved back to the Texas border with a large force. He deployed his men at La Bolsa Bend, a point on the south bank of the Rio Grande about thirty-five miles north of Brownsville. Using his artillery, he intended to control the river traffic and eventually shut Brownsville off from the upper river.

On February 4, shortly after Ford's newly reorganized company surprised and attacked a party of Cortina's men at the river crossing, the steamship *Ranchero* came under fire from Cortina's main camp. The *Ranchero* was steaming downriver toward Brownsville loaded with a cargo estimated to value over $200,000. The capture of this cargo would have allowed Cortina to fund a large mercenary force.

Mounted as naval guns aboard the *Ranchero* were two of the field pieces the Rangers had captured from

Cortina in December. By opening up with these guns to suppress enemy fire, U.S. artillery Lt. Lomis Langdon gave the steamer time to back out of range. It was only a temporary measure. Unless they could put Cortina's guns out of action, the ship couldn't move downriver past the bend.

Ford rode up to the ship where it had anchored on the American side of the river and convinced the captain, John Martin, to ferry himself and fifty of the Rangers across the river into Mexico. Ford sent spy companies ahead, then once he received their reports on the enemy position he advanced to attack the buildings where Cortina had placed his artillery. Using the riverbank as cover, the Rangers took position and began firing. As a detail of a dozen riflemen kept the Mexican cavalry from charging, Ford and the rest of his command advanced on foot to engage the Mexican infantry.

The firing from the Mexican lines intensified, but the Rangers took their time, picked their targets, and made each shot count. Ford sent back an order for Captain Martin to bring up the *Ranchero* so Lieutenant Langdon's guns could bear on the enemy. The Rangers who were still on the American side moved up to the river to lay in cover and fire from across the water.

The Mexican cavalry was first to leave the field as the relentless Rangers moved in close enough to use their deadly six-shooters on the troops guarding the palisade. The infantry center began to crumble around Cortina. Although he mounted his horse, fired his pistol at the Rangers, and tried to rally his men for a charge, his three-hundred-man force broke and ran, leaving him the last Mexican on the field. Only then did Cheno Cortina retreat, wheeling his horse into the chaparral as Ranger bullets cut close to his ears.

The battle of La Bolsa Bend was the last fight of any significance between the Texas Rangers and Cortina before the Civil War. Ford's small company of Rangers had killed twenty-nine of Cortina's men and wounded many more, suffering only one fatality and four wounded in the process. Never again would the

Robert E. Lee learned some of the Rangers' tactics during the Mexican War.
Brady-Handy Collection, Library of Congress

charismatic leader be able to muster a sufficient force to invade Texas in strength. Even so, the small raids he did mount kept Ford's Rangers and two regular cavalry units under Capt. George Stoneman on patrol along the Rio Grande for another month. On March 18, Ford and Stoneman crossed into Mexico to hit Cortina's stronghold at La Mesa, but the elusive leader once more escaped their grasp. After this last attack, Cortina's followers deserted him, leaving him to go into hiding to escape his enemies.

As it had on the northern frontier in the campaigns against the Comanche, the new cooperation between the U.S. forces and the Texas Rangers proved to be the answer to the problem of frontier defense. It was not a perfect solution; some U.S. officers still refused to learn from the Ranger example, while some of those who did learn from the Cavalry of the West, like Earl Van Dorn, claimed credit for creating the new tactics. Lt. Col. Robert E. Lee of the U.S. 2nd Cavalry not only learned but gave credit where it was due.

By mid-May of 1860, the state mustered out the companies of Rangers who had been gathered to fight

Cortina. For Ford, it was the end of his long career as a combat leader of the Texas Rangers in the service of the United States. It was not the last time he would lead Texas forces in combat, nor was it the end of his involvement with the Texas Rangers. Ford would once again lead the Cavalry of the West into battle, this time wearing a gray uniform.

In April of that year, the U.S. commander of the Texas Military District, Lt. Col. Robert E. Lee, came to tour the scenes of the Cortina War. Lee, who had first-hand knowledge of the Texas Rangers from his service in the Mexican War, was eager to learn more about the recent conflict from the Ranger commander. In his visits with Lee, Ford found much to admire in the officer from Virginia:

> He evinced an imperturbable self-possession, and a complete control of his passions. To approach him was to feel yourself in the presence of a man of superior intellect, possessing the capacity to accomplish great ends and the gift of controlling and leading of men.

In less than a year, Ford and Lee would be leading men into battle against the Union they'd fought to preserve.

7

IN BLUE AND GRAY

AS ABRAHAM LINCOLN LATER SAID, THE UNITED STATES WAS A house divided against itself, Democrat against Republican, South against North. By 1860, the social and economic differences between the states of the American Union expanded into a vicious political struggle between the radicals on both sides. The final dissent that shattered the Union led Texas, with her ties to the South, into the heart of a destructive civil war against the American nation she had so proudly joined only fifteen years before.

The Texas Rangers exerted a profound influence on that conflict, directly and indirectly, as individuals and as an organization. The effects of their expertise in frontier warfare reached far beyond the borders of Texas to touch almost every battlefield of the American Civil War. Frontier Texas had served as the training ground, with her Rangers as the instructors, for many of the officers who later commanded forces on both sides in the war. Whenever a Union or Confederate commander employed modern cavalry tactics pioneered by Ranger leaders like Hays and Ford, the fighting spirit of Texas rode forth.

The Texas yell, the war cry of the West, joined in with the Rebel yell as Texans fought side by side with their brothers in gray. Sometimes, the Texas yell rang out from the ranks in blue, from the Texans who remained loyal to the Union. The "Brother-Brother War," as the Indians called it, divided old friends, former comrades in arms, and relatives into opposing camps.

Texas Rangers who had served with and protected U.S. troops during the Mexican War and the Indian Wars found themselves fighting against some of their former comrades. Rip Ford and the other experienced Rangers, among them Benjamin and Henry E. McCulloch, Edward Burleson Jr., George B. Erath, and Lawrence Sullivan Ross, emerged as the premiere leaders not only of the Texas state forces but regular Confederate troops in Texas, in the Indian Territory, and in the great battles farther east.

In *The Texas Rangers, A Century of Frontier Defense*, historian Walter Prescott Webb dismisses the Civil War service of the Rangers and their wartime efforts as negligible. This is a notable and regrettable

Abraham Lincoln led the United States through the difficult years of the Civil War.
Dictionary of American Portraits

omission in an otherwise definitive work. The war drew many of the veteran leaders and men of the Texas Rangers into regular Confederate service, leaving behind the almost impossible task of frontier defense to the few men who remained. The settlers on the Texas frontier suffered because their most capable defenders had joined the Confederate war effort, as Texas Gov. Francis Richard Lubbock said in 1863, "leaving their wives and children to be butchered by savages." Despite these losses, the remaining Rangers fought against the Indians who threatened to overrun the unguarded frontier, against federal troops and Kansas guerrillas, and against the bandits, deserters, and renegades who flourished in the wartime atmosphere of political and moral confusion.

The Ranger companies who remained in Texas served bravely, but not always wisely or well. In one of the darkest chapters in Texas Ranger history, the state

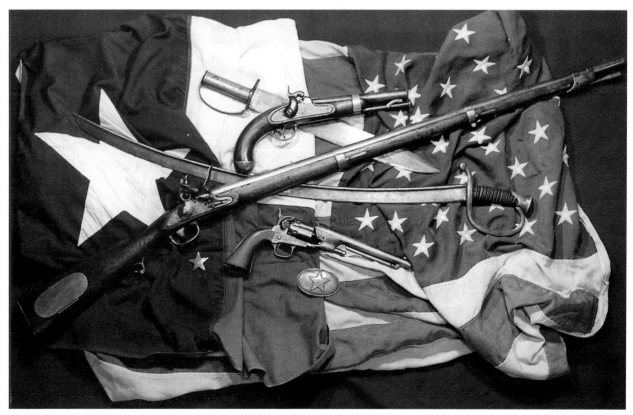

The Civil War—U.S. Common Rifle (military rifled musket), Model 1842 Palmetto Armory U.S. Model pistol in .54 caliber; Texas military belt buckle; Texas Confederate "D-grip" bowie knife; Confederate Texas silver star worn on caps by Texas Confederate partisan volunteers, originally worn by J. T. Cyrus of Houston; fluted-cylinder Colt 1860 Army Model revolver; Texas Confederate artillery sword marked "B Co.-15."
Photo by Tom Knowles, Texas Ranger Hall of Fame and Museum

maintain order in a time of general chaos. They failed, often at the cost of their lives, but they never gave up. For that alone, they deserve to be remembered.

As difficult and divisive as the war itself proved for the Texans, the aftermath would be even more destructive. In one way or another, the Civil War put an end to the careers of many of the veteran Rangers. For seven long years, the anti-Confederate bias of the post-war Reconstruction government would exile the Texas Rangers from the service of the Lone Star. In that dark age, the light kindled in 1823 by the first Defenders of the West would flicker and fade to embers, and would come close to extinction.

The Reckless Spirit of Revolution

Former Ranger Noah Smithwick, fifty-two, and a settled, prosperous farmer and businessman at the time of the 1860 presidential election, was a true Jacksonian Democrat, loyal to the Union. Smithwick found he could not support the Democratic Party when it became

An engraving of a caricature of a Texas Ranger, published in *Harper's Weekly* magazine, July 6, 1861.
UT Institute of Texan Cultures at San Antonio

set the untrained and undermanned Ranger units to chasing deserters, draft evaders, and war protesters under the edicts of the hated Confederate Conscription Bureau. These Rangers volunteered for an inglorious duty, to act as policemen for the Confederate government that ignored them. While they fought desperate battles against Indians and relatively unimportant federal forces, others won fame and honors in the "real" battles that took place in the East. Unsupported and forgotten, they struggled to

"the party of secession." As Smithwick leant his voice to Gov. Sam Houston's campaign against secession, the valiant old Ranger received death threats from men who had, as he wrote, "never set foot in the country till all the danger from Mexicans and Indians had passed."

Unwilling to fight for a cause he couldn't support but just as unwilling to fight against his fellow Texans, Smithwick had already determined to move to California if the Ordinance of Secession passed. It did

so by an overwhelming majority on February 1, 1861. Conspicuous in their dissent were Gov. Sam Houston and convention delegates John and George Hancock, E. J. Davis, A. J. Hamilton, David Burnet, E. M. Pease, and James W. Throckmorton. As Smithwick later wrote, Throckmorton rose from his seat to deliver his vote, saying, "Unawed by the reckless spirit of revolution around me, in the presence of God and my country and my own conscience, which I fear more than either, I vote 'No.'"

Noah Smithwick sold out his interests and went to the capital to purchase the supplies he would need for his move to California. During his last visit with Sam Houston he offered to stay, to raise a company of men to fight to preserve the Lone Star as a republic independent of the South and the North. Smithwick later wrote of their conversation in *The Evolution of a State*:

> "General," said I, "if you will again unfurl the Lone Star from the capitol, I will bring you 100 men to help maintain it there."
>
> "My friend," said he, "I have seen Texas pass through one long, bloody war. I do not wish to involve her in civil strife. I have done all I could to keep her from seceding, and now if she won't go with me I'll have to turn and go with her."

When the popular vote approved the Ordinance of Secession by a three-to-one margin, Houston refused to take the Confederate oath of office. He stepped down as governor on March 16 and withdrew from the political battlefield to retire to his home in Huntsville, in East Texas.

Sam Houston died there in July 1863, at the age of seventy-one, even as thousands of his fellow Texans fought a desperate, losing battle against the tide of Union victories. Three months after his death, the Texas State Legislature mourned his passing with a special resolution praising his devotion to Texas.

Rip Ford, the most prominent Texas Ranger leader, threw his support behind the secessionist cause, playing an instrumental role in convening the secession convention in Austin on January 28, 1861. Ford

had often employed his eloquent pen to defend the actions of his ally and friend, Sam Houston, but on this fateful point the two great Texas leaders found themselves as divided as was the nation itself.

From June 1862 through December 1863, he served as head of the Texas office of the Confederate Conscription Bureau, applying the criteria for conscription fairly, trying to keep the conflict from becoming a "rich man's war but a poor man's fight." His sense of honor and his belief in personal liberty would not allow him to force Union men into Confederate military service against their beliefs. After Ford turned his attention to his battlefield command in the Rio Grande country, less honorable men in the new government used conscription as a weapon to punish Union sympathizers and political enemies.

Before war broke out, many Southerners and many Texans were caught up in the "reckless spirit of revolution," believing that the Yankees would not have the stomach for a fight. Rip Ford, always a good judge of warriors, knew that the North would fight and that secession would certainly produce "a terrible war."

The split between the Unionists and Confederates in Texas would fragment the independent Texans more deeply than it would the people of the more culturally cohesive Southern states. Although an overwhelming majority of Texans favored secession, Union sentiment remained strong in some areas of the state, particularly in the capital city of Austin, among the citizens of the German communities of Central Texas, and in the western frontier settlements where slave owners were scarce.

Texan would fight Texan, Unionist against Confederate, radical against radical. Under the Confederate colors, the Texas Rangers would ride to defend the frontier not only against Indians and bandits but their own countrymen.

A Terrible Foreboding of Civil War
Immediately after the Ordinance of Secession passed by popular vote, Judge O. M. Roberts, president of the

Secession Convention, directed Rip Ford to take over command of the state forces. His first mission was to convince the federal commander, Capt. B. H. Hill, to surrender Fort Brown on the Rio Grande. Even as he traveled from Austin to the Rio Grande, Ford began to recruit commanders for three new Ranger companies, drawing on the experienced leaders he'd trained. Brothers Ben and Henry McCulloch were the first Texas Ranger leaders to answer Ford's call.

Rip Ford took personal command of the Rio Grande district, the southern frontier that stretched from Brownsville to Fort Duncan. Ben McCulloch took command of the Central Texas district, including San Antonio and Austin. Henry McCulloch took command of the major Indian frontier in the north, from Fort Chadbourne to the Red River.

A photograph of Gen. David E. Twiggs, Commander of the Department of Texas at the time of secession. Twiggs worked with Rip Ford and other Texas leaders to allow the peaceful withdrawal of federal troops, thus preventing the first shots of the Civil War from being fired in Texas.
Prints and Photographs Collection, Center for American History, University of Texas at Austin

Brig. Gen. Edmund Kirby Smith, captain of the 2nd U.S. Cavalry unit that surrendered to Henry McCulloch's Rangers at the beginning of the Civil War. He later became McCulloch's commander when they both served the Confederacy.
UT Institute of Texan Cultures at San Antonio

Gen. David Twiggs, the U.S. commander for the Department of Texas, was a Georgian who had already communicated to his superiors his desire to resign his post in order to offer his services to his home state. Twiggs issued orders that U.S. military units in Texas offer no resistance to state forces. The U.S. forces were to retain their individual arms but to withdraw when requested to do so by Texas authorities, leaving most of their supplies, their heavy equipment, and the military facilities for the Texans. Twiggs directed the federal troops to report to the Texas coast, there to board ships to return to U.S. territory.

Henry McCulloch recruited one hundred men from the militia companies in the North and West Central Texas counties, including militia lieutenants James "Buck" Barry of Bosque County, B. B. Holley of Coryell County, D. C. Cowan of San Saba County, and Thomas C. Frost of Comanche County. McCulloch's first objective was to assume control of the headquarters of the U.S. Cavalry Company B, commanded by Capt. Edmund Kirby Smith and based at Camp Colorado, located in Coleman County not far from the town of Brownwood.

By February 22, McCulloch had recruited two hundred men, including civilian volunteers from Brownwood. McCulloch positioned his forces around the fort, then offered Captain Smith surrender terms. In return for allowing the cavalry to withdraw peacefully, the Texans demanded that they leave behind all ordinance, mounts, supplies, and equipment.

Captain Smith replied that he would fight rather than accept terms he felt would dishonor his command. If Henry McCulloch had been a hasty man, the Civil War would have started with a battle between the Texas Rangers and the U.S. Cavalry. As it was, McCulloch continued to negotiate with Smith for the

After annexation, the U.S. Army Quartermaster Corps used the partially-restored Alamo as a garrison post, arsenal, and supply depot. When Texas seceded from the Union in 1861, Ben McCulloch led his Rangers to the Alamo to force the surrender of the federal post and arsenal.
The San Antonio Light Collection, UT Institute of Texan Cultures at San Antonio

better part of two days. Finally, Smith agreed to turn over the fort if McCulloch allowed the federal cavalry to keep their horses, their individual weapons, and enough supplies to sustain them for the ride to the Texas coast. U.S. Cavalry Company B withdrew from Camp Colorado on February 26, leaving it in the possession of Henry McCulloch's Rangers.

In one of those ironic twists of history, Kirby Smith would later rise to the rank of general in the Confederate Army and take command of the entire Trans-Mississippi District. In 1863, he would appoint Henry McCulloch as the commander of the Northern Sub-District of Texas, the very area from which McCulloch had forced him to retreat in 1861.

Ben McCulloch had not remained idle in South Central Texas while his brother secured the northern frontier. On February 16, he led his force of Rangers and volunteers into San Antonio. Marching to the Alamo under the colors of a Lone Star flag, McCulloch demanded that the U.S. arsenal located there be turned over to the Texans. The 8th U.S. Infantry in San Antonio obeyed a direct order from General Twiggs to surrender control of the city to McCulloch. McCulloch also performed another vital service for Texas, convincing Samuel Colt to make one more large shipment of two thousand of the 1860 Army Colt revolvers to the Texas Rangers, just before the U.S. government banned weapons sales to the Southern states.

In the south, Rip Ford persuaded Captain Hill to withdraw from Fort Brown in compliance with General Twiggs's general order. Gen. E. B. Nichols brought in a recently formed unit of state troops, recruited and commanded by Benjamin Franklin Terry of Brazoria, to take possession of the vacated fort. This force later became the nucleus for the 8th Texas Cavalry Regiment, better known as "Terry's Texas Rangers" (see "Terry's Texas Rangers").

The efforts of Twiggs, Ford, and the McCulloch brothers allowed the federal troops stationed in Texas to withdraw peacefully. Judge Roberts later said of Ford's diplomatic work with the U.S. forces, "...but for

A cabinet card photograph of former Texas Ranger Henry McCulloch, circa 1875.
John N. McWilliams Collection

his prudence and masterly management of the troops, and his address with the United States officers," the war would have opened in Texas even before the state had seceded.

The majority of the federal forces marched unmolested to the mouth of the Rio Grande and other Texas ports, where they boarded steamships for transport back to the United States. On March 20, 1861, Rip Ford said his last farewells to those federal officers with whom he had served during his Old Company's campaigns against Indians and bandits in the Rio Grande country. He later wrote:

Each one of us felt a dread of what might befall us. A terrible foreboding of civil war warned us that we might meet as foes and, under a sense of duty, might take the life of a valued friend.

Ford's fears of what would come proved correct. The coming war would be the first "modern war," one in which the use of radical new tactics and weapons would foreshadow the destruction and mass slaughter of the World Wars of the twentieth century. The American Civil War introduced trench warfare, heavy artillery bombardment of civilian population centers, rapid-fire weapons, ironclad naval vessels, and aerial observation platforms. The innovations in cavalry techniques and tactics developed by the Texas Rangers expanded the role of cavalry units from conventional scouting and harassment to include strike force and guerrilla operations.

Many of the U.S. officers and men who had served with the Texans, from the Mexican War to the Cortina War, had at least begun to learn the tactics of frontier warfare from the Texas Rangers. Whether they decided to wear blue or gray, they applied those terrifying tactics against one another in the conflict. Union Maj. Gen. George Stoneman, who had served so well with Rip Ford in the Cortina War, would face Hood's Texas Brigade and Sul Ross's 3rd Texas Cavalry in Sherman's battle to take Atlanta.

Some of the best commanders of Union and Confederate cavalry came out of the cadre of 2nd U.S. Cavalry who served in Texas in the time between the Mexican War and the Civil War. Lt. Col. Robert E. Lee of the 2nd Cavalry was a veteran of the Mexican War who had served almost his entire military career in Texas. When he resigned his commission with the Union forces to take command of the Confederate Army of Virginia, he took with him the experience he'd gained from fighting alongside Jack Hays and Rip Ford.

Lee was not alone in his admiration for the Texans and their combat skills. The long list of Civil War commanders who had learned their trade from the

A photo of Benjamin Franklin Terry, the original commander of Terry's Texas Rangers.
Texas State Library & Archives Commission

Texans included men like Edmund Kirby Smith, Earl Van Dorn, and John Bell Hood. Hood, a West Point graduate from Kentucky who had served with the 2nd Cavalry on the Texas frontier, would rise to command the famous Texas Brigade at the bloody battles of Antietam, Chickamauga, and Second Manassas, and in the desperate assault on Little Round Top at Gettysburg.

In the first months of the conflict, the Confederate authorities believed that the war would be over shortly, that there would be no need to recruit regular units from the frontier state of Texas. They were wrong; the war would last until the spring of 1865, when the ragged remnants of Confederate resistance would surrender to a victorious Union. Out of a population of about 400,000 citizens, Texas contributed more than 60,000 soldiers to Confederate service, a higher percentage of her able-bodied men than any other Confederate state.

For the duration of the war, the tactics of frontier

TERRY'S TEXAS RANGERS

Terry's Texas Rangers: A Civil War photo of five troopers of the 8th Texas Cavalry.
Texas State Library & Archives Commission

In the shadow of the Texas capitol in Austin stands a statue of a horse and rider, a tribute to one of the most famous military units to serve in the American Civil War — the 8th Texas Cavalry, better known as Terry's Texas Rangers. The statue was erected in 1867 by the survivors of this Confederate unit as a tribute to their fallen comrades.

The 8th Texas Cavalry was not an official part of the Texas Ranger organization, but it proved so adept at using Ranger tactics in the great cavalry battles of the Civil War that no one questioned its use of the famous name. One Union officer who saw Terry's men in action paraphrased Rip Ford's description of the original Texas Rangers: "They ride like Arabs, shoot like archers at a mark, and fight like devils."

Not long after the Texas Secession Convention of 1861, Benjamin F. Terry, a prominent planter; John A. Wharton, attorney and politician; and Thomas S. Lubbock, a veteran of the Texas Revolution, decided to raise a cavalry unit for Confederate service. As Wharton began recruiting volunteers, Terry and Lubbock traveled to Virginia, where they signed on as staff officers to Gen. Pierre G. Beauregard and participated in the first Battle of Bull Run. They returned to Texas with a commission to recruit a regular Confederate cavalry regiment.

Much like a Texas Ranger unit of the time, the men of the 8th Texas Cavalry elected their own officers; they were volunteer Texans who provided their own clothing, weapons, and horses, although they would exchange these to some extent for military-issue weapons and mounts later in the war. The first companies came from Brazoria and from Fort Bend County; early in 1861, these original elements supported Rip Ford's troops in the peaceful removal of federal troops from the Rio Grande district and then took over garrison duty at Fort Brown. In June 1861, after Terry sent out a call for volunteers to report to him in Houston, more than four thousand men showed up to apply. At the mustering-in ceremony on September 9, Terry accepted approximately 1,200 of them, selected for their ability to ride and shoot.

Gen. Albert Sidney Johnston.
Texas State Library & Archives Commission

They were men from all walks of life — farmers, cowboys, professionals — and many of them had ridden with Texas volunteer companies and militia units in fights against Indians and bandits. At first they wore civilian clothes, from broadcloth suits to buckskins, and they carried an assortment of weapons, from six-shooters to shotguns, from sabers to Bowie knives. Some of them wore Mexican sombreros, sashes, and serapes. It was little wonder that, when the citizens of the Southern states first saw them as they made their way to Virginia, they called them "Texican Rangers." The name stuck with them, and though the Texas Ranger legend was a difficult reputation to live up to, they never did anything to bring shame to it.

The regiment traveled to Bowling Green, Kentucky, to sign on with Gen. Albert Sidney Johnston, commander of the Confederate Army of the West. Johnston, a veteran of the Mexican War and a former Secretary of War of the Republic of Texas, was a close friend of Terry's family. There they formally mustered in, organized into ten companies, and held officer elections. Even though they set aside their regular commissions to stand for election, Terry and Lubbock were elected as the commanding officers at the rank of colonel and lieutenant colonel.

Confederate Gen. Nathan Bedford Forrest fought alongside Terry's Texas Rangers.
Library of Congress

Their first major action took place at the bloody battle near Woodson, Kentucky, on December 17, 1861. The 32nd Indiana Volunteers withered before the Texans' deadly charge as Terry's Rangers inflicted casualties six times

Union Gen. George Crook's cavalry fought Terry's Texas Rangers at the Battle of Chickamauga.
Brady-Handy Collection, Library of Congress

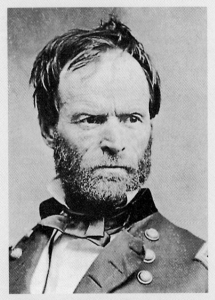

Union Gen. William Tecumseh Sherman accepted the surrender of the surviving members of Terry's Texas Rangers in April 1865.
New-York Historical Society

heavier than their own. Colonel Terry himself was among the four members of the 8th Cavalry killed in the battle. The Texans elected Lubbock to take Terry's place, but then he died of illness at Nashville in January 1862. John A. Wharton, who had been wounded but survived, took over the command, with John G. Walker as the lieutenant colonel.

The 8th Texas Cavalry continued to fight through most of the major battles of the west, at Shiloh, Bardstown, Chickamauga, and Knoxville. At the Battle of Shiloh in April 1862, Wharton was wounded once again, and Clinton Terry, the brother of the slain colonel, was also killed.

On July 13, 1862, Terry's Rangers joined Nathan Bedford Forrest's brigade in an attack that drove the Union troops out of Murfreesboro, Tennessee. In the fall of 1863, they joined up with members of Hood's Texas Brigade at the Battle of Chickamauga, where they killed, wounded, or captured 140 members of Gen. George Crook's cavalry brigade. Throughout 1864 and 1865, they remained in the thick of the fighting, coming to the aid of several of the Confederacy's commanders. After they finally surrendered to Gen. William Tecumseh Sherman in April 1865, of the 1,200 men who had originally joined, only 248 survived to return to Texas.

Author's note: Terry's 8th Cavalry was only one of many Confederate units formed during the war that used the term "Ranger" in its informal designation. The men of the 5th Texas Cavalry, a consolidation of the 9th and 10th Texas Cavalry Battalions, were better known as the Texas Partisan Rangers. After entering Confederate service at Fort Washita in February 1863, the Partisan Rangers served primarily in combat against Union forces in the Indian Territory, Oklahoma, and Arkansas. As partisan cavalry, they were sometimes subject to summary execution when captured by Union regulars.

Terrell's 34th Texas Cavalry, organized in April 1863 by Lt. Col. Alexander W. Terrell, began as a battalion but shortly afterward increased to a regiment. Among the officers and troopers of the 34th were a number of Indians, *Tejanos,* and black Texans, including Capt. José Rodriguez and 3rd Sgt. James Washington. A young Clay Allison, one of the most notorious gunmen of the post-Civil War period, got his start as a trooper in the 34th.

Walter P. Lane's Texas Confederate Rangers, Gen. John Bell Hood's Texas Brigade, Ben McCulloch's 3rd Texas Cavalry, and other Texas groups used the Ranger name in their official and unofficial unit designations. The name and the reputation of the Texas Rangers had become so

This statue at the Texas state capitol building is dedicated to the 8th Texas Cavalry, the Confederate unit known as "Terry's Texas Rangers."
Photo by Tom Knowles

nationally recognizable because of their service in the Mexican War that the average American, North and South, tended to consider any Texas cavalryman a "ranger." The Texas Confederates did their best to live up to that reputation.

Confederate Gen. John Bell Hood served with the 2nd Cavalry on the Texas frontier before he commanded the famous Texas Brigade during the Civil War.
Dictionary of American Portraits

Robert E. Lee had served almost his entire military career in Texas when he took command of the Confederate Army in Virginia.
National Archives and Records Administration

warfare and the men who knew how to use them replaced cotton and beef as the main exports from Texas.

The Forgotten Frontier

On the northwestern frontier, Henry McCulloch saw a devastated country of burned farms and homes, the results of Comanche and Kiowa raids. The Indians took advantage of the confusion of the secessionist movement to hit the frontier settlements. The McCulloch brothers and Rip Ford submitted reports on frontier conditions, recommending that the forces in the field be increased and given more of a permanent status.

By March 1861, the new state government confirmed the McCullochs and Ford as the commanders of the Ranger forces in the field. The Confederate Secretary of War, Leroy P. Walker, sent a request to Ben McCulloch that he raise a regiment of ten compa-

nies, a thousand men to defend the Texas borders. Anxious to join a regular Confederate unit, Ben McCulloch declined the command, suggesting that his brother, Henry, take over the responsibility for recruiting the regiment.

On May 11, 1861, Ben McCulloch left the Texas Ranger service to accept a commission as a brigadier general in the regular Confederate Army, taking command of the Confederate forces in the Indian territories. It was the end of McCulloch's long and brilliant career as a Texas Ranger. His command won a series of victories against Union forces in the Indian territories, but his habit of scouting behind enemy lines and the reckless daring that had made him famous in the Mexican War finally proved his undoing. In Arkansas on March 7, 1862, as he commanded elements of the 3rd Texas Cavalry Regiment at the Battle of Pea Ridge, McCulloch decided to run a reconnaissance of a dug-in enemy position that had blocked his advance. Ben McCulloch, the veteran leader of a dozen deadly scouts through Mexico, fell to a Union sniper's bullet.

Riding in that same battle was Lawrence Sullivan Ross, who at the time was the major in command of a detachment of the 6th Texas Cavalry Regiment. In May 1861, Ross resigned from the Texas Ranger service to join the Confederate Army as a private. Near the end of the war, after he'd fought in almost 140 battles, he'd risen to the command rank of brigadier general. Ross survived the war to return to Texas, but although he would later serve as a peace officer, as governor of the state, and as the president of Texas A&M College, he never returned to service with the Rangers.

Every experienced fighting man drawn to the battles in the east left the border country just that much more open to Indian raiders. Most of the Confederacy's military efforts were directed toward the war against the Union, and the Confederate Conscription Act of April 16, 1862, the first military draft law to be enacted in North America, would make a bad situation even worse.

Edward Clark, who replaced Sam Houston as

Engraving of former Texas Ranger leader Benjamin McCulloch in his uniform as a Confederate general, published in *Harper's Weekly* magazine, September 7, 1861. *UT Institute of Texan Cultures at San Antonio*

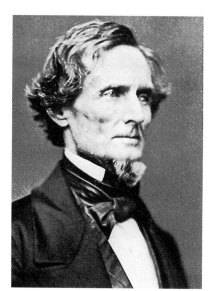

During the Civil War, Jefferson Davis was President of the Confederacy. Texas found itself facing the same lack of support for frontier defense from his government as it had as part of the United States. *Brady Collection, National Archives*

Texas Governor, appealed directly to President Jefferson Davis, asking that the Confederate government assume responsibility for the defense of the frontier. Clark's appeals and Davis's negative response to them began a bitter states' rights controversy between Texas and the Confederate government. The lack of adequate military support by the United States was one of the major reasons Texas had seceded, but the same disagreement developed between Texas and the Confederacy.

For the entire period of its existence as a nation, the Confederacy refused to authorize Texas state troops or to provide the necessary Confederate troops to defend the Texas frontier. Every time Texas formed a Ranger unit or a state militia regiment for frontier defense, the Confederate Conscription Bureau tried to draft it into the regular army. To the Confederate central government in Virginia, the murders of civilians on the frontier were easily lost and forgotten in the mass carnage of the war.

Governor Clark proceeded to authorize the new frontier Ranger unit without approval from President Davis or the Confederate Legislature. On March 4, 1861, Henry McCulloch accepted the rank of colonel and began recruiting for a regiment supposedly in Confederate service but actually controlled by the State of Texas. Veteran Ranger Buck Barry signed on as the captain of one of McCulloch's ten companies. Edward Burleson Jr., one of Ford's most experienced Ranger captains, joined as McCulloch's major.

James "Buck" Barry, long-time Texas Ranger and major of the Frontier Regiment.
UT Institute of Texan Cultures at San Antonio, Courtesy of Mr. S. W. Pease

By early April, the 1st Regiment, Texas Mounted Riflemen, reached its full strength of 1,000 men. McCulloch sent six companies to operate near San Antonio in South Central Texas, keeping four companies stationed near Camp Colorado, Camp Cooper, and Fort Chadbourne on the northern frontier.

McCulloch's regiment was the first major Texas force to take service under the Confederate flag. They operated much as had Rip Ford's Old Company in the 1850s, but they were more similar in organization to the Texas Mounted Rifles of the Mexican War. The 1st Texas differed from previous frontier Ranger units in that they enlisted a full regiment of ten companies for a year, not six months. No matter what they were called, no matter that they served under Confederate orders, the Texans saw the men of the Texas Mounted Riflemen as Rangers.

Flying the Colors

One of Henry McCulloch's first actions with the 1st Texas was a tour through the Indian territories across the Red River. Guided by Charles Goodnight and accompanied by a large force of Tonkawa allies, the Ranger leader visited not only with the more peaceful tribes but with Eagle Chief and Red Bear of the Comanche, and Satanta, Lone Wolf, and Satank of the Kiowa.

The Kiowa and Comanche refused to talk peace, but McCulloch expected no more positive results from his meetings with the horse lords. He was showing the Lone Star flag, delivering the message that any of them he caught raiding into Texas could expect a fight. Upon his return to Texas, McCulloch deployed his forces along the defensive line from Camp Jackson at the junction of the Red River and the Big Wichita River to Fort Mason, northwest of Austin. McCulloch began running regular patrols along the frontier and into the fringes of Indian territory, an action designed to put an end to raids across the Red River.

While some tribes signed treaties, and some, like the Cherokee and Chickasaw, even formed their own regiments to fight in Confederate service, the Comanche and the Kiowa merely took advantage of the situation to raid into Texas. Former enemies, by the time of the Civil War the Kiowa and the Comanche had become staunch allies against their common enemy, the Texans.

Federal attacks on the coast and the war in the east drew away the regular troops and put a strain on supplies available to the 1st Texas. In one instance, McCulloch's men were forced to withdraw from a battle with Comanche raiders because they'd run out of ammunition. The long supply lines from the major cities and regular shortfalls in promised supplies meant that men of the 1st Texas often had to live off the land.

One Ranger tactic — using grain-fed horses that had the stamina to run down Comanche ponies — fell prey to the lack of adequate supply. Long patrols so weakened their mounts that on more than one occasion McCulloch's men were forced to break off a pursuit. In August 1861, forty Indians intercepted ten men of Captain Buck Barry's Company C between Camp Jackson and Camp Cooper. The poor condition of their horses left the Rangers surrounded on the open prairie, where they managed to hold off the Indians for five hours. Six Rangers were wounded in the fight.

Just a week later, a detachment under Lt. Col. Thomas Frost engaged another band of raiders in a running battle. The Rangers killed two Indians in the fight, but Capt. Green Davidson and a private were also killed. When the Rangers' horses began to tire, the Comanche turned to fight. Seldom did Rangers refuse such a challenge, but on this occasion they were seriously outnumbered, their horses exhausted. Frost wisely withdrew his command from the battlefield.

Despite the difficulties they faced, the 1st Texas continued to run regular patrols. On November 1, Captain Barry's company of thirty-five men defeated a much larger force of Comanche in a running battle near Camp Colorado. These patrols discouraged some of the raiders, reducing the damage to frontier settlements throughout the regiment's period of service.

In December, Henry McCulloch was appointed as the Confederate commander of the new Western Military District of Texas. Edward Burleson resigned as major of the 1st Texas shortly after McCulloch received his new appointment. The regiment elected Buck Barry to hold that position, which he did until the 1st Texas mustered out at Fort Mason in April 1862. Because the Confederate Conscription Act went

Maj. Edward Burleson, Jr., Texas Ranger and officer in the Frontier Regiment. From Lewis Worthan's *A History of Texas.* *UT Institute of Texan Cultures at San Antonio*

into force on April 16, most of the former members of the 1st Texas Mounted Rifles enlisted in the regular Confederate Army at that time. A number of them served with the 8th Texas Cavalry Battalion, which later became a part of the 1st Texas Cavalry Regiment.

The Rangers stationed in the Red River district faced another problem in addition to Indian raids — political dissent in the Red River district. Several of the northern counties in the region between Dallas and the Red River that had voted for the Union in the secessionist election remained antisecessionist strongholds. There were few slave holders among the small farmers of these counties, and while they weren't necessarily pro-Union or abolitionist, they resisted the Confederate conscription laws and taxation that they felt violated their rights as Texans. As the section of the population hardest hit by Indian raiders, they were angered by the indifference of the Confederate central government toward frontier defense.

As the war continued to divide the people of Texas, Red River country became haven and refuge for many embittered, desperate men who had good reason to hate anyone in Confederate service. Increasingly, the job of maintaining civil order in these counties fell to the Rangers.

On the Rio Grande

The 1st Texas took the place of U.S. troops on the northern and central frontiers, but the southern frontier remained open after the federals vacated the Rio Grande country. In March 1861, at the same time as McCulloch was recruiting for his regiment in the north, Rip Ford accepted the rank of colonel in command of the 2nd Regiment, Texas Mounted Rifles. He recruited former Rangers and seasoned volunteers as his company commanders. Ford, who had decided to settle back into private life after he'd married Addie Smith in 1860, could not ignore the Lone Star's call to service.

As commander of the military district of the Rio Grande, Ford took on the responsibility for defending a thousand miles of border from the mouth of the river to El Paso. He sent seven companies commanded by Lt. Col. John R. Baylor and Maj. Ed Waller to patrol the upper river and El Paso area, then he took the remaining three companies to set up his own headquarters on the lower river.

His first major concern was that Mexico might use the conflict between North and South to advance against Texas, but the revolutionary turmoil in Mexico gave Ford the opportunity to prevent this. The old Ranger had friends in Mexico, and he used these contacts to strengthen ties with Mexican leaders, including the nationalist patriot leader, Benito Juarez. Ford was also instrumental in opening Mexican ports for trade between the Confederacy and European nations, a move that allowed the Confederacy to avoid the Union naval blockade.

Juan N. Cortina, still smarting from his earlier defeat under the guns of Ford's Old Company, declared war on the Confederacy and began causing trouble along the border near Rio Grande City. Cortina's raiders fought a number of skirmishes with Texas state troops and Ranger companies in March and April of 1861. After one of Cortina's lieutenants, a man named Ochoa, seized and hanged the Zapata County judge, Señor Vela, a volunteer Ranger company under Capt. Santos Benavides rode from Laredo to attack Cortina near Carrizo. Captain Benavides, who later rose to the rank of colonel in service with Rip Ford, soundly defeated Cortina.

The Texas coast, Ford's district, remained the most likely venue for a federal attack. With the assistance of the citizens of Brownsville, he immediately set his men to rebuilding and expanding old Fort Brown. As Ford had expected, the Union Navy moved in to blockade Texas ports and to land troops on the island of Brazos Santiago at the mouth of the Rio Grande River. After a tour of the area, Ford realized that the desolate island was indefensible against naval bombardment; he ordered Confederate and state forces to evacuate.

The Union forces declined to move further into the Texas interior, but by July 1861, the Union naval blockade of the Texas coast had closed down Galveston and most of the other Texas ports. Bagdad, a sleepy fishing village on the Mexican side of the mouth of the Rio Grande, changed almost overnight into a major port. Massive shipments of Texas and Confederate cotton moved through the neutral port to England and other European destinations.

By the fall of 1861, Ford had organized and set the necessary forces in place to guard the border country against all of the enemies of Texas. He was unable to command the 2nd Texas for the full enlistment because his malarial fever had returned. Before he left for San Antonio to take a much needed rest, he temporarily turned his command over to Col. Philip N. Luckett.

While Ford was otherwise occupied in running the conscription service, the Confederate authorities made a shambles of his carefully constructed frontier organization. When Col. Charles G. Torkelin, the new commander appointed by the governor, arrived in the Rio Grande country, he immediately mustered out all of Ford's Texans who didn't wish to join the regular Confederate Army. This move so weakened the Rio Grande district's defensive capabilities that the federals were able to make small-scale landings all along the Texas coast, from Sabina City to Aransas Pass, from Corpus Christi to Galveston. In the fall of 1862, they launched a major offensive, bombarding Galveston harbor, destroying coastal fortifications at Sabine Pass, and landing troops to occupy Beaumont. Federal gunboats sailed into Galveston harbor, leading the way for the Union troops who would occupy the port city. Brownsville and Fort Brown fell to the federal advance, which also threatened Laredo.

Before the defenses of the Rio Grande District fell apart, Capt. John R. Baylor took most of Ford's 2nd Texas off adventuring into the southwest, where he linked up with three regiments commanded by Confederate Brig. Gen. Henry H. Sibley. Together they attempted to secure Colorado, New Mexico, and Arizona for the Confederacy. Baylor should have considered what had happened to the Texans during the expedition to Mier and in the Carbajal uprising. Foreign adventures, long supply lines, and unreliable reinforcements almost always ended in disaster for the Rangers.

Several large Union forces moved in from California and Colorado to oppose Baylor's Rangers and Sibley's Confederates in two major battles. The federals first destroyed a Confederate supply train at the battle of Apache Canyon in New Mexico on March 26, 1862. Two days later they ambushed Sibley and Baylor at Glorietta Pass. Cut to pieces in the fierce battle, sometimes called the "Gettysburg of the West" because it put an end to Confederate expansionist dreams, the pitiful remnants of the 2nd Texas and Sibley's command were forced to retreat through miles of arid, rugged country to escape.

Ford was angered by the shortsighted way in which the Confederates had handled the 2nd Texas,

but that wouldn't prevent him from returning to Confederate service to clean up the mess they'd left him. He had not yet led his last campaign in the service of the Lone Star.

The Frontier Regiment

As the 2nd Texas fell apart under Confederate command, Gov. Francis Lubbock realized that the northern frontier would need a replacement for the 1st Texas when its one-year enlistment expired. In January 1862, the state created that replacement, the Frontier Regiment. It consisted of nine companies that would serve at the frontier posts closest to the counties from where they were recruited, and a tenth company recruited directly by the governor, which would patrol the area where it was most needed.

By the time the 1st Texas Mounted Riflemen

A portrait of Texas Governor Francis Lubbock by William Henry Huddle.
Texas State Library & Archives Commission

TEXAS RANGERS.

ATTENTION!

DO NOT WAIT TO BE DRAFTED.

The undersigned having been authorized by his Excellency, the Governor, to raise a company of Rangers, under the provisions of an act entitled "An act to provide for the protection of the frontier of Texas," and approved Dec. 21, 1861, has been granted the privilege to receive men from any portion of the State, with a view to select the very best materia the country affords, that efficient service may be rendered.

The act requires each man to furnish his own horse, arms and accoutrements, and I need not say that I wish them to be of the best kind obtainable---double-barreled shot guns, light rifles and six-shooters, if possible.

The pay offered by the State Government is very liberal and equal to the most favored troops in the service---equal to the pay of any troops of the same class in the Confederate Army.

All persons desirous of availing themselves of this last opportunity of serving their State, are invited to rendezvous at Concrete, De Witt co., on the Guadalupe r.ver, on the last day of February, 1862, for the purpose of enrollment and organization the following day, from which time they will be provided for by the Government.   JOHN J. DIX.

McMullen Co., Feb. 11, 1862.

A Civil War era recruiting poster, February 11, 1862, urging Texans to sign up for the Texas Ranger Frontier Regiment. The Texas state government enlisted these Rangers for frontier defense despite a complete lack of support from the central Confederate government. *UT Institute of Texan Cultures at San Antonio/UT Archives, Texas Ranger Scrapbook*

doning Camp Jackson, some of the forts farther west, the outer settlements, and all of Clay County. The Rangers consolidated along a line at the western edge of Central Texas and stationed the bulk of their forces between Fort Belknap and the Red River station, the major route taken by Kiowa and Comanche war parties on their raids into Texas. For the first time, because of diminished resources and support, the Rangers were forced to give up territory they'd claimed from the Indians.

In February 1863, Governor Lubbock reorganized the regiment by allowing the men to exercise the time-honored right

mustered out in April 1862, Frontier Regiment companies took station at eighteen camps and forts from the Red River to the Rio Grande. The remainder of the former 2nd Texas recruited by Rip Ford made up the required tenth company. The Frontier Regiment would serve through three enlistment periods until the end of the war in 1865. It began one thousand strong, but by the end of the war, the remnants under Lt. Col. Buck Barry's command mustered less than three hundred Rangers.

The Frontier Regiment's deployment pulled it back about fifty miles from the previous frontier, aban-

of Rangers to elect their own officers. They replaced the ineffective Col. James N. Norris with James E. McCord, elected Buck Barry as lieutenant colonel, and chose W. J. Alexander as major. Colonel McCord, who had previously served as the first lieutenant for Capt. Edward Burleson's company in 1860 and as a scout for Col. William Dalrymple's Texas Ranger regiment in 1861, proved to be an able leader.

His second in command, Buck Barry, was a veteran Ranger who had served in the Mexican War and had fought Indians in Texas for years. Between them, the two experienced officers whipped the reorganized

Big Tree, a Kiowa chief, photo by William S. Soule.
UT Institute of Texan Cultures at San Antonio/Barker Texas History Center, University of Texas

two hundred stolen horses. By the winter of 1862 to 1863, however, the Comanche and Kiowa had learned the pattern of the thin Ranger patrols and began to slip by them. Their raids increased in ferocity and daring, and in February 1863, a large war party defeated a Frontier Regiment company sent to pursue it. At the instigation of federal forces and Kansas guerrillas in the Indian territories, the Kiowa and Comanche also began stealing cattle and other supplies, which they traded to the federals for modern weapons, ammunition, and good horses. For the first time since Jack Hays supplied his men with Paterson revolvers, the Comanche and Kiowa had mounts and weapons equal to those used by the Rangers.

On July 19, on the Clear Fork of the Brazos, Capt. M. B. Lloyd and fifteen men engaged an equal number of Indians in a short, deadly cavalry battle. The Texans lost one man and four were wounded, but they defeated the Indians. Most of the engagements the Frontier Regiment fought in 1863 occurred in this fashion, a number of small fights that nonetheless discouraged Comanche and Kiowa raiders to some extent. In a relatively short time, McCord's Rangers engaged the enemy in more successful battles than had McCulloch's 1st Texas, recapturing more stolen horses and cutting short more Comanche raids.

Frontier Regiment into the best fighting condition possible under the circumstances.

Despite supply and equipment shortages, low morale, and a lack of munitions, the Frontier Regiment managed in its first six months to kill twenty-one hostiles in combat and to recapture over

Although McCord planned to mount a major expedition to strike at the Indian strongholds in the north in the fall of 1863, the Rangers were forced to turn some of their attention from fighting Indians to the onerous duty of chasing down deserters and draft

Satanta, or White Bear, a Kiowa chief, photo by William S. Soule.
UT Institute of Texan Cultures at San Antonio/Barker Texas History Center, University of Texas

evaders. The number of deserters increased as the Confederate war effort faltered and federal troops pushed deeper into Arkansas and the Indian Territory, retaking territory from the Confederates. Bands of outlaws, deserters, angry Unionist draft evaders, and guerrillas began to use the frontier and Indian Territory as hideouts and staging areas for raids into the Texas settlements.

Like the frontier Ranger companies that preceded it, the Frontier Regiment was originally designed to fight Indians. Their willingness to face new enemies created by the Civil War heralded the first major shift in focus of the basic Ranger mission from military operations to law enforcement. For years to come, the Rangers would continue to fight Indians and to guard against border incursions from Mexico, but from 1863 on, their mission would never again be purely one of frontier defense.

A Forlorn Hope

The Texas Mounted Riflemen and the Frontier Regiment were only the beginning of a succession of Ranger units raised by Texas in defiance of Confederate apathy toward frontier defense (see "The Texas Rangers of the Confederacy"). In 1863, Col. James Bourland's Texas Cavalry, also known as the Border Regiment, assembled five hundred men specifically to combat the Indian menace in the Red River country. As the Confederate brigadier general in command of the Northern Sub-District, Henry McCulloch used promises of amnesty to recruit former deserters for the "Brush Battalion." Bourland's Borderers proved invaluable in the fight against the Indians, but the Brush Battalion eventually became so troublesome that McCulloch was forced to disband it.

As the Confederacy crumbled, the Texans fell back on the militia system to form the Frontier Organization. Under the last Confederate governor of Texas, Pendleton Murrah, the state reorganized and strengthened the defense forces by drafting the resi-

dents of the frontier counties into old-fashioned minutemen or volunteer Ranger units. Each county provided a company of no less than twenty-five and no more than sixty-five men to the new Frontier Organization. The effected counties included the entire western half of settled Texas, from the Red River to the Rio Grande, from the western frontier to the edge of the Central region. Although the major of each region wasn't expected to keep more than one-fourth of his men on duty at any given time, the entire force could be called out in emergencies.

The governor appointed a major for each of three subdistricts of the western frontier: William Quayle for the 1st Frontier District in the north; veteran Texas Ranger commander George B. Erath for the 2nd Frontier District in the Central region; and James M. Hunter for the 3rd Frontier District in the south. Of a muster strength of about four thousand men, one thousand would be on duty at any given time. One company in the 1st Frontier District was made up of forty-five Tonkawa Indians, commanded by their chief, Castile.

Made up almost exclusively of old men, boys, and former Confederate soldiers who had been mustered out because of wounds or illness, the companies of the Frontier Organization represented the last, forlorn hope for the forgotten frontier. Through the long, dark years of the Reconstruction, the local companies it created would nurture the last spark of the Texas Ranger tradition, preserving it for the day when the Frontier Battalion would reclaim it.

The Cavalry of the West Reborn

In a December 22, 1863, letter to Rip Ford, the Confederate district commander of Texas, Gen. J. B. "Prince" Magruder, outlined a plan to repulse the federal troops who had invaded the coast to take Galveston, Brownsville, and Fort Brown. He asked Ford to take part in this plan. Ford gladly left his despised post with the Conscription Service to raise a new regiment for action in the Rio Grande country.

THE TEXAS RANGERS OF THE CONFEDERACY

This list shows the series of units that served as Texas Rangers, or in a Ranger capacity, on the frontier during the Civil War:

Enlistment Term	Unit Designation/District	Commanding Officers	Strength
Dec. 1860–Mar. 1861	Texas Ranger Regiment, State of Texas, Northern Indian Frontier	Col. William C. Dalrymple, Capt. John R. Baylor	500
Feb. 1861–April 1861	Texas Ranger Company, by authority of the Committee of Public Safety, Béxar and Central Texas region	Capt. Benjamin McCulloch	100
Feb. 1861–April 1861	Texas Ranger Company, by authority of the Committee of Public Safety, Northern Indian Frontier	Capt. Henry E. McCulloch	200
Feb. 1861–April 1861	Texas Ranger Company, by authority of the Committee of Public Safety, Rio Grande District	Col. J. S. "Rip" Ford	200
April 1861–April 1862	1st Regiment, Texas Mounted Riflemen, state forces in Confederate service, Northern Indian Frontier	Col. Henry E. McCulloch, Lt. Col. Thomas C. Frost, Maj. Edward Burleson, Jr. Maj. James "Buck" Barry	1,000
April 1861–Sept. 1861	2nd Regiment, Texas Mounted Riflemen, state forces in Confederate service, Rio Grande District	Col. J. S. "Rip" Ford, Col. John R. Baylor, Maj. Ed Waller	1,000
April 1862–Feb. 1863	Texas Rangers, Frontier Regiment (1st enlistment), Confederate State of Texas	Col. James N. Norris, Lt. Col. Alfred Obenchain, Maj. James E. McCord	1,200
Feb. 1863–March 1864	Texas Rangers, Frontier Regiment (2nd enlistment), Confederate State of Texas	Col. James E. McCord, Lt. Col. James "Buck" Barry, Maj. W. J. Alexander	1,000

Enlistment Term	Unit Designation/District	Commanding Officers	Strength
Aug. 1863–May 1865	Texas Cavalry Border Regiment in Confederate service, Northern Indian frontier and Indian Territory	Col. James Bourland, Lt. Col. John R. Diamond, Maj. C. L. Roff	500
Nov. 1863–May 1865	The Brush Battalion irregulars in Confederate service, Northern Sub-District	Brig. Gen. Henry E. McCulloch, Maj. John R. Diamond, Capt. John R. Baylor	500
Jan. 1864–June 1865	Texas Rangers, Frontier Organization, Confederate State of Texas 1st District, Northwest	Brig. Gen. J. W. Throckmorton, Maj. William Quayle	1,400
Jan. 1864–June 1865	Texas Rangers, Frontier Organization, Confederate State of Texas 2nd District, Central West	Maj. George B. Erath	1,400
Jan. 1864–June 1865	Texas Rangers, Frontier Organization, Confederate State of Texas 1st District, Southwest	Brig. Gen. J. D. McAdoo, Maj. John H. Brown, Maj. James Hunter	1,200
March 1864–May 1865	Ford's 2nd Texas Cavalry, Confederate State of Texas Rio Grande District	Col. John S. Ford	1,500
April 1864–May 1865	Texas Rangers Frontier Regiment/Battalion (3rd enlistment), Confederate State of Texas	Lt. Col. James "Buck" Barry, Capt. Henry Fossett	300

Ford experienced great difficulty in securing adequate supplies and arms for his troops, but he was accustomed to overcoming that kind of obstacle. By March 1864, Ford had managed to recruit and provision enough men to begin operations. A number of the volunteers were too old or too young for regular Confederate service, but the Ranger leader applied the honored name of the Cavalry of the West to this force, his last major command. He coordinated operations with Confederate forces already in place, adding the existing forces under Col. Santos Benavides, Lt. Col. Daniel Showalter, and Col. George H. Giddings to his command. With 1,300 men, mostly volunteers, Ford moved out of San Antonio and headed for the border.

Within a week of their departure, Ford's regiment reached San Fernando west of Corpus Christi, where they joined with a Confederate force under Maj. Mat

Nolan. As a youngster, Nolan had served as a bugler with the U.S. forces in the Mexican War; he'd later served as lieutenant in Ford's command during the Cortina War. Before Ford's arrival, Nolan's command had fought a major battle with Cecilio Balerio's Mexican guerrillas near Patricio.

By the time Ford's cavalry established its base camp on the King ranch, Ford received reports of a Union attempt to invade Laredo. Confederate forces under Colonel Benavides, along with local companies, managed to muster less than one hundred men to face more than two hundred Union regulars. Benavides's force held off the Union troops until nightfall. During the night Confederate reinforcements arrived, and after a sharp fight the next day, the Union force retreated.

On March 30, Ford's command began its march to Brownsville; they reached Laredo on April 17. They converged on Rio Grande City, where Ford set up headquarters at the old Ringgold Barracks. There they were joined by troops from the 4th Arizona Regiment and some of the old 2nd Texas Riflemen. The Ranger leader's fame induced a number of men who had deserted from Confederate units to leave their refuges in Mexico to join him. Ford accepted these men and other volunteers, including some French artillerymen and some Mexican nationals who were fleeing the French Imperialists, all without questioning their past actions.

Between his cavalry unit and the other Confederate units attached to his command, he had just over 1,500 men to face the estimated 7,000 federal troops commanded by Gen. Francis J. Herron. Leaving the artillery and other dismounted troops at the Ringgold Barracks, he took his cavalry on a scout toward Brownsville in June. He stuck to the river road because it was the only area with sufficient grass and water to sustain his horses in the drought-stricken countryside. During this scout, he learned that the federals had decided to pull the major portion of their troops back to the coast, leaving a force only somewhat larger than his own to defend Fort Brown.

Gen. John B. Magruder was the Confederate district commander of Texas.
Dictionary of American Portraits

The first battle of the campaign took place on June 25 on the road at Carricitos ranch, south of Las Ruicas, as Ford mounted a major scout in force. The advance element of Ford's cavalry, led by Capt. James Dunn, a veteran of the Vásquez incident of 1842, ran into a troop of federals commanded by Capt. Philip G. Temple. The federals killed Dunn and several of his men in the first minutes of the fight, but Colonel Showalter immediately moved to support Dunn's embattled company. As Capt. Refugio Benavides and Capt. Thomas C. Cater attacked, the tide of the battle turned. Advancing through the chaparral into the outskirts of the village, using the *jacales* and the brick walls as cover while they fired, the Texans drove the federals back until they broke. Captain Temple was wounded in the retreat; most of his men escaped across the river into Mexico.

Despite the death of Captain Dunn, it was an overwhelming victory. The battle set 200 of Ford's Texans against a well-armed force of 250 Union regulars, which included two companies of Texas Unionists from the troop commanded by Col. E. J. Davis, future governor of Texas during Reconstruction. The Union troops suffered comparatively heavy casualties to the three killed and four wounded on the Confederate side. Ford's men took thirty-six prisoners and captured two wagon loads of badly needed supplies and munitions. Ford heard reports that only eight soldiers from the entire Union force managed to make their way back to Fort Brown.

Ford fully expected to meet stronger resistance along the way, but even though the Texans passed within twenty-four miles of the main Union force at Brownsville and stopped to rest for a day at Edinburg, the federals declined the opportunity to do battle. The scout force returned to the Ringgold Barracks without further incident, where Ford and his company commanders began preparing for their assault on Fort Brown.

For the Cavalry of the West, the fight at Carricitos was only the beginning of the offensive. The task of driving the invaders into the sea still lay ahead.

The Cooke County Raid

As the Cavalry of the West moved against Union troops in the Rio Grande district, Henry McCulloch did his best to meet the demands of his appointment as commander of the Northern Sub-District. His Confederate force of about two thousand regulars was stretched thin, fighting guerrillas and renegades, arresting deserters, and supporting the dwindling combat forces in the Indian Territory. He had no troops left to fight the Indians, who were waging their own major offensive on the counties of Northwest Texas, riding under the Comanche moon to kill and burn.

In October 1863, a Comanche raiding party of about twenty-five warriors headed toward the Indian Territory after killing several settlers, kidnapping children, and stealing cattle and horses in Montague and Cooke Counties. A company of the Border Battalion commanded by Capt. F. M. Totty cut the war party's trail. They were joined in the scout by a detachment from Company C of the Frontier Regiment from the Red River station. When they caught up with the Indians, the Rangers attacked, killing several of the raiders. One Ranger lost his life in the fight.

As the two organizations began to coordinate their actions, they became more effective. As part of the Confederate command, Colonel Bourland's men could scout into the Indian Territory, whereas Lt. Colonel Barry's state troops were limited to specific pursuits. The Ranger leaders recruited spies from among the friendly tribes to scout the movements of the Kiowa and Comanche. Bourland kept one of his companies on station deep in the Indian Territory, at Fort Arbuckle, and two others at the Red River north of Clay County, the main entry point used by the raiders. Barry pulled in his scouts and gathered his men so he could respond to a major raid in regimental strength. Acting on intelligence gathered by Bourland's spies in the Indian Territory, the Border Battalion, the Frontier Regiment, and the Confederate Chickasaw Battalion began preparing to defend against a major raid that they knew was coming.

Unfortunately, the Comanche moved before the Rangers finished establishing the planned patrol line. On December 21, the Comanche began their biggest raid since the days of the Republic. Three hundred warriors crossed the river into Montague County near Red River Station, then struck the homesteads and ranches near the Illinois Bend of the river. The Comanche had come to Texas not just to raid for cattle or horses, but to kill. They burned several ranches and outposts, killing the occupants, then moved swiftly on toward larger targets.

Capt. James Rowland, commander of the Frontier Regiment company at Red River Station, set out with thirty men to meet the attack. The Comanche crossed back over the Red River at Mountain Creek, outdistancing the Rangers. Word of the raid had spread; close behind Rowland's company, Capt. Samuel P. Patton's company of twenty-five men rode from Gainesville to the river crossing.

The Comanche crossed back into Texas and into

"THE BONNIE BLUE FLAG"

Terry's Texas Rangers' flag. *Texas State Library & Archives Commission*

This song was the unofficial Confederate anthem of the Texas troops in the Civil War, the favorite marching tune of Terry's Texas Rangers and Hood's Texas Brigade.

> *We are a band of brothers and native to the soil*
> *Fighting for the property we gained by honest toil*
> *And when our rights were threatened, the cry rose near and far*
> *Hurrah for the Bonnie Blue Flag that bears a single star!*
>
> *Hurrah! Hurrah!*
> *For Southern rights, hurrah!*
> *Hurrah for the Bonnie Blue Flag that bears a single star.*
>
> *As long as the Union was faithful to her trust*
> *Like friends and brethren, kind were we, and just*
> *But now, when Northern treachery attempts our rights to mar*
> *We hoist on high the Bonnie Blue Flag that bears a single star.*
>
> *Hurrah! Hurrah!*
> *For Southern rights, hurrah!*
> *Hurrah for the Bonnie Blue Flag that bears a single star.*

First gallant South Carolina nobly made the stand
Then came Alabama and took her by the hand
Next, quickly Mississippi, Georgia, and Florida
All raised on high the Bonnie Blue Flag that bears a single star.

Hurrah! Hurrah!
For Southern rights, hurrah!
Hurrah for the Bonnie Blue Flag that bears a single star.

Ye men of valor gather round the banner of the right
Texas and fair Louisiana join us in the fight
Davis, our loved President, and Stephens statesmen are
Now rally round the Bonnie Blue Flag that bears a single star.

And here's to brave Virginia, the Old Dominion State.
With the young Confederacy at length has linked her fate.
Impelled by her example, now other States prepare
To hoist on high the Bonnie Blue flag that bears a single star.

Then here's to our Confederacy, strong we are and brave,
Like patriots of old we'll fight, our heritage to save.
And rather than submit to shame, to die we would prefer
So cheer for the Bonnie Blue flag that bears a single star.

Then cheer, boys, cheer, raise a joyous shout
For Arkansas and North Carolina now have both gone out;
And let another rousing cheer for Tennessee be given
The single star of the Bonnie Blue Flag has grown to be eleven!

Cooke County. They first attacked the Elmore settlement, shooting and burning as they rode. The fleeing settlers and the Ranger companies could track the war party's movements by the plumes that rose from burning homesteads. This time, the Indians slowed down a bit to plunder the houses, steal horses, and take captives, moving to consolidate their loot at Elm Creek, just six miles west of Gainesville. They stopped there to plunder the Bonner home and set it on fire.

The Rangers had picked up citizen volunteers along the way, which slowed them down even more than their tired horses. The Comanche had brought their *remuda* with them, and had also captured horses to switch out, so they moved more quickly. When the Rangers rode out ahead of the volunteers, they caught up with the Comanche ten miles northwest of Gainesville, on a ridge near the Potter settlement.

Although they were vastly outnumbered, the Rangers formed up for a charge. The Comanche countercharged, splitting their force into two wings to attack the Rangers on both flanks. Rowland knew that he couldn't allow the Indians to surround his command, so he halted his charge and turned his men to run for cover. The Comanche, who were armed with good rifles, shot several Texans from their saddles. Most of the company made it to a split-rail fence that gave them basic cover. The Comanche, who had learned how costly it could be to attack once the Rangers got into a defensive position, withdrew from the field.

Rowland's men and their horses were exhausted; they'd suffered much heavier casualties than the Comanche. According to Bourland's report, the war party had killed more than fifteen settlers, had taken several young women captive, had burned ten homes, and had stolen a large number of horses. Major James J. Diamond and the other Ranger companies arrived too late to reinforce Rowland and Patton, and although hundreds of Texans joined in the pursuit, the Comanche crossed the Red River and disappeared into the Wichita Mountains.

Fire and Murder from the North

In the summer of 1864, Colonel Bourland spread his Border Battalion thin to take in the additional area vacated by Buck Barry's men, who were on detached duty in the south, and the disbanded Brush Battalion. He attempted to compensate for this by working closely with Major Quayle and the 1st District organization. He was also assisted by Chief Castile's Tonkawa scout company.

Also during that summer, the men under George B. Erath in the 2nd Frontier District fought numerous small-company actions against the Indians through the rolling prairies, canyons, and hill country near northern forks of the Brazos River. On August 8, a scout party from the Frontier Organization company stationed at Eastland commanded by Lt. Singleton Gilbert cut the trail of an Indian horse-stealing party. The scouts tracked the raiders to Ellison Springs, some miles west of the town of Gorman, then sent word back to Lieutenant Gilbert. Gilbert led several of his men out to join the scout, which raised the Texan force to about fifteen men against thirty-five Comanche.

Lieutenant Gilbert ordered a charge; the Comanche gunfire killed him and one other Ranger, wounding three more. Despite the loss of their commander, the men of his company continued to pursue the Indians, recovering some of the fifty horses they'd captured near Stephenville. The Indians eventually outdistanced the Eastland company and split into two groups. A few days later the main group, twenty Indians, ran into an eight-man squad of 2nd District Rangers commanded by Sgt. A. D. Miller. Miller's men pursued the Indians in a fifteen-mile chase, and in a battle that lasted for an hour, they killed two Indians and wounded several others. The Rangers suffered no casualties in the fight, and they recaptured seventy-three horses and several pack loads of other loot.

In the fall, poor health led Major Quayle to resign from the 1st Frontier District post. He recommended as his replacement James W. Throckmorton of McKinney, the man who had spoken out so eloquently against secession in 1861. Unlike some other antisecessionists, Throckmorton had continued to serve Texas in the war effort under the Confederacy. As a member of the legislature, he'd regularly served on the Committee for Frontier Defense.

Throckmorton took command just in time for the 1st District's first real Indian fight. Because he'd planned to attend the second legislative session, he'd not yet traveled to the frontier when the Indians struck. The Indians picked a perfect time to ride out under the Comanche moon. McCord was in the south, Quayle had resigned but was still in command, Throckmorton had not yet arrived, Buck Barry's company was still on detached duty on the coast, and Bourland's Borderers were running themselves ragged trying to cover the gaps. The Cooke County raid of the previous December would pale beside the raid on Elm Creek.

For several months, the Comanche and Kiowa had been raiding Union convoys destined for New Mexico and California, threatening to cut the Union supply line to the far West. The Kiowa and Comanche needed horses to replace those destroyed by Kit Carson's Union artillery in the Battle of Adobe Walls, especially if they were going to continue fighting the Union forces that guarded the western wagon trails. Texas was a natural target for a raid, and the Comanche enjoyed nothing more than stirring up a little trouble with the Texans. On October 12, 1864, under the light of a full autumn moon, the Comanche war chief Little Buffalo led a combined Kiowa and Comanche force of more than seven hundred men across the Red River into Texas. They moved south into Young County and camped several miles north of Fort Belknap, there to await the morning to begin their attack on the community near the fort. The Indians had somehow managed to avoid every Ranger patrol set out to watch for them. The settlers and defense forces were completely unaware that a Plains Indian army had invaded Texas, until they attacked.

On October 13, the Indians moved into the Elm Creek area south of the Brazos River, then split up into several smaller bands. At noon, these groups began to hit the settlement clusters, farms, and isolated ranches along the river. Plumes of smoke from burning buildings soon alerted the settlers along the Brazos River to the raiders' presence. The settlers began retreating to two strong points — the Bragg ranch, which was built in stockade fashion of solid logs with a palisade surrounding it, and Fort Murrah (named after the governor), another ranch stockade that was even more heavily constructed and protected.

A group of women and children who were cut off from these strong points took refuge in the two-story house at the Fitzpatrick ranch. Indians broke down the door as Millie Durkin, age twenty-one, fired at them with her shotgun in an attempt to hold them off. The Indians killed and scalped her, which was actually a sign of respect because she'd taken the role of a warrior. They then tortured and killed several of the other occupants, including an infant and a seven-year-old boy. This group decided to take its captives and leave the fighting to the other bands. They tied five children and the two surviving women, Mrs. Fitzpatrick and Mary Johnson, to stolen horses and headed for the Pease River, riding for two days without stopping to make camp. When they noticed that Mrs. Fitzpatrick's thirteen-year-old son was too ill to ride, they burned him to death in a brush bonfire, forcing his mother to watch as he died.

The twenty men of Border Battalion Company D, commanded by a lieutenant named Carson, were in camp some thirteen miles west of Fort Belknap when they heard of the assault. They immediately rode to the Bragg ranch stockade, where they ran into a large band of warriors who had laid siege to the fortress. Twenty Rangers against three hundred Indians was pretty long odds; the Rangers had to turn and ride for their lives. The Indians killed five Rangers in the running battle and wounded several of their horses. Despite their losses, the Rangers managed to beat the Indians to the McCoy ranch. They picked up the civilians who were hiding at the ranch, then crossed the Brazos River to the relative safety of the Murrah outpost.

The civilians at the Bragg ranch managed to hold off the Comanche and Kiowa in six desperate hours of fighting. Finally, after a rifle bullet fired from the Bragg stockade killed Little Buffalo, the Indians decided to break off the siege. They pulled in their smaller raiding parties and moved back toward the river. The civilians and Rangers at Murrah fully expected to be attacked in force at dawn, but the Indians had decided to leave. The Texans at Murrah were able to observe two large groups of Indians, one to the east and one to the west, as they passed by, driving their stolen cattle and horses. One Ranger and one civilian volunteered to make the twelve-mile ride to Fort Belknap for help, an act of considerable daring. The two frontiersmen avoided the Indians, who were busy celebrating their successful raid.

There were only twenty-five men at Fort Belknap because the rest of the Rangers had recently left on a scout patrol — looking for Indians, no less! They'd already learned of the attack and had sent word to Major Quayle in Decatur. Quayle, who was still in poor health, dragged himself into his saddle and pulled together as many volunteers, Frontier Organization men, soldiers, and Rangers as he could find, about two hundred men in all. They made the eighty-mile ride to Fort Belknap at top speed, but they were too late to join in the fighting. The news of the raid didn't reach Bourland's headquarters in Gainesville until the morning of October 15. The Border Battalion commander immediately dispatched three of his four companies stationed in the Red River country to Fort Belknap to aid the 1st District men.

Most of the Ranger forces arrived too late. The Indian expedition declined to make a serious attack on the Murrah stockade. Instead, they gathered up their loot and captives and began moving for the Red River at a fast pace. Captain White's Company D of the Border Battalion and some volunteers, a force of about sixty men, chased after the Indian force, but the raiders had a good head start. Even burdened as they were by their loot, they were able to lose their pursuers after about a hundred miles. Captain White reported that his men were able to pick off some straggling raiders.

The raid was a complete success, from the Indian viewpoint. They'd killed at least five Rangers in battle; they'd taken a huge haul of horses and cattle. They'd killed and scalped seven settlers and had taken seven women and children captive. If they'd intended to sow terror in the hearts of the North Texans, they'd certainly accomplished that goal with their brutal murders of the women and children who had taken refuge at the Fitzpatrick ranch. They'd slipped past the Texans' patrols, they'd hit their targets, they'd accom-plished their objectives, and they'd made good their escape.

For the Texas forces, it was an almost complete failure — they were a day late and a dollar short, as the old saying goes. Again, Bourland and Quayle attempted to raise support for a mission in force to strike at the Comanche in their Indian Territory strongholds. Once again, the lack of government support caused plans for retaliatory raids to come to nothing — there would be no major Indian-fighting expeditions across the Red River until well after the Civil War. Throckmorton took command as Quayle stepped down; Barry's companies came back from the coast to fill out the rest of their time chasing deserters through the brush country.

The Dove Creek Fight

In their last year of service, Major Erath's men of the 2nd District also spent more of their time chasing deserters than in fighting Indians. The last major Indian battle the Texans fought in the Confederate period took place on January 8, 1865, and it was a tragedy nearly equivalent to Lamar's campaign against the Cherokee. Second District scouts mistook a large group of Kickapoo Indians camped at Dove Creek for a hostile war party. The Kickapoo, an entire village of men, women, and children, were attempting to pass through Texas in order to migrate to Mexico. They weren't looking for trouble, but they were armed with Enfield rifles and willing to use them to defend themselves.

At the Battle of Dove Creek, near the Middle Concho River, a combined force of Confederates, Tonkawa, and 2nd District men assaulted the Kickapoo in what was essentially a perfect defensive position. The Kickapoo spotted the Texans well before the attack. Their warriors dug in rifle pits along the banks of the creek, and they set up their main camp in the protection of the brush and trees. When Capt. Silas Totten's Rangers charged through the water, the Kickapoo riflemen mowed them down. Capt. Henry

Fossett's cavalry attacked the horse herd from the opposite side of the camp. As the cavalry rounded up the horses and started to drive them off, Kickapoo warriors rose up out of the brush to ambush them. The Indians used their rifles to deadly effect, cutting the cavalry down and recovering their horses. Twenty-six Texans were killed and as many were wounded; the Kickapoo lost eleven warriors and had seven wounded. The Kickapoo, who had tried several times to stop the battle by signaling to the Texans that they weren't Comanche or Kiowa, became the implacable enemies of the Texans. In the years to come, they would launch a number of raids into Texas from their Mexican stronghold.

Back in the 1st Frontier District, General Throckmorton made a final important contribution on the part of the Frontier Organization, this time a diplomatic action. Leaving Maj. John W. Lane in command of the 1st Frontier District, Throckmorton traveled to the Indian Territory in May 1865 to a major conference of the tribes near Elm Springs on the Washita River. He managed to meet with the chiefs of all but one of the major bands of Kiowa and Comanche. In this meeting and in subsequent meetings in May and August, he convinced the Indians to sign treaties; in trades and in good faith gestures, the Indians returned most of their white captives, including some that were taken in the Elm Creek raid.

Throckmorton was an effective and able leader. He might have pulled the entire Frontier Organization together into the defense force it had been designed to become, but he never got the chance. When he returned to his headquarters at Decatur after his successful trip into the Indian Territory, he found that the Confederate authority of the Trans-Mississippi District had surrendered to the U.S. government on May 26, two weeks before.

Relieved of his command of the district, Henry McCulloch left his headquarters at Bonham on May 28 to return to his home at Seguin. Several Rangers accompanied him to protect him from the renegades and deserters who had sworn to kill him.

Once the Union took control of Texas, those who had served in the forces under the Confederacy would no longer be allowed to bear arms in their own defense. Frontier defense would be left to a Union army more concerned with punishing former Rebels than in protecting those Rebels against the Indians. The Kiowa-Comanche alliance would resume its assault by the end of the summer of 1865, bringing blood and fire to Texas under the Comanche moon.

The Last Battle

Rip Ford met with much greater success in his campaign against the federal forces in the Rio Grande district. By July 22, 1864, Ford had moved his army to within eleven miles of Fort Brown. At the Ebonal ranch, eight hundred Texans defeated a larger force of Union troops and drove them back to the city limits of Brownsville. As Ford wrote of his men, "...they raised the Texas yell and went in." Wherever the Cavalry of the West attacked, the federal troops retreated.

On July 25, Ford's men moved on Brownsville and engaged the Union troops in heavy fighting within the outskirts of the city. By July 29, the federals evacuated Brownsville and Fort Brown, falling back toward their strong point on the island of Brazos Santiago. General Herron had been ordered to send most of his troops back to that point from which they could board Union naval vessels; the trooops were needed because the major battles in the east were draining the Union's resources. The Union had decided not to make a serious fight for South Texas, at least for the time being. Herron's force still outnumbered Ford's, and the Union commander had a decided advantage in artillery, but as Ford said, "They were too weak to attack us."

Although he could barely sit upright in his saddle because of an attack of malaria, Ford rode with his troops into Fort Brown on July 30. He found the fort's defenses in good condition, but he couldn't spare any artillery for the garrison he left there. He intended to use all of his resources in an immediate attack on

General Herron's forces that were camped downriver. Ford sent Captain Refugio Benavides to scout the enemy's forward defenses, and as he wrote, "Benavides executed the order, struck a party of the enemy, attacked, and drove them."

That was the order of the day — "strike the enemy and drive them." The federals retreated slowly, but each time they stopped, the Texans hit them. On August 4, Captain Robertson's company attacked Herron's troops fifteen miles downriver from Brownsville, killing two and taking two prisoners. Shortly after this fight, the remaining federal troops withdrew to Brazos Santiago, leaving the Texas mainland to the victorious Cavalry of the West.

Ford and his troops spent the next few months maintaining their siege of Brazos Santiago and occasionally skirmishing with the ever-present Cortina, who conspired with a few Union officers to mount attacks from Mexico. The federals attempted several times to break out of the siege, with Cortina's assistance. On September 9, 600 federals and 300 of Cortina's Mexicans engaged a force of 370 men under Colonel Giddings in a battle at Palmito ranch. The Confederates defeated the Union advance guard, killing eighty to ninety men in the first stage of the battle; some of the survivors retreated into Mexico. The rest of Ford's command arrived to reinforce Giddings, then hit the main body of troops further downriver at San Martin ranch. Captain Benavides and Capt. W. H. D. Carrington led their men into a charge into the center of the federal lines as other companies hit the enemy flanks. The combined Union-Mexican force broke and ran, some of them tossing aside their weapons and supplies. Ford estimated the federal and Mexican casualty list for the battle at 550 men killed. Only three Texans were killed in the fight.

Giddings caught up with the main body of the federals as they neared Brazos Santiago, but he allowed them to withdraw when they were heavily reinforced from the federal position. The Texans followed the federals all the way to Boca Chica, the river channel between the mainland and the island. The Confederate commander of the district, Gen. James E. Slaughter, later approached Ford with a plan to attack Brazos Santiago across the Boca Chica, and Ford agreed to try it. In November, he led 1,500 men to the river's mouth and sent out scouts to probe the enemy defenses. He eventually concluded that the enemy artillery was too well dug-in for a daylight attack to succeed. A night attack would have resulted in too many deaths from drowning, and those men who did survive the cold, rushing water of the channel would have been rendered unable to fight by the time they reached the island. An amphibious assault would have been an easy target for the federal artillery. Ford decided not to attack, thus ending the hostilities between his force and the federals for the year. He withdrew most of his forces to spend the winter at Fort Brown and Palmito ranch, leaving only a scout force to stand watch on the federals.

The final battle of the Civil War took place five weeks after Robert E. Lee surrendered the Army of Virginia to Grant at Appomattox, and it took place on Texas soil. For Rip Ford it was his last battle as the commander of the Cavalry of the West; ironically, it was a stunning Confederate victory. On May 12, a scout from Capt. John H. Robinson's company rode into Fort Brown with a report that the federals had broken out of Brazos Santiago and were advancing upriver to assault Fort Brown. Ford ordered Robinson to fight a delaying action while the rest of the Texans gathered at Fort Brown. He sent out couriers to alert the units stationed at Palmito ranch and other camps, then informed General Slaughter of the breakout.

When Ford realized that Slaughter was commandeering wagons and horses, not preparing his men to attack, he asked the general to explain his intentions. When Slaughter replied that he intended to retreat, Ford shouted:

> You can retreat and go to hell if you wish! These are my men, and I am going to fight. I have held this place against heavy odds. If you

lose it without a fight the people of the Confederacy will hold you accountable for a base neglect of duty.

Slaughter agreed to support Ford in the fight, but the Confederate commander failed to meet Ford at the appointed staging area. Despite this, Ford and his men moved out on May 13 to intercept the Union troops at San Martín ranch. The federals, under the command of Col. T. H. Barrett, were waiting for him on the road south of the ranch — three regiments of Union regulars, including the 34th Indiana and the 62nd Colored, supported by two companies of the Texas Unionist cavalry. Ford deployed his artillery to cover and support his infantry and cavalry, then sent out several companies to flank the enemy position. For the last time, the main force of the Cavalry of the West rode directly into enemy fire.

It turned into a running battle, moving toward Palmito ranch as Ford's artillery and his cavalry charges broke the enemy lines. Captain Robinson's men cut off and captured the enemy skirmishers; as Ford's artillery and rifle companies gained the heights that overlooked the road, the fight turned into a Union retreat. Ford's cavalry drove the enemy dragoons and infantry from each strong point at which they stopped to fight. The artillery broke up enemy cavalry charges before they started. Finally, after a pursuit that ran for seven miles, Ford recalled his men. As General Slaughter arrived too late for the battle, the federals, what remained of them, retreated to Brazos Santiago.

Twelve of Ford's men were killed in winning this last, futile victory, not for the Confederacy, but for Texas. Barrett, who had disobeyed a direct order from his superiors to remain inactive, had marched out from Brazos Santiago intending to end his Civil War service with a Union victory. He'd lost 30 of his own men to the guns of the fierce Texans, and a great many more were wounded; some drowned while swimming the river to escape into Mexico. Ford's men took 113 of the federals prisoner, including members of the 62nd Colored Regiment. The black soldiers expected to be shot or returned to slavery — some of them were escaped slaves from the Austin area — but Ford's Texans showed them the same courtesy as they did the other Union prisoners of war.

The Texans found their positions reversed as the news of the Confederate surrender reached the Rio Grande country within days of the Battle of Palmito Ranch. Ford and Slaughter met with Union officers in Brownsville and Matamoros to discuss surrender terms. The Union men received them with hospitality and courtesy. Not all such meetings would be as pleasant, as other officers from the east, men who had not met the Texans on the battlefield, would march into Texas as they would into a conquered nation.

Many Confederates refused to surrender, or they fled because they feared prosecution by federal authorities for the roles they'd played in the rebellion. Shortly after the surrender, General Slaughter took a company of his men into Mexico, joining up with five hundred Missouri cavalrymen and Gen. E. Kirby Smith. As the Missourians crossed the Rio Grande, they buried their bullet-shredded battle flags in the waters of the Big River. Governor Murrah and General Magruder fled the country as well. Rip Ford, fearing that he'd be singled out for retribution, took his family to Matamoros. Although Ford shortly returned to Texas and swore an oath of loyalty to the United States, it was no longer the same country. Texas was, for all intents and purposes, a conquered nation.

The last border had been crossed; the Confederacy was no more.

~ Afterword ~

FROM THE ASHES

"In all the elements of true courage, earnestness, and activity, in ready obedience
to the orders of their chosen leaders, and in efficiency and patriotic devotion to
the public service, these different bodies of earlier Rangers were seldom equaled
and never excelled by any purely military organization in any part of the world."

— Texas Adj. Gen. W. H. King,
from *A Comprehensive History of Texas*

THE SERVICE RECORD OF THE TEXAS RANGERS OF THE EARLY
nineteenth century remains unchallenged by history. As the Defenders
of the West and the knights of the Lone Star, they served longer,
endured more rapid social changes, and exerted a deeper influence than
any other band of citizen soldiers. Their traditions of duty, honor, and sacrifice survived multifronted wars, revolutions, and chaotic political evolution

to shape the destiny of Texas and the American
West.

I found in researching the saga of the Texas
Rangers that I couldn't possibly compress 175 years of
dramatic history into a single volume. Because the
Rangers have survived through so many drastic
changes, almost any dividing point will appear to be
an arbitrary choice. I decided to break the story at the
end of the American Civil War because its devastating
social aftermath, the era of Reconstruction, came
closer to extinguishing the Texas Ranger tradition
than any other catastrophic event in their history. The
Frontier Battalion's rise from the ashes of war marked
the beginning of the most radical evolution in the

basic nature of the Texas Rangers, from citizen soldiers to peace officers.

Even though Texas was spared most of the devas-
tation suffered by the other states, the economic
depression that hit Texas after the war destroyed most
of the state's business, agriculture, and professional
systems. The Texans had lost not a single battle they
fought against the Union, and the Union commanders
who had fought against them respected the Texans,
but the radical military and political officials sent to
reclaim the Rebel state had their own agenda. After
the assassination of President Abraham Lincoln, the
Radical Republicans took control of the U.S. legislature and overpowered Lincoln's successor, President

Texas Rangers George Black and J. M. Britton of Company B in the post-Civil War Frontier Battalion.
Gonzaullas Collection, Moody Texas Ranger Memorial Library

Andrew Johnson. They set out to exact retribution for the rebellion.

In 1867, J. W. Throckmorton, the Unionist who had gone on to fight for the Confederacy and to command the 1st District Rangers, became the first legally-elected post-war governor of Texas. At the same time, the Radical Republicans passed the Reconstruction Act against President Johnson's veto. This illegal and unconstitutional piece of legislative misconduct allowed the military authorities to assume complete political control of the Southern states, including Texas. Military rule would remain in force until the Rebel states complied with all of the act's requirements for readmission to the Union. When Governor Throckmorton objected to the act on constitutional grounds and defied the U.S. authorities, Gen. Charles Griffith, the Union military commander in Texas, sent in U.S. troops under Gen. Phil Sheridan to depose the lawfully elected Texas government.

Sheridan removed from office not only Throckmorton but every Texan who opposed the Reconstruction process. Reconstruction edicts barred from service any Texan who had served in the Confederate military or had in any way played a part in the state's affairs from the Secession Convention to the Confederate surrender, including all civil officials down to the county and city level — postmasters, clerks, mayors, peace officers, and members of the local militia groups. Even to serve on a jury, a Texan was required to swear by the "ironclad oath" that he had not been involved in Confederate activity.

Except for the minority of Union loyalists who had managed to avoid conscription, the oath excluded virtually all of the male citizens of Texas from holding office or voting in state elections. This disenfranchisement destroyed the political and civil structure of the state, disrupting not only the courts and the legal system but the remaining frontier defense forces. Under Reconstruction rules, no Texan who had served in the Frontier District organization, the Frontier Regiment, the Mounted Rifles, or any other Ranger unit active from 1860 to 1866 was eligible to serve in

any official capacity. Rip Ford, Henry McCulloch, Buck Barry, and all of the other experienced Texas Rangers were stripped of their rights as citizens. They were forced to stand by and watch as the organization they had sacrificed so much to maintain was dismantled, while the frontier they had guarded with their lives was laid open to the border bandits and the fierce Comanche raiders.

The election of 1869, dominated by the Radicals, swept aside the few Conservative Republicans eligible to run, and put E. J. Davis in power as the Reconstruction governor. Davis, one of the original Unionists who had voted against secession, had spent the war leading his Texas Union cavalry in losing battles against Rip Ford in the Rio Grande district. There was no question that most Texans detested the radical policies of the Reconstruction, but the iron-fisted rule Davis exercised made him almost universally hated, even by his former Unionist colleagues. Davis responded to this enmity by pushing through legislation that extended his own term of office, postponing the next election until November 1872.

To consolidate his power, Davis designed legislation that would bring the state militia and law-enforcement agencies under his direct control. When the few Conservative Republicans and Democrats in the state senate attempted to block passage of these bills, Davis had them arrested and expelled until he had pushed through the entire series of Radical proposals, including the Police and Militia bills. Former Unionists and Conservative Republicans, including A. J. Hamilton, J. W. Throckmorton, and E. M. Pease, appealed in vain to the U.S. Congress to block Davis's unconstitutional actions. For this act of Texas patriotism, the Radical Republicans labeled them as traitors.

The Police and Militia bills allowed Davis to create his own police force, the Texas State Police, to take the place of the disenfranchised Texas Rangers. The State Police functioned as the law-enforcement arm of Reconstruction oppression, as the officers of what was essentially a police state. With a few notable

Frontier Battalion Texas Rangers on a scout through the creek bottoms at Bosque Bonito, circa 1900.
Moody Texas Ranger Memorial Library

exceptions, the activities of this organization more closely resembled the terrorist tactics of the bandits and raiders of the frontier than they did the actions of the Texas Rangers. So hated did they become that they set back law-enforcement and race relations in Texas for years.

No doubt many of the men who participated in the Reconstruction government in Texas were personally honorable. Much of what they accomplished in the enfranchisement and advancement of the former slaves was astonishingly positive, given the nature of the situation. Unfortunately, the Reconstruction process was morally and legally corrupt, not only unconstitutional but socially destructive. In such a climate of chaos, scoundrels and fanatics flourish, and the damage they do negates any constructive results that may occur during their rule. As T. R. Fehrenbach says in his history of Texas, *Lone Star*, "Even the good things were intensely unpopular, because the regime itself was universally held in contempt." Whatever good the Reconstruction government accomplished in Texas would be washed away by the explosive racial hatred and the social and economic destruction it left in its wake.

The story of the Texas Rangers could have ended at that point, were it not for those Texans who risked their lives and their freedom to preserve the tradition. Rip Ford, the men of the Frontier Organization companies, and even one officer of the State Police, Leander H. McNelly, held to the ideal, striving to serve the Lone Star as if she'd never been defeated. In the local militia companies, in the selfless actions of a few brave men, and in the hearts of those Texans who remembered their former glory, the spark endured for six long years of repression. Even though Reconstruction laws prohibited large gatherings of armed men, local companies like the Milam County

Minute Men defied these laws to fight desperate battles against Indian raiders.

When the Texans overthrew the Reconstruction government in the elections of 1873, they turned to the Texas Rangers to set things right. Answering the desperate pleas of Texas citizens, in 1874, Gov. Richard Coke and the Texas legislature created a new Texas Ranger organization, the Frontier Battalion. Originally mustered in to fight Indians on the western frontier, after the end of the Indian Wars the Frontier Battalion turned its attention to quelling civil disorder and to dealing with outlaws, bandits, and gunmen. They were the first group of Rangers actually empowered to make legal arrests in civil matters, and the first to begin the tradition of wearing the circle-star silver badges that became a Ranger trademark. The evolution of the Frontier Battalion Rangers from a paramilitary defense force into a unique band of peace officers sprang from this change in their mission.

The Frontier Battalion formed the nucleus of the Texas Ranger organization that endures to this day. As they survived so many wars, disasters, and revolutions before, the Texas Rangers endured the long, dark road of Reconstruction to emerge once more as the defenders of the Lone Star.

Appendix

IN THE LINE OF DUTY

Texas Rangers Killed in Action in the Service of the Lone Star, 1823-1865

T HIS PARTICULARLY SAD MUSTER ROLL IS INCOMPLETE AND WILL probably remain so. It's unlikely that we will ever determine the exact number of Texas Rangers killed in the line of duty, if for no other reason than the lack of hard documentation. Some early companies failed to keep complete muster rolls or to file detailed casualty reports, and some of the surviving casualty reports list only the numbers and not the names of the men

killed or wounded in action. Many records were lost to fire, accident, or neglect. For example, the trunk containing the original records Rip Ford kept of Hays's Company of Texas Mounted Rifles during their service in Central Mexico was lost, left behind on the ship that carried Hays and Ford back to Texas. Ford also sent detailed reports from Mexico to his newspaper office in Austin, but when he returned he found that those letters had been thrown out. In writing his memoirs years later, he recreated some of the information from memory. Faded memories and recollections are often the only available historical reference to the death of a Texas Ranger in combat with Indians or Mexicans.

Not all of the Texas Rangers who died while on duty did so as a result of intentional violence or violent accident. Disease, bad food, bad water, stress-related illnesses, and other hardships killed many

Rangers. During the Mexican War, yellow fever, malaria, and other ills common to the deserts, jungles, and mountains of Mexico killed more Texans and other American soldiers than did bullets and bayonets. These deaths are not listed here.

This list does not rigidly follow the standard criteria defining "in the line of duty" as it applies to peace officers. That definition doesn't quite fit the diverse nature of the services performed by Texas Rangers through their 175-year history. Because of their involvement in the Indian Wars and revolutionary strife on the Mexican border, until the 1920s Rangers performed services both military and civilian, often at the same time. Even up into the 1930s, the state government often called upon the Rangers in times of emergency to enforce martial law. This list includes those Texas Rangers killed in combat from 1823 to 1865, including the Texans who served as state troops in federal service before, during, and after the Mexican War, and as state troops under the Confederacy.

This list does not include civilian volunteers who were killed while riding with the Rangers, nor does it include Rangers killed in action while serving with regular Union or Confederate military units. Samuel H. Walker, one of the most famous of the Hays-era Rangers, was a Captain of the U.S. Army Mounted Rifles at the time of his death at the Battle of Humantla on October 9, 1847. Benjamin McCulloch was killed as he commanded elements of the Confederate 3rd Texas Cavalry Regiment at the Battle of Pea Ridge in Arkansas on March 7, 1862. Notable exceptions, they are not listed here because they were not serving as Texas Rangers at the time of their deaths.

Colonial Rangers and Republic of Texas Rangers 1823–1845

John Jackson Tumlinson, *alcalde* of the Colorado River colony	July 6, 1823	Serving with Capt. Moses Morrison's company, killed by a Karankawa Indian at the Guadalupe River crossing en route to San Antonio for supplies
José Toribio Losoya	May 6, 1836	Former member of the *Alamo de Parras* company under Mexican rule, serving with Capt. Juan Seguin's ranging company, killed at the fall of the Alamo
Philip Martin	Jan. 1837	Killed in action against the Comanche on the Colorado River while serving with Capt. Micah Andrews
Pvt. David Clark Frank Childress (civilian volunteer)	Jan. 7, 1837	Killed in action against Indians while serving on the Brazos River with Capt. Thomas Barron and George B. Erath
Pvt. Julius Bullock Pvt. J. W. Carpenter Pvt. Thomas M. Scott Pvt. John Wilson	Oct. 12, 1838	Serving under Capt. S. Brown, killed in action against Indians and Mexican agents during the Cordova Revolt
Joseph Martin	Feb. 14, 1839	Wounded serving under John H. Moore in action against the Comanche on the San Saba River; died a few weeks later

Capt. John Bird 1st Sgt. William H. Weaver Pvt. Thomas Gay Pvt. H. M. C. Hall Pvt. Jesse E. Nash	June 26, 1839	Killed in action against the Comanche and other Indians at the Battle of Bird Creek
Pvt. John Stein	July 21, 1841	Serving under Capt. John Coffee Hays, killed in action against the Comanche
Pvt. A. T. Smith unnamed Huaco scout	Aug. 5, 1841	Serving in the Milam County Minute Men under Capt. George B. Erath, killed in action against Indians in a battle on the Brazos River at the upper edge of the crosstimbers
Pvt. Peter Fohr	June 8, 1844	Serving under Capt. John C. Hays, killed in action against the Comanche at the Battle of Walker Creek

Texas Rangers in Federal Service, Mexican War Period 1845–1848

1st Regiment of Texas Mounted Riflemen, 1845–1846
Col. John Coffee Hays, Commander

J. W. D. Austin	Sept. 21, 1846	Serving with Company E, Capt. C. C. Herbert, killed in action at the Battle of Monterrey
Herman S. Thomas	Sept. 22, 1846	Serving with Company A, Capt. Ben McCulloch, killed in action while storming the second height at the Battle of Monterrey
Daniel McCarty	Sept. 22, 1846	Serving with Company D, Capt. Ballowe, killed in action at the Battle of Monterrey
Capt. R. A. Gillespie	Sept. 22, 1846	Serving as commander of Company I, killed while storming the second height at the Battle of Monterrey

Cpl. John M. Fullerton	Sept. 22, 1846	Serving with Company K, Capt. Eli Chandler, killed in action at the Battle of Monterrey
J. Buchannan H. P. Lyon C. W. Tufts	Sept. 1846	Serving with Company H, Capt J. B. McGown, missing in action, supposed killed by bandits or guerrillas

2nd Regiment of Texas Mounted Riflemen, 1845–1846
Col. George T. Wood, Commander

George Short Thomas Gregory	Sept. 22, 1846	Killed in action at the Battle of Monterrey

Ben McCulloch's Company, Texas Mounted Volunteers, 1847

William H. Anderson	Feb. 23, 1847	Killed in action at the Battle of Buena Vista

Maj. Michael Chevallie's Battalion, 1847–1848
(muster roll unavailable)

1 unnamed Ranger	Feb. 1847	Assassinated at Monterrey
1 unnamed Ranger	July 29, 1847	Killed in action against guerrillas at Papagallos
1 unnamed Ranger	Aug. 1847	Assassinated at Monterrey
4 unnamed Rangers	Aug. 5, 1847	Killed in action against Indians at Los Tablas
1 unnamed Ranger	Sept. 1847	Killed in action against guerrillas at Carmargo
1 unnamed Ranger	Oct. 1847	Assassinated at Monterrey
1 unnamed Ranger	Nov. 21, 1847	Killed in action against Indians at Agua Noche
2 unnamed Rangers	Dec. 1847	Killed in action against guerrillas at Parras
1 unnamed Ranger	May 25, 1848	Killed in action against bandits at Concepción

Texas Mounted Riflemen, 2nd Service, 1847–1848
Col. John Coffee Hays, Commander

Lt. Herndon Ridgely	Nov. 24, 1847	Killed in action against lancers in a fight at Galaxa Pass
Adam Allsens	Feb. 13, 1848	Died from wounds inflicted earlier by assassins in Mexico City
Jacob M. Horn	Feb. 25, 1848	Killed in action against Juarata's guerrillas at the battle of Zacualtipán (Sequalteplan)

State of Texas Rangers in Federal Service, 1848–1861

Pvt. William Gillespie	May 29, 1850	Serving with Capt. J. S. Ford, killed in action against the Comanche at Agua Dulce–Amargosa
Pvt. D. C. "Doc" Sullivan Pvt. John Wilbarger	June 1850	Serving with Capt. J. S. Ford, killed by Indians near Santa Gertrudis while returning to camp after a furlough
1 unnamed Ranger	Jan. 25, 1851	Serving with Lt. Andrew J. Walker in Ford's Old Company, killed in action against the Comanche at Arroyo Gato
Pvt. Baker Barton Pvt. William Lackey	Jan. 27, 1851	Serving with Lt. Edward Burleson in Ford's Old Company, killed in action against the Comanche near the Nueces River
Pvt. Henry J. Willis	Sept. 15, 1851	Serving under Capt. Henry McCulloch, killed in action against Indians on the San Saba River
Pvt. Robert Nickles	May 12, 1858	Killed in action against Indians during the Callahan expedition into Mexico
Pvt. Fountain B. Woodruff	Feb. 4, 1860	Serving with Capt. J. S. Ford, killed in action against Juan Cortina's Mexican irregulars at the Battle of La Bolsa Bend on the Rio Grande River

Confederate-Era Texas Rangers, 1861–1865

Capt. Green Davidson 1 unnamed Ranger	Aug. 1861	Serving under Lt. Col. Thomas Frost, 1st Texas Mounted Rifles, killed in action against Indians in North Texas
1 unnamed Ranger	July 19, 1863	Serving under Col. James E. McCord, Frontier Regiment, killed in action against the Comanche on the Clear Fork of the Brazos
1 unnamed Ranger	Oct. 1863	Serving under Capt. F. M. Totty, Border Regiment, killed in action against Indians on the Red River
4 unnamed Rangers	Dec. 21, 1863	Serving under Captain Rowland, Frontier Regiment, killed in action against Comanche and Kiowa in the Cooke County raid
Capt. James Dunn 2 unnamed Rangers	June 25, 1864	Serving under Col. J. S. Ford in the Cavalry of the West, killed in action against federal troops at the battle of Carricitos ranch
Lt. Singleton Gilbert 1 unnamed Ranger	Aug. 8, 1864	Serving with the Eastland Company of the Frontier District, killed in action against Indian raiders at Ellison Springs
5 unnamed Rangers	Oct. 13, 1864	Serving with Company D of the Border Regiment, killed in action against the Kiowa and Comanche in the Elm Creek raid
26 unnamed Rangers	Jan. 8, 1865	Serving with Maj. George B. Erath, Frontier District, killed in a battle with the Kickapoo at Dove Creek
12 unnamed Rangers	May 13, 1865	Serving with Col. J. S. Ford, killed in action against federal troops at the battle of Palmito ranch

Bibliography

BOOKS

Barker, Eugene C. *The Life of Stephen F. Austin*. Austin: University of Texas Press, 1985.

————, and Amelia W. Williams, eds. *The Writings of Sam Houston 1818–1863*. 8 vols. Austin: University of Texas Press, 1938.

Brown, Dee, with Martin F. Schmitt. *Fighting Indians of the West*. New York: Charles Scribner's Sons, 1974.

Conger, Roger N., James M. Day, Joe B. Franz, Billie Mac Jones, Ben Procter, Harold B. Simpson, Dorman H. Winfrey. *Rangers of Texas*. Waco, Tex.: Texian Press, 1969.

Cox, Mike. *Texas Ranger Tales: Stories That Need Telling*. Plano, Tex.: Republic of Texas Press, 1997.

Dobie, J. Frank. *I'll Tell You a Tale*. Austin: University of Texas Press, 1931.

Erath, George B. *The Memoirs of Major George B. Erath, 1813–1891*. Ed. Lucy A. Erath. Waco, Tex.: The Heritage Society of Waco, 1936.

Fehrenbach, T. R. *Comanches: The Destruction of a People*. New York: Alfred A. Knopf, 1974.

————. *Lone Star: Texas and the Texans*. New York: American Legacy Press, 1983.

Ford, John Salmon. *Rip Ford's Texas*. Ed. Stephen B. Oates. Austin: University of Texas Press, 1994.

Gallaway, B. P., ed. *Texas, the Dark, Corner of the Confederacy*. Lincoln, Neb.: University of Nebraska Press, 1994.

Green, Rena Maverick, ed. *Memoirs of Mary A. Maverick*. San Antonio, Tex.: Alamo Printing, 1921.

Greer, James Kimmins. *"Buck Barry": Texas Ranger and Frontiersman*. Waco, Tex.: Texian Press, 1978.

————. *Colonel Jack Hays*. New York: E. P. Dutton, 1952.

Hale, Douglas. *The Third Texas Cavalry in the Civil War*. Norman, Okla.: University of Oklahoma Press, 1993.

Hardin, Stephen L. *Texian Illiad: A Military History of the Texas Revolution*. Austin: University of Texas Press, 1994.

Kilgore, Dan E. *A Ranger Legacy*. Austin: Madrona Press, 1973.

McDowell, Catherine W., ed. *Now You Hear My Horn—The Journal of James Wilson Nichols, 1820–1887*. Austin: University of Texas Press, 1967.

McMurry, Richard M. *John Bell Hood and the War for Southern Independence*. Lincoln, Neb.: Bison Books, University of Nebraska Press, 1982.

Newcomb, W. W., Jr. *The Indians of Texas*. Austin: University of Texas Press, 1961.

Reid, Samuel C., Jr. *The Scouting Expeditions of McCulloch's Texas Rangers*. Philadelphia: J. W. Bradley, 1860.

Robinson, Duncan W. *Judge Robert McAlpin Williamson, Texas' Three-Legged Willie*. Austin: Texas State Historical Society, 1948.

Simpson, Col. Harold B. *Cry Comanche: The Second U.S. Cavalry in Texas 1855–1861*. Hillsboro, Tex.: Hill Junior College Press, 1979.

Smith, David Paul. *Frontier Defense in the Civil War: Texas Rangers and Rebels*. College Station, Tex.: Texas A&M University Press, 1983.

Smithwick, Noah. *The Evolution of a State, or Recollections of Old Texas Days.* Austin: University of Texas Press, 1983.

Tijerina, Andrés. *Tejanos and Texans Under the Mexican Flag, 1921–1836.* College Station, Tex.: Texas A&M University Press, 1994.

Tumlinson, Samuel H. *Tumlinson: A Geneology.* British Columbia, Can.: published privately.

Wallace, Ernest, and E. Adamson Hoebel. *The Comanches: Lords of the South Plains.* Norman, Okla.: University of Oklahoma Press, 1952.

Webb, Walter Prescott. *The Texas Rangers: A Century of Frontier Defense.* Boston: Houghton Mifflin, 1935.

Wilkins, Fredrick. *The Highly Irregular Irregulars: Texas Rangers in the Mexican War.* Austin: Eakin Press, 1990.

———. *The Legend Begins: The Texas Rangers 1823–1845.* Austin: State House Press, 1996.

ARCHIVES AND COLLECTIONS

Barker Texas Library. University of Texas, Austin.

Baylor Texas Collection. Baylor University, Waco Heritage Society Collection, Waco, Tex.

Institute of Texan Cultures, San Antonio.

The McCulloch Family Papers. Library of the Daughters of the Republic of Texas, San Antonio.

Moody Texas Ranger Memorial Library. Texas Ranger Hall of Fame and Museum, Waco, Tex.

Adjutant General Records, The Texas Ranger Papers, The Samuel H. Walker Papers. Texas State Archives, Texas State Library, Austin.

OTHER SOURCES

Arts & Entertainment Network. *The Story of the Gun.*
KUHT Houston Public Television. *The Texas Rangers: Six Brave Men.*

❧ Index ❧

Illustrations and photographs are indicated by *italic* page references.

A

Abenaki Indians, 9
Acklin, Christopher "Kit", 73, 90, 119
   on muster roll, *112*
Agaton, 65, 83, 94
agencies, Indian, 165
Agua Dulce, Battle of, 158, 159
   Rangers killed at, 219
Agua Fria, 136–37
Agua Noche, 218
Alamo, the, 41, *42*, *111*, *180*
   Battle of Béxar, 33–35
   in Civil War, 181
   flying squadrons of, 6–7
   Long Barracks at, 7
   siege of, 38–40, *39*, 216
   under Spanish rule, 5
   Woll's cavalry in, 89–90
Alamo de Parras company, 5, 6–7
Alexander, W. J., 167, 193, 197
Alf, Tom, 162
Allison, Clay, 185
Allsens, Adam, 144, 219
Alston, Fielding, 136, 137
Amangual, Francisco, 6
Ampuida, Pedro, 92, 123, 128, 135
Anderson, William H., 218
Andrews, Micah, 55, 56, 60, 63, 98
annexation of Texas, 103–4, *104*
Apache Indians, 8, 50, 165
   artifacts of, *13*
   See also Lipan Apache Indians
Arista, Mariano, 115, 118–19
armistices, with Mexico, 93, 130, 135
Arredondo, Joaquín de, 7
Arrington, William A., 30
Arroyo Gato, Battle of, 161–62, 219
Arroyo Seco, 60, 71
Austin (city), *74*, 88, 153
Austin, J. W. D., 217

Austin, Moses, 15, *15*
Austin, Stephen F., 5, 16, 32, *108*
   call to war by, 28
   colonization by, 15–16
   as diplomat, 16, 25, 26–27
   early ranging companies of, 19–21, 25, *50*
   friends of, 7, 32
   imprisonment of, 27
   meeting with Santa Anna, 26–27
   Texas Ranger vision of, realized, 29–30
Austin Colony Rangers, *50*
Avalos, Francisco, 164

B

Bagdad, 191
Ballowe, Captain, 217
bandits, 65, 79, 83, 94, 149
Barnett, T. H., 208
Barragan, Manuel, 92
Barron, Thomas H., 59
   Rangers killed under, 216
Barry, James "Buck", 125, 129, *189*
   at Camp Colorado, 180
   in Elm Creek raid, 203–4, 205
   Ranger companies of, 189, 193–94, 197, 198
   in Reconstruction era, 211
   in Red River raid, 190
Barton, Baker, 162, 219
Bastrop, 35–36, 40, 52
Battle of Agua Dulce, 158, 159
Battle of Arroyo Gato, 161–62, 219
Battle of Béxar, 7, 33–35
Battle of Bird Creek, 68, 70–71
   Rangers killed at, 217
   song about, 69–70
Battle of Buena Vista, 137–38, 218
Battle of Chickamauga, 185
Battle of Dove Creek, 205–6
   Rangers killed at, 220

Battle of La Bolsa, 173–74
  Rangers killed at, 219
Battle of Monterrey, *110*, 122–26, 128–30
  Rangers killed at, 217–18
Battle of Paint Rock, 115, 116–17
Battle of Palmito Ranch, *113*, 207–8
  Rangers killed at, 220
Battle of Palo Alto, 118–19
Battle of Pea Ridge, 187–88
  Rangers killed at, 216
Battle of Plum Creek, 77–79, *78*
Battle of San Jacinto, 44–46
Battle of Shiloh, 185
Battle of Walker Creek, 99–101
  Rangers killed at, 217
  song about, 69–70
battles. *See specific battles (e.g.* Battle of Bird Creek). *See
    under* Civil War; Comanche Indians; Mexican War;
    Mexico, military conflicts with; Texas Revolution
Baylor, John R., 165, 191, 192
  Ranger companies of, 197, 198
Beason's Ford, 43
Bell, Jesse, *xvi*
Bell, John, *187*
Bell, Peter H., 151, *151*
Bell, Robert, *xvi*
Benavides, Refugio, 199, 207
Benavides, Santos, 191, 198, 199
Béxar
  the Alamo. *See* Alamo, the
  Battle of, 7, *33*–35
  flying squadrons of, 6–7
  presidio, 4, 5
  See also San Antonio de Béxar
Big Tree (Kiowa), *194*
Billingsley, Jesse, 90
Bird, James, 77–79, 89
Bird, John, 68, 70, 217
Bird Creek, Battle of. *See* Battle of Bird Creek
Bishop's Palace, 123, 124, 128
Black, George, *210*
Black Fort, 123, 126
"Bonnie Blue Flag" (song), 201–2
Border Regiment, 196, 198, 200, 203, 204, 205
  Rangers killed in, 220
border treaties, 94, 106
Bosque Bonito, *212*
Bourland, James, 196, 198, 200, 203
Bowie, James, 27, *27*, *33*, 38
Bowles, John, 27, 61, 66
Bragg ranch, 204
Brazos River, 30, 44, 59, 194
  Rangers killed at, 216, 217, 220
  reservations on, 165

Brazos Santiago, 191, 207
Britton, J. M., *210*
Brooke, George M., 153
Brooks, A. J., *xvi*
Brookshire, Nathan, 68, 70–71
Brown, John H., 198
Brown, S., 216
Brownsville
  in Civil War, 192, 196, 199, 206
  in Cortina War, 169, 171–74
Brownwood, 180
Brush Battalion, 196, 198
Brushy Creek, 36, 40, 57
Bryan, Moses, 46
Bryant, Benjamin, 60
Buchannan, J., 218
Buena Vista, Battle of, 137–38, 218
Buffalo Hump (Comanche), 167–68
Bullock, Julius, 216
Burleson, Edward, Jr., *190*
  in campaign against Comanche, 154, 161, 162–63,
    165, 166
  in Civil War, 175, 189, 190
  Ranger company of, 197
  Rangers killed under, 219
Burleson, Edward, Sr., *33*
  as aide to Governor Henderson, 119
  in Austin, 88
  in Battle of Plum Creek, 77–79
  in campaign against Cherokee, 63, 66
  on Flacco's death, 81
  in Mexican War, 124
  in Texas Revolution, 33–35, 46
Burnet, David G., 32, *32*, 178
Burton, Isaac, 30, 45, 46
Bustamante, Anastasio, 26

C

Caddo Indians, 60
  in Canadian River fight, 166, 168
  on reservations, 165
Cage, A. C., 69
Caldwell, Matthew, 77, 89, 91
Callahan, James H., 83
  Ranger killed under, 219
Calvert, Susan, 94, 101, 138, 147, 152
Cameron, Ewan, 88, 89, 92
Camp Colorado, 180–81
Canadian River fight, 165–69
Canales, Antonio, 88, 89, 91
Cano (Stephen Austin's dog), *108*
Carbajal, José María Jesús, 164–65
Carmargo, 218
Carne Muerto (Comanche), 158, 160, 162

Carpenter, J. W., 216
Carr, Jim, 162
Carricitos fight, 199–200
Carrington, W. H. D., 207
Carson, Lieutenant, 204
Carter, James, 66
Casa Blanca River, 77
Casteñeda, Francisco, 7
Castile, Chief (Tonkawa), 196, 203
Castro, Juan, 66, 67–68, 79
Cater, Thomas C., 199
Cavalry of the West, 150, 198–200, 207, 208, 220
Cedar Creek, 40
Centralists, 26, 79, 87, 135, 163–64
Chandler, Eli, 60, 83, 121
    Rangers killed under, 218
Cherokee Indians
    campaign against, 63, 66
    in Civil War, 189
    policies and views towards, 61
    as ranger scouts, 66
    in Salado Creek ambush, 89–90
Chevallie, Michael, 73, 77
    in Battle of Plum Creek, 92, 95
    in campaign against guerrillas, 144, 146
    in Mexican War, 119, 121, 126, 138, 139
    on muster roll, 112
    Rangers killed under, 218
    in San Antonio raid, 87
Chickamauga, Battle of, 185
Chickasaw Indians, 189, 200
Chihuahua-El Paso expedition, 151
Childress, Frank, 59, 216
Childs, Colonel, 128
Choctaw Indians, 61, 66
Chul-le-quah (Shawnee), 167
Cibolo River, 30
    "civilized" Indians, policies and views towards, 61, 63, 66
Civil War, 113, 175–208
    Battle of Dove Creek, 205–6, 220
    Battle of Palmito Ranch, 113, 207–8, 220
    Battle of Pea Ridge, 187–88, 216
    Carricitos fight, 199–200
    Cooke County raid, 200, 202–3, 220
    early days of, 178–82
    Elm Creek raid, 203–5, 206, 220
    Indians in, 189–91, 194, 196, 200, 202–6
    Ordinance of Secession, 177–78
    Ranger companies in, 197–98
    Rangers' role in, 175–77
    Reconstruction, 209, 211–13
    recruiting poster, 193
    Rio Grande area, 191–92, 196, 198–200, 206–8

Terry's Texas Rangers, 183, 183–85, 186
    weapons, 114
Clark, David, 59, 216
Clark, Edward, 188, 189
Clear Fork, 165, 194, 220
    clothing, of Rangers, 121
Coke, Richard, 213
Coleman, John A., 35
Coleman, Robert M., 52, 55, 59
Coleman's Fort, 52, 54–56, 55
Cole's Settlement, 44
Colonial Rangers, killed in action, 216–17
colonization
    American, 8, 13, 15–16
    Spanish, 1–5
    by Stephen F. Austin, 15–16
Colorado River, 24, 30, 43, 216
Colored Regiment, 208
Colt, Samuel, 96–98, 130, 131, 131–34, 181
Colt firearms, 95–99, 101, 131–34, 181
    Army model, 114, 176
    Navy model, 152
    Paterson model
        "Baby" model, 96
        carbine, 99
        holster model, 100
        pocket model, 100
        rifle, 99
        "Texas" model, 95, 96, 99, 100, 129
    Walker model, 133, 140, 150
    wooden model parts for, 132
Comanche (ship), 46
Comanche Indians, 3, 12, 50, 51–52, 67
    in Arroyo Seco raid, 60
    artifacts of, 13
    in Battle of Bird Creek, 68, 70–71
    in Battle of Paint Rock, 115, 116–17
    in Battle of Plum Creek, 77–79, 78
    in Battle of Walker Creek, 69, 99–101
    in Canadian River fight, 165–69
    in Civil War, 187, 189–91, 194, 200, 202–6
    Colt pistols used against, 98–99
    in Cooke County raid, 200, 202–3
    in Council House fight, 76
    culture of, 8, 11, 57–58
    early colonists and, 13
    in Elm Creek raid, 200, 203–5
    in Enchanted Rock battle, 84, 86
    fighting style of, 11, 17, 21, 52
    Ford's campaign on, 152–62
    in Fort Coleman raid, 55–56
    in Frio River battle, 82
    in Great Raid, 76–77

language of, 58
low birth rate of, 36
in Nueces Strip, 153–63
in Parker's Fort raid, 53
Quanah Parker, *14*, 53–54, *54*
Rangers killed by, 216–17, 219, 220
on reservations, 165
in San Antonio raid, 83, 86
in San Saba River battle, 67–68
Texans living among, 56, 57–58, 60
treaties with, 56, 206
village of, *11*
in Walnut Creek ambush, 36–37
Williamson ambush of, 32
compañía volantes, 5, 6–7
Concepción, 218
Confederate Conscription Act, 178, 190
Congressional acts, 63, 92, 94, 95
conscription, for Civil War, 178, 188, 190
Cooke, W. G., 95
Cooke County raid, 200, 202–3, 220
Copana Bay, 46
Cordova, Vicente, 89–90
Cordova Revolt, 89–90, 216
Corpus Christi, 106, 115
Cortez, Ignacio, 65, 83
Cortina, Juan N., 169, *170*, 171–73, 191
Cortina War, 169, 171–74
Cós, Martín Perfecto de, 28, 33–35, 45
    circular by, *29*
Council House fight, 76
Cowan, D. C., 180
Coy, Antonio, 64, 87, 91, 95
    on muster roll, *65*
Crockett, David, *35*, 35–36, 38
Crook, George, *185*
Crowder, T. S., *xvi*
Cuero, Otto, 158, 159
currency, *45*, 66
Curtis, Jimmy, 43
Curtis, Lieutenant, 59

D

Daggett, E. M., 146
Dalrymple, William, 197
Daniels, Marcellus, *xvi*
Davidson, Green, 190, 220
Davis, E. J., 178, 199, 211
Davis, George Washington, 30
Davis, James, 88
Davis, Jefferson, 188, *188*
Dawson, Nicholas, 90
Delaware Indians, 61, 66, 166

"Devil Jack" (Jack Hays), 73
    See also Hays, John Coffee (Jack)
Diamond, James J., 203
Diamond, John R., 198
Dickinson, Almeron, 38
Dominguez, Manuel, 146
Dove Creek, Battle of, 205–6
    Rangers killed at, 220
Duncan, James, 125–26, 162
Dunn, James, 87, 199, 220
Durkin, Millie, 204

E

Eagle Chief (Comanche), 189
Eastland, Thomas, 67–68
Eastland, William M., 56, 63, 90
Ebonal ranch, 171, 206
edicts of 1830, 26, 27
Edmundson, James, 40, 43
Ehlers, John, 96, 98
8th Texas Cavalry Regiment. *See* Terry's Texas Rangers
Ellison Springs, 203, 220
Elm Creek raid, 203–5, 206, 220
El Paso wagon trail, 151
El Plan de Loba, 164–65
El Soldado, 123, 126
Enchanted Rock, 84–86, *85*, *110*
epidemics, 27
Erath, George B., *x*, *59*, 63, 83
    in Civil War, 175, 196, 203, 205
    in Indian raid, 59
    Ranger company of, 198
    Rangers killed under, 216, 217
Erskin, Andrew, 100
Evans, W. G., 68
executions, of Texans, 40, 44, 92, *93*

F

Falls on Brazos River, 59
fandango, *111*
Fannin, James, 40, 44
Fanny Butler (ship), 46
"Father of Texas". *See* Austin, Stephen F.
Federalists, 25–26, 87, 163–64
Federation Ridge, 126, 128
Filisola, Vicente, 61
Fisher, William S., 91
Fitzpatrick, Mrs., 204
Flacco, Chief (son), *82*, 86
    death of, 80–81
    friendship with Hays, 66, 80–82, 83
    in Frio River battle, 82
    on Mier expedition, 91

Ranger company of, 83
in San Saba River battle, 67–68
Flacco, old (father), 81
flags, *50*, *107*, *201*
Flores, Manuel, 60–61
Flores, Juan, 139
flying squadrons, 5, 6–7
Fohr, Peter, 69, 100, 217
Ford, John S. "Rip", *vi,* xvi, *xvi,* 103, 106, *139,* 143, *171,* 175
    background of, 150
    in Battle of Palmito Ranch, 206–7
    blazing of El Paso wagon trail, 151
    in Canadian River fight, 165–67, 169
    with Carbajal's forces, 164–65
    in Carricitos fight, 199–200
    as commander of state forces, 179
    as Conscription Bureau head, 178, 196
    in Cortina War, 171–74
    fears concerning Civil War, 181–82
    Fort Brown negotiations by, 179, 181
    horse of, 157, 159, 161
    illness of, 161, 162–63, 191
    in Mexican War, 139–40, 143, 144, 146, 147
    nickname of, 139
    in Nueces Strip, 152–62
    Ranger companies of, 197, 198
    Rangers killed under, 219, 220
    in Reconstruction era, 211
    records of, 215
    retirement of, 163
    on Rio Grande in Civil War, 191–92, 206–8
Ford, William, 166
Ford's Old Company, 153, 163
Ford's 2nd Texas Cavalry, 198
Forrest, Nathan Bedford, *184,* 185
Fort Belknap, 204, 205
Fort Brown, 191, 192, 196, 199, 200, 206–7
    Hill's withdrawal from, 179, 181, 184
Fort El Soldado, 123, 126
Fort Independence, 123
Fort Liberty, 123, 124
Fort Merrill, 156, 157
Fort Murrah, 204–5, 205
Fort Paredes, 164
Fort Prairie, 59–60
Fort Smith, 68
Fossett, Henry, 198, 205–6
Friar, Daniel, 89
Frio River, battle on, 82, *82*
Frontier Battalion, 66, *210,* 213
Frontier Organization, 196, 198, 203, 205, 206
Frontier Regiment, 192–94, 196, 197, 198, 200
    Rangers killed in, 220

Frost, Thomas C., 180, 190, 197
    Rangers killed under, 220
Fry, James H., 172
Fryar, D. B., 30
Fullerton, John M., 218

G
Galaxa Pass, 141, 219
Galveston, 191, 192, 196
Gaona, Antonio, 43
Gay, Thomas, 70, 217
"Gettysburg of the West", 192
Gibbons, Emory, 117
Giddings, George H., 198
Giddings, Luther, 123–24, 125, 207
Gilbert, Singleton, 203, 220
Gillespie, R. A. "Ad", 73, 92, 217
    in Battle of Walker Creek, 100
    in Mexican War, 119, 121, 122, 123, 126, 128–29
    on muster roll, *112*
    Ranger companies of, 115
Gillespie, William, 157–58, 159, 219
Glen Springs, *2*
Glorietta Pass, 192
Goliad, 40, 44
Gonzales, battle at, 28–29
Gonzaullas, Manuel "Lone Wolf", 65
Goodnight, Charlie, *53,* 54, 168, 189
Goss, Pete, 144
Great Raid, 76–77, 79
Greenwood, Garrison, 30
Griffin (Samuel Maverick's servant), 90
Griffith, Charles, 211
Grumbles, John J., 153, 163
Guadalupe River, 24, 216
Guererro, 91
guerrillas, 136, 138, 139, 140–41, 144, 146
    Rangers killed by, 218, 219
guns
    Civil War era, *114, 176*
    Colt firearms. *See* Colt firearms
    long rifles, 17–19, *18*
    Spanish colonial era, *3*
Gutierrez-Magee affair, 6–7

H
Hall, H. M. C., 70, 217
Hamilton, A. J., 178, 211
Hancock, George, 178
Hancock, John, 178
Harris, Tupper, *xvi*
Hays, John Coffee (Jack), *vi,* 71, *74, 104, 123, 152*
    appointment by Lamar, 79

background of, 73
in Battle of Monterrey, 122–26, 128–30
in Battle of Plum Creek, 77–79
in Battle of Walker Creek, 99–101
in campaign against guerrillas, 144, 146
on Chihuahua-El Paso expedition, 151
company's muster roll, *112*
courtship and marriage of, 94, 101, 130, 138
at Enchanted Rock, 84, 86, 97–98, *110*
friendship with Flacco, 66, 80–82, 83
in Frio River battle, 82, *82*
in second campaign against Texas, 88–91
invasion of Mexico by, 91–92
in Laredo attack, 73–74, 76, *112*
in Mexico City, 143–44
in Nueces Strip, 64–65, 83, 86
Ranger companies of, *92–93*, 95, 99, 115, 117, 119, 121
Rangers killed under, 217–18
reputation of, 86–87
retirement of, 146–47, 150–52
in San Antonio raid, 87–88
training of Rangers by, 94
in Vera Cruz, 138, 139
Heintzelman, Samuel P., 171, 172
Henderson, James P., 117, *117*, 119, 122, 130, 141
Herbert, C. C., 217
Herrera, Pedro, *33*, 45
Herron, Francis J., 199, 206–7
Hibbons, Sara, 36–37
Higgins (Ford's horse), 157, 159, 161
Highsmith, Malcijah J., 154, 160, 161
Hill, B. H., 179, 181
Hitchcock, Ethan Allen, 121
Hockley, George W., 98
Holland, James K., 123
Holley, B. B., 180
Hondo Creek, battle on, 90–91
Hood, John Bell, 182, 185
Horn, Jacob M., 146, 219
Hornsby Station, *35*, 36
"horse marines", 46
Houston, Sam, 28, *33*, 88, 91
    against secession, 177–78
    background of, 27
    call to war by, *35*
    Comanche treaty and, 56
    death of, 178
    declaration of martial law by, 94
    expansion of Rangers by, 95
    on Flacco's death, 81
    Lamar's animosity towards, 61
    in Texas Revolution, 32, 38, *44*, 44–47
    on value of rangers, 64

    views on annexation, 103
Howard, G. T., 95
Huaco Indians, 24, 57–58
    in Canadian River fight, 166, 167
    on reservations, 165
    scout killed, 217
Hughes, John R., *xvii*, 54
Humantla, battle at, 143
Hunter, James M., 196, 198
Huston, Felix, 77

I
immigrants
    early colonists, 3–4, 8
    Mexico's ban on, 26
    prejudice of, 49
    Tejanos at disadvantage from, 87
    variety of, 50–51
independence
    debating question of, 32–33
    early days of, 50–51
Independence, War of. *See* Texas Revolution
Independence Hill, 124, 128–29
Indians
    allies of Texans, 166
    policies and views toward "civilized", 61, 63, 66
    public opinion on, 165
    Ranger companies of, 65–66
    reservations and agencies, 165
    See also *specific tribes* (*e.g.* Comanche Indians)
Iron Jacket (Comanche), 166
Izucar de Matamoros, 141

J–K
Jackson, Andrew, *28*
Jalapa, 141
Johnson, Andrew, 211
Johnson, Francis W., *32*, 34
Johnson, Mary, 204
Johnston, Albert Sidney, 119, 184, *184*
Jones, Anson, 115, *115*
    in annexation ceremony, *104*
Jones, Tommy Lee, *xviii*
Juarata, Padre Celedonia de, 144, 146, 219
Juarez, Benito, 191
Karankawa Indians, 8, 24, 25
    Tumlinson killed by, 24, 216
Karnes, Henry Wax, 28, 45, 63
    at Arroyo Seco, 60, 71
    illness and death of, 77
Keechi (Indian scout), 166
Kelly, William, H., 136
Kennedy, Miflin, 169

Kickapoo Indians, 68, 205–6, 220
Kicking Bird (Kiowa), *3*
Kimbell, George, 38–39
King, W. H., 209
Kiowa Indians, *3*, 50, *94*, 165, *195*
    artifacts of, *13*
    in Civil War, 187, 189–91, 194, 203–5, 206
    early raids by, *3*, 8
    Rangers killed by, 220
    treaties with, 206
Kuykendall, Robert, 24–25

L
La Bolsa, Battle of, 173–74
    Rangers killed at, 219
Lackey, William, 162, 219
La Libertad, 123, 124
Lamar, Mirabeau B., *61*, *113*
    campaign against Cherokee by, *63*, 66
    formation of Ranger companies by, 79
    house of, *74*
    as inspector, 119
    in Mexican War, 135
    military policy of, *63*, 67
    views toward "civilized" Indians, 61
lancers, 7, *40*, *107*
    in Mexican War, 115, 117–19, 122–26, 141, 143
land grants, 49
Lane, John W., 206
Lane, Joseph, 141, 142–43, 146
Lane, Walter P., *138*, 139, 185
Langdon, Lomis, 173
Laredo, 91
    attack on, 73–74, 76, *112*
    in Civil War, 199
    Comanche in, 158, 160
Las Ruicas, 199
Lee, Robert E., *173*, 174, 182, *187*
Lee, W. B., 100
léperos, los, 144
Level, David M., 154–55, 156, 158, 161–62
Lewis, Mark B., 83
Lincoln, Abraham, 175, *176*
Linney, Jim, 166
Linville, 76
Lipan Apache Indians, *3*, 83
    Chief Flacco. *See* Flacco, Chief
    Flacco's death and, 81–82
    in Great Raid, 79
    Ranger companies of, 66, 83
    in San Saba River battle, 67–68
Little Buffalo (Comanche), 203
Little River, 68

Lloyd, M. B., 194
Lockhart, Matilda, *67*, 68
"Lone Ranger", *xvii*
Lone Wolf (Kiowa), 189
Long Barracks, 6, *7*
long rifles, 17–19, *18*
Los Ojuelos, 161, 162–63
Losoya, José Toribio, 38, 216
Los Tablas, 218
"Lottery of Death", 92
Lubbock, Francis R., 176, 192, *192*, 193
Lubbock, Thomas S., 183–84, 185
Luckett, Philip N., 191
Lusk, Patrick, 92
Lynch's Ferry, 45
Lyon, H. P., 218
Lytle, James T., 145

M
Magruder, J. B. "Prince", 196, *199*, 208
Manchaca, Antonio J., 64, 88, 91, 95
maps, *viii*, *51*, *105*, *109*
Marcy, William L., 122, 132, 136, 138
María, José Casa, 60, 166
martial law, in Nueces Strip, 94
Martin, John, 173
Martin, Joseph, 68, 216
Martin, Philip, 55–56, 216
Martinez, Lieutenant "Padre", 146
Matamoros, 115, 117, 122, 164–65
Maugricio, Roque, 154–55, 157–58
Maverick, Samuel, 151, *151*
    servant of, 90
May, Charles, 137
McAdoo, J. D., 198
McCarty, Daniel, 217
McCord, James E., 193–94, 197, 220
McCulloch, Benjamin, *vi*, 45, 95, *119*
    in Battle of Plum Creek, 77–79
    in Civil War, 175, 179, 181, 185, 187–88, *188*
    death of, 187–88, 216
    in Great Raid attack, 76–77
    in invasion of Mexico, 92
    in Mexican War, 106, 119, 121, 122, 124–26, 136–38, *138*
    on muster roll, *112*
    Ranger companies of, 83, *112*, 115, 196, 197, 198
    Rangers killed under, 218
    in San Antonio raid, 87–88
    in second campaign against Texas, 90
McCulloch, Henry, 45, 175, *181*
    in Civil War, 179, 180–81, 189–90, 196, 200, 206
    at Enchanted Rock, 84
    in second campaign against Texas, 89, 90

in Nueces Strip, 153, 163
    Ranger companies of, 165, 179, 189, 196, 197, 198
    Rangers killed under, 219
    in Reconstruction era, 211
    request for increased forces by, 187
McCurly, Plas, 164
McGown, J. B., 218
McLochlan, Sergeant, 59
McMullen, John, 124
McNeil, Wallace, 161
McNelly, Leander H., 66, 213
Medicine Lodge Creek Council, 11
Medina, 80–81
mercenaries, 137, 164
Mexican government
    aid promised by, 24, 25
    debating question of independence from, 32–33
    edicts issued by, 26, 27
    incitement of Indians by, 60–61, 79
    resentment towards, 25
    tensions between Texas and, 87, 103
Mexican War, 103–6, *107*, 115, 117–47, *120*, 122–26, *127*
    Agua Fria, 136–37
    armistice agreement, 134
    Battle of Buena Vista, 137–38
    Battle of Monterrey, *110*, 124–26, 128–30
    Battle of Palo Alto, 118–19
    Humantla battle, 143
    Matamoros invasion, 115, 117, 122
    Mexico City, 136, 139, 140–41, 143–44
    Nueces Strip dispute, 115, 117
    Puebla, 141, *142*, 143
    Vera Cruz, 136, 138–40
    volunteers for, 119, 121–22
Mexico, military conflicts with
    Cortina War, 169, 171–74
    Laredo attack, 73–74
    Matamoros attack, 164–65
    Mexican War. *See* Mexican War
    San Antonio raid, 43, 87–88
    second campaign against Texas, 88–91
    Texas Revolution. *See* Texas Revolution
Mexico City, 136, 139, 140–41, 143–44
Mier expedition, 91–92, *93*
Milam, Ben, 7, 33–35, *34*
Milam County Minute Men, 59, 213
    killed in action, 217
military policies, 63, 67, 79
Miller, A. D., 203
Miracle, Pedro Julian, 61
missions, Spanish, 3, 5, 6–7
Mission Valero, 5, 6–7
Mississippi Rifles company, 126, 129
Mohee (Comanche), 167

money, *45*, 66
    See also wage, of Rangers
Montagna, Colonel, 146
Monterrey, Battle of, *110*, 122–26, 128–30
    Rangers killed at, 217–18
Moore, Clayton, *xvii*
Moore, Jim "Nest Egg", *xvi*
Moore, John H., 67–68, 71, 79, 90
    Ranger killed under, 216
Morgan, Tom, 51
Morrison, Moses, 24–25
    Ranger killed under, 216
Mounted Gunmen, 62, 64, 95
Mounted Riflemen. *See* Texas Mounted Riflemen
Mounted Volunteers, 115, 117, 218
Muguara (Comanche), 56, 57
Murrah, Pendleton, 196, 208
muster rolls, *62, 63, 65, 112*

N
Nacogdoches, 4
Nacona, Peta (Comanche), 53
Naconi Indians, 53
Naduah. *See* Parker, Cynthia Ann
Nájera, Juan, 126
"Napoleon of the West". *See* Santa Anna, Antonio
        López de
Nash, Jesse E., 70, 217
Navarro, Antonio, 81
Navarro, Nepomuceno, 45
Neal, Adelphus D., 156–57
Neches River, 66
Neighbors, Robert S., 151, 165
Newman, Joseph, 24
Nichols, E. B., 181
Nickles, Robert, 167, 219
Nolan, Mat, 198–99
Norris, Chuck, *xviii*
Norris, James N., 193, 197
Nueces River, 154–55, 162
Nueces Strip
    bandits in, 79, 83, 94
    Comanche in, 153, 154–55, 157–58, 160–63
    dispute over, 49, 93–94, 106, 115, 117
    martial law in, 94
    Rangers killed in, 219
Nuestra Señora del Carmen lancers, 7

O–P
Obenchain, Alfred, 197
Ochoa, Lieutenant, 191
Old Higgins (Ford's horse), 157, 159, 161
Ordinance Department, 95, 97

Ordinance of Secession, 177–78
Owen, Clark, 76–77
Paint Rock, Battle of, 115, 116–17
Palmito Ranch, Battle of, *113*, 207–8
    Rangers killed at, 220
Palo Alto, Battle of, 118–19
Palo Duro Canyon, 54
Panther, Captain, 65–66
Papagallos, 218
Paredes, Mariano, 144, 146
Parker, Cynthia Ann, 53, *53,* 169
    children of, *53*
Parker, Isaac M., *53*
Parker, John, 53
Parker, Quanah, *14,* 53–54, *54*
Parker, Silas M., 29–30, 54
Parker's Fort, *53*
Parras, 218
Partisan Rangers, *113,* 185
Paschal, Frank, 92, 95
Paschal, George W., 167
Paterson firearms. *See* Colt firearms
Patterson, Robert, 140
pay, of Rangers, 30, 80, 95, 149, 153
Pea Ridge, Battle of, 187–88
    Rangers killed at, 216
Pease, E. M., 178, 211
Perez, Antonio, 64, 91, *112*
    discrediting of, 79
    muster roll of, *65*
    in Nueces Strip, 65, 83
Perry, Rufus (on muster roll), *112*
Peter, Fohr, 101
Petty, George M., 44
Phillips, Billy, 137
Pitts, John D., 153
Pitts, William A., 165
Placido, Chief (Tonkawa), 77, *77,* 166
Plan de Loba, El, 164–65
Plum Creek, Battle of, 77–79, *78*
Plummer, J. B., 157
Po-bish-e-quash-o (Commanche), 166
Polk, James K., 131, *135,* 136
Polk, William H., 141, 146
presidios, system of, 3
Price, John T., 73, 79, 83, 118–19
provisional government, 29–30, 32
    president of, *32*
Puebla, 141, *142,* 143
Puestia (Comanche), 56

Q–R

Quayle, William, 196, 198, 203, 205
Quinaseico (Comanche), 56

Quitman, John A., 126
Radical Republicans, 209, 211
raids, Indian. See *specific raids (e.g.* Great Raid). See under
    specific Indian tribes (e.g. Comanche Indians)
Ranchero (ship), 172–73
rancheros, 4–5
Rancho Salado, 92
Rangers. *See* Texas Rangers
ranging companies, 5, *20*
    early, 19–21, 29, *50*
    function of, 64
Reconstruction, 209, 211–13
Reconstruction Act, 211
"Redback" (currency), *45*
Red Bear (Comanche), 189
"Red Caps" (soldiers), 92
Red River, 200
    Comanche village near, *11*
    Indian raids on, 61, 189–91, 220
Republic of Texas Rangers, killed in action, 216–17
reservations, Indian, 165
resolutions of 1835, 29–30
Revolution. *See* Texas Revolution
Reynosa, 122
Rice, James O., 60
Richardson, Sam, *113*
Ridgely, Herndon, 219
rifles
    long, 17–19, *18*
    U. S. Common, *176*
Ringgold, Sam, 118
Ringgold barracks, 171–72, 199, 200
Rio Grande, as border, 94, 106, 115
    See also *specific places on Rio Grande (e.g.* Brownsville)
Rio Grande City, 171, 199
Robel, Lieutenant, 55
Roberts, Jacob, 141
Roberts, O. M., 178–79, 181
Robertson, Captain, 207
Robinson, John H., 207, 208
Rodger, Jo, 40
Rodriguez, José, 185
Roff, C. L., 198
Rogers, C. L. "Kid", *xvi*
Rogers, Charles, *xvi*
Rogers, John H., *xvi*
Rogers, Robert, *9,* 9–10
Rogers's Rangers, 8, 9–10
Rohrer, Conrad, 37, 45
Ross, Elizabeth, 168
Ross, Lawrence Sullivan, 53, 167–69, *168,* 175, 188
Ross, Shapley P., 165, 166, 167
Rowland, James, 200, 203
Ruiz, José Francisco, 7

Runaway Scrape, 40, 43–44, 49
Runnels, Hardin R., 165, 169, 171
Running Bird (Comanche), *12*
Rusk, Thomas J., 63

S
Salado Creek ambush, 89–90
Saltillo, 92, 136–37
San Antonio company, 73
San Antonio de Béxar (San Antonio), 5
    the Alamo. *See* Alamo, the
    Battle of Béxar, 7, 33–35
    Comanche fight near, 83, 86
    during second campaign against Texas, 88–91
    first battle of Revolution at, 24–25
    flying squadrons of, 6–7
    presidio of, *4*, 5
    Seguín as governor of, 41
    Vásquez's raid on, 43, 87–88
San Antonio Viejo, 154, 158, 160–61
Sanches, Antonio (on muster roll), *65*
Sanches, Lewis, 64, 66
    company's muster roll, *62*
San Felipe de Austin, 29, 31
San Gabriel River, battle at, 60–61
San Jacinto, Battle of, 44–46
San Luis Potosi, 92
San Saba River, battle on, 67–68, 71
    Rangers killed in, 219
Santa Anna, Antonio López de, *26*, 28, *135*
    in Battle of San Jacinto, 44–46
    execution orders by, 40, 44, 92, 93
    imprisonment of Seguín by, 43, 87
    invasion of Texas by, 35
    meeting with Austin, 26–27
    in Mexican War, 135–38, 139, 143, 146
    return to power of, 49–50
    siege of the Alamo by, 38–40
    victory over Bustamante, 26
Santa Catarina River, 126
Santa Gertrudis, 156, 219
Satank (Kiowa), 189
Satanta (Kiowa), 189, *195*
Scott, Thomas M., 216
Scott, Winfield, *135*, 136, 138, 139, 140–41, 144
Searcy, Oliver, 167
secession, 177–78
second campaign against Texas, 88–91
Seguín, Juan N., 7, 28, *41*, *111*
    at the Alamo, 39
    in Battle of Béxar, 33
    in Battle of San Jacinto, 45
    discrediting of, 79, 87, 91

    imprisonment of, 43, 87
    life of, 41, 43
Segunda Compañía Volante, La, 5, 6–7
Seis, Juan, 67
Seminole Indians, 164
Sequalteplan, battle at, 146, 219
Shawnee Indians, 61, 65–66
    in Canadian River fight, 166, 167
    on reservations, 165
Sheridan, Philip, 211
Sherman, William Tecumseh, 185, *185*
Shiloh, Battle of, 185
ships, capture of Mexican, 46
Short, George, 218
Shot Arm (Huaco), 166
Showalter, Daniel, 198, 199
Sibley, Henry H,, 192
Slaughter, James E., 207–8
Smith, A. T., 217
Smith, Addie, 191
Smith, C. F., 125
Smith, Edmund Kirby, *179*, 180–81, 182, 208
Smith, Erastus "Deaf", 28, 45, *45*
Smith, Henry, 32
Smithwick, Noah, 52, *57*, 63
    against secession, 177–78
    at Coleman's Fort, 52, 54–56
    on Comanche raids, 36–37, 67–68
    friendship with Williamson, 32
    living among Comanche, 56, 57–58
    Runaway Scrape and, 40, 43
    as scout for Bowie, 33
    in Texas Revolution, 35–36, 46
    treaty negotiations by, 56
Somervell, Alexander, 80, 88, 91–92
songs, Texas Ranger, 145, 201–2
Spain, colonization by, 1–5
Spencer, Jack, 162
Stark, John, *9*, 9–10
statehood
    annexation, 103–4, *104*
    separate from Coahuila, 26–27
State Police, 211–12
Steele, David, 155, 158
Stein, John, 217
Stoneman, George, 173, 182
Sullivan, D. C. "Doc", 154, 155, 156, 219
surveyors, 52, 86, 151
Swenson, S. M., 98

T
Tarin, Manuel, 45
Tarin, Vicente, 6

taxation, lack of support for, 79
Taylor, Zachary, 106, 115, 117, *121*
    in Agua Fria, 136–37
    armistice agreement of, 130, 135
    in Battle of Buena Vista, 137–38
    in Battle of Monterrey, 122–26, 129–30
    in Battle of Paint Rock, 116–17
    in Battle of Palo Alto, 118–19
    in Mexico City, 143–44
    request for volunteers by, 119
Tejanos
    early, 4–5
    Ranger companies of, 64–65
    tensions between U. S. immigrants and, 13, 15, 49, 87
    Texians unified with, 35
Temple, Philip G., 199
Tenewa Indians, 166
Terrell, Alexander W., 185
Terry, Benjamin Franklin, 181, *182*, 183–85
Terry, Clinton, 185
Terry's Texas Rangers, *114*, 181, *183*, 183–85, *186*
    flag of, *201*
Texas Mounted Riflemen (or Rifles)
    in Civil War, 189, 191, 197
    killed in action, 217–18, 219, 220
    in Mexican War, 119, 122, 126, 129, 135, 146
Texas Mounted Volunteers, 115, 117, 218
"Texas Ranger, The" (song), 69–70
Texas Rangers, *107*, *160*
    after annexation, 104, 115
    appearance of, *121*, 143
    caricature of, *177*
    character and mission of, xvi–xviii, xx, 1
    companies in Civil War, 197–98
    confusion surrounding, 64–66
    first companies of, 29–30, *50*
    governmental funding and support for, 29–30, 63, 94
    killed in action, 215–20
    ranging companies as predecessor of, 19–21
    in Reconstruction era, 211, 213
    role in Civil War, 175–77
    role in frontier society, 54
    role in Texas Revolution, 37–38
    wage of, 30, 80, 95, 149, 153
    See also *specific companies (e.g.* Texas Mounted
        Riflemen); *specific conflicts (e.g.* Civil War); *specific
        Rangers (e.g.* Walker, Samuel H.)
Texas Revolution, 28–47
    Battle of Béxar, 7, *33*–35
    Battle of San Jacinto, 44–46
    capture of ships, 46
    Goliad, 40, 44
    Gonzales battle, 28–29

Houston's routes during, *44*
Runaway Scrape, 40, 43–44, 49
siege of the Alamo, 38–40, *39*, 216
Texas at close of, *51*
Texians
    early, 8, 13, 15
    fighting style of, 21
    Tejanos unified with, 35
Thernon, Tom, 81
Thomas, Herman S., 128, 217
Thorton, Seth, 115
"Three-Legged Willie". *See* Williamson, Robert M.
Throckmorton, James W.
    against secession, 178
    in Civil War, 203, 205, 206
    Ranger company of, 198
    in Reconstruction era, 211
Tobin, W. G., 171, 172
Tonkawa Indians
    in Battle of Plum Creek, 77
    in Canadian River fight, 166, 167
    Chief Placido, 77, *77*, 166
    in Civil War, 189, 196, 203, 205
    on reservations, 165
Torkelin, Charles G., 192
Torrejón, Anastacio, lancers of, 115, 117–19, 122–26
Totten, Silas, 205
Totty, F. M., 200, 220
trade restrictions, 26
Travis, William Barret, 32, *38*, 38–40
treasury, 49, 66, 79
treaties
    border, 94, 106
    with Indians, 56, 206
    Mexican War, 130, 135, 146
    Treaty of Guadalupe Hidalgo, 146
    Treaty of Velasco, 94, 106
Trespalacios, José, 24
Trespalacios Creek, 24
Trimble, Lee, *xix*
Trinity River, 30
truce, Mexican War, 130, 135
Trueheart, John O., 64
    on muster roll, *65*
Truett, Alfred M., 146
Tufts, C. W., 218
Tumlinson, David, 45
Tumlinson, George W., 38
Tumlinson, Joe, 25, 45
Tumlinson, John (cousin), 45
Tumlinson, John J. (son), 24, 25, 28, 52
    in Battle of San Jacinto, 45, 46
    election to captain, 30, 35

in Great Raid attack, 76–77
Runaway Scrape and, 40, 43
in Walnut Creek ambush, 36–37
Tumlinson, John Jackson (father), 24, 25, 216
Twiggs, David E., 126, 179, *179*, 181

U–V

Ugartechea, Domingo de, 28
Van Camp, Cornelius, 167
Van Dorn, Earl, 167, 173, 182
vaqueros, 5, *108*, 150
Vásquez, Rafael, 43, 76, 87–88
Vela, Señor, 191
Vera Cruz, 49–50, 136, 138–40
Veramendi, Mariá Ursula de, 27
Victoria, 76
Vince's Bridge, 45
Vinton, Colonel, 128

W

wage, of Rangers, 30, 80, *95*, 149, 153
Wahqua (Noah Smithwick), 57, 58
See also Smithwick, Noah
Walker, Andrew J., 154, 158, 162–63, 164
Rangers killed under, 219
Walker, Leroy P., 187
Walker, Samuel H., *vi, xviii, 95, 110, 131, 141*
in Battle of Monterrey, 124, 128, 130
in Battle of Palo Alto, 118–19
in Battle of Walker Creek, 69, 100
in campaign against Comanche, 161–62
death of, 143, 216
friendship with Colt, 97, 130, 131–34
imprisonment of, 106, 141–42
in second campaign against Texas, 90
as lieutenant colonel, 121
in Mexico City, 139
on Mier expedition, 91–92
on muster roll, *112*
reputation of, 130
spy mission of, 115, 117
Walker Creek, Battle of. *See* Battle of Walker Creek
Wallace, William "Bigfoot", 73, *75*
in Battle of Plum Creek, 77
friendship with Williamson, 32
in second campaign against Texas, 88, 89, 90
on Mier expedition, 91–92
Waller, Ed, 191, 197
Walling, Van, 144
Walnut Creek
ambush, 36–37
Coleman's Fort on, 52, 54–56, *55*
Ward, Lafayette, 77

War of Independence. *See* Texas Revolution
War Party convention, 28
wars. *See* Civil War; Mexican War; Texas Revolution
"War Song of the Texas Rangers", 145
Washington, James, 185
Washington-on-the-Brazos, 30, 38, 40, 95
Watchman (ship), 46
weapons, *ii,* 30, 121
Civil War era, *114, 176*
Colt firearms. *See* Colt firearms
of Indians, *13*
of lancers, *40*
long rifles, 17–19, *18*
Spanish colonial era, *3, 6, 40*
Weaver, William H., 70, 217
Wells, J. P., 121
Wharton, John A., 183–84, 185
Wheeler, Alfred, 161
White, Captain, 205
White Bear (Kiowa), *195*
Whitney, Eli, 132
Wichita Mountains, 167
Wilbarger, John, 156, 219
Wilkinson, Jim, 162
Williamson, Robert M., *31*
election to captain, 30
life of, 31–32
in Texas Revolution, 38, 40, 43–44, 45
Willis, Henry J., 163, 219
Wilson, John E., 161–62, 216
Woll, Adrian, 88–91, 97
Wood, George T., 121, 153
men killed in action under, 218
Woodruff, Fountain B., 219
Woodson, Kentucky, 184–85
Wool, John, 137, *137*, 138–39
Worth, William J., 124, *124*, 129, 130
Wren, Nicholas, 55, 90
Wynkoop, F. N., 141–42

Y–Z

Ytúrria, Francisco, 169
Zacualtipán, battle at (Sequalteplan), 146, 219

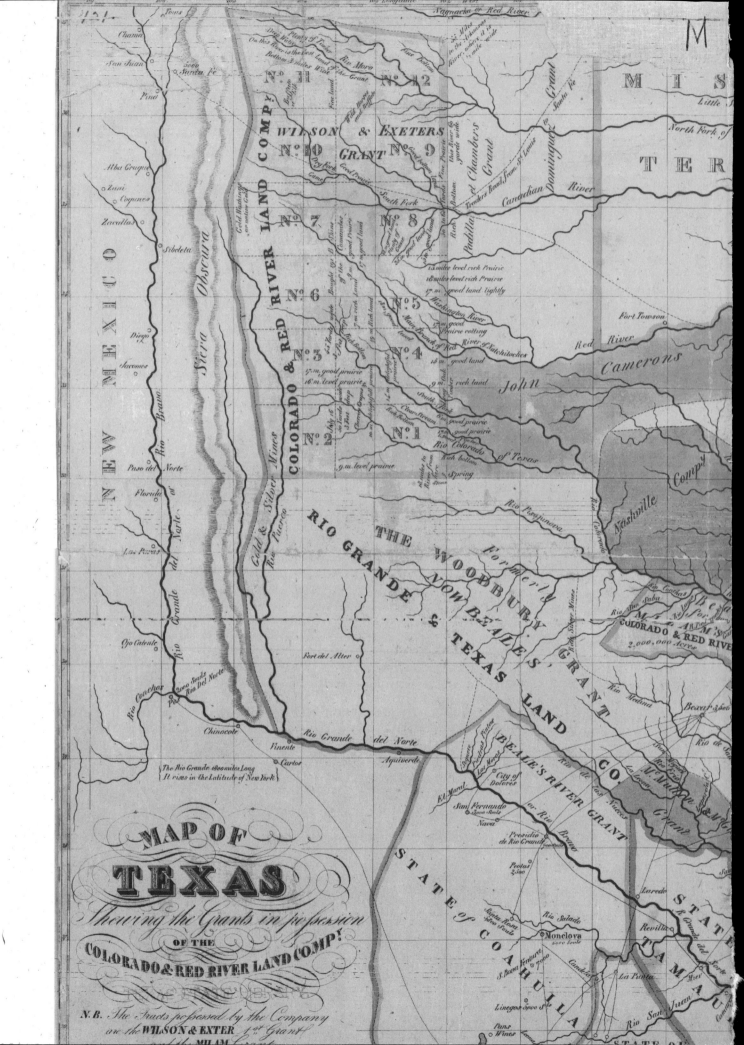

MAP OF
TEXAS
Shewing the Grants in possession
OF THE
COLORADO & RED RIVER LAND COMP!

N.B. The Tracts possessed by the Company
are the WILSON & EXTER 1st Grant